CONTENTS

Cover Picture: Mago Estate Hotel,
Soufrière, St Lucia, West Indies (see page 165).

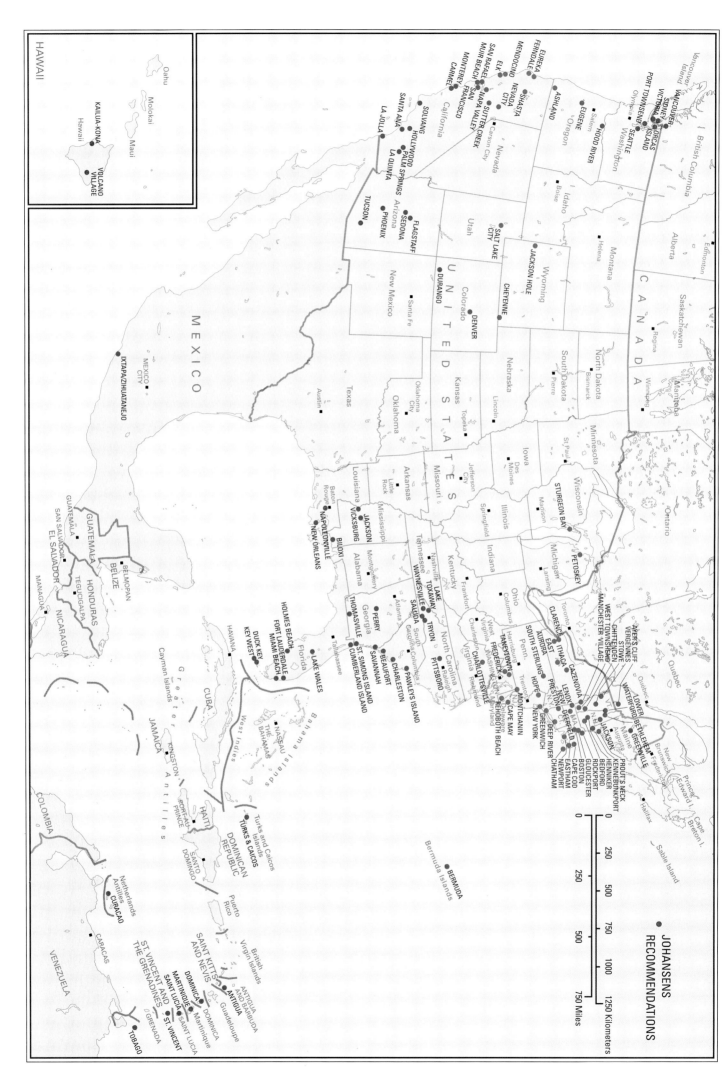

FOREWORD

In 1999 we were delighted to present three new 'Annual Awards for Excellence' to establishments featured in 'Recommended Hotels & Inns – North America, Bermuda & The Caribbean'. The winners were selected from nominations based on the many thousands of 'Guest Survey Forms' that you send us each year.

Our inspectors annually visit every recommended establishment in addition to the many hotels, inns, country houses and business meeting venues which regularly apply for inclusion. Only those that match our standards of diversity and excellence can be recommended.

The new millennium editions of our guides include the launch of 'Recommended Hotels & Game Lodges – Southern Africa, Mauritius & The Seychelles'. You will find these exciting new recommendations together with those for Europe & The Mediterranean in a new illustrated listing at the back of this guide.

A complete reference to our year 2000 recommendations representing 40 countries may be found together with a direct on line availability service (DOLAS) on our Internet site www.johansens.com The guides are also available on CD-ROM.

Your experience has proved that to mention that you use Johansens when making a booking is a positive benefit to the enjoyment of your stay.

We wish you many more of them.

Andrew Warren
<u>**Managing Director**</u>

Published by

Johansens Limited, Therese House, Glasshouse Yard, London EC1A 4JN

Tel: +44 20 7566 9700 Fax: +44 20 7490 2538

Find Johansens on the Internet at: **http://www.johansens.com**

E-Mail: admin@johansen.u–net.com

Publisher:	Jane Valentine
Editorial Manager:	Yasmin Razak
North American Executive:	Sally Howarth
Inspectors:	Christine Calloway-Holt
	Suzanne Flanders
	Susannah Macpherson
	Paul Stanislas
Production Manager:	Daniel Barnett
Production Controller:	Kevin Bradbrook
Senior Designer:	Michael Tompsett
Designer:	Sue Dixon
Copywriters:	Simon Duke
	Norman Flack
	Trudie Le Marie
	Aarish Shah
Map Ilustrations:	Linda Clark
Sales and Marketing Manager:	Laurent Martinez
Marketing Executive:	Stephen Hoskin
Sales Executive:	Susan Butterworth
Special Projects Editor:	Fiona Patrick
Webmaster:	John Lea
P.A. to Managing Director:	Glenda Walshaw
Managing Director:	Andrew Warren

Copyright © 1999 Johansens Limited

Johansens is a member company of Harmsworth Publishing Ltd, a subsidiary of the Daily Mail & General Trust plc

ISBN 1 86017 7123

Printed in England by St Ives plc
Colour origination by Icon Reproduction

Distributed in the UK and Europe by Johnsons International Media Services Ltd, London (direct sales) & Biblios PDS Ltd, West Sussex (bookstores). In North America by Hunter Publishing, New Jersey. In Australia and New Zealand by Bookwise International, Findon, South Australia

HOW TO USE THIS GUIDE

The Contents section on page 1 illustrates how this guide is set out.

A small scale map on page 2 indicates where Johansens Recommended Hotels and Inns are situated in North America, Bermuda and The Caribbean. Their actual locations are shown more precisely on the larger scale maps of different regions as they appear in the guide.

If you want to find a hotel whose name you already know, look for it in the Indexes on page 172.

If you want to find a Hotel or Inn in a particular area, first turn to the map on page 2 then to the Contents section on page 1 and select the region in which you wish to stay: Bermuda, Canada, The Caribbean or a named individual state of the U.S.A. Each Hotel or Inn appears on a regional map with a number that correlates to the page on which its description is published. Due to the geographical grouping of the states they are not arranged in alphabetical order.

Mini Listings on pages 173–176: You will find the names, locations and telephone numbers of all Johansens Recommendations in Great Britain & Ireland.

Illustrated Mini Listings on pages 177–196: You will find the names, locations, telephone numbers and pictures of all Johansens Recommendations from the guide to Europe & The Mediterranean and the guide to Southern Africa, Mauritius & The Seychelles.

The Johansens guides in which these recommendations appear are described fully on the outside back cover. Copies of these guides are obtainable direct from Johansens by calling +44 990 269397 or by using the order coupons on page 197–200.

Prices: throughout the guide the majority of prices listed refer to 'room' rate, not 'per person rate'. These prices are correct at the time of going to press, but should always be checked with the establishment when you reserve your accommodation. You may, in addition, wish to note that prices are subject to state tax.

We occasionally receive letters from guests who have been charged for accommodation booked in advance but later cancelled. Readers should be aware that by making a reservation with a hotel, either by telephone or in writing, they are entering into a legal contract. A hotelier under certain circumstances is entitled to make a charge for accommodation when guests fail to arrive, even if notice of the cancellation is given.

"FOR BEST BEFORE DATE SEE CAP"
Bottled at source, Broughton, Hampshire
750mle
WELL... DE GUSTIBUS NON EST DISPUTANDUM
HILDON
AN ENGLISH
Hildon Ltd., Broughton, Hampshire SO20 8DG, ☎ 01794 - 301 747

KEY TO SYMBOLS

14 rms	Total number of rooms	Nombre de chambres	Anzahl der Zimmer
MasterCard	MasterCard accepted	MasterCard accepté	MasterCard akzeptiert
VISA	Visa accepted	Visa accepté	Visa akzeptiert
AMERICAN EXPRESS	American Express accepted	American Express accepté	American Express akzeptiert
Diners Club	Diners Club accepted	Diners Club accepté	Diners Club akzeptiert
other	Other Credit Cards accepted	Autres cartes de crédit acceptées	Anderen Kredit Karten akzeptiert
	Quiet location	Lieu tranquille	Ruhige Lage
	Access for wheelchairs to at least one bedroom and public rooms	Accès handicapé	Zugang für Behinderte

(The 'Access for wheelchairs' symbol (&) does not necessarily indicate that the property fulfils National Accessible Scheme grading)

24	24 hour room service	Service en chambre à toute heure	24 Std. Service
M 20	Meeting/conference facilities with maximum number of delegates	Salle de conférences – capacité maximale	Konferenzraum-Höchstkapazität
8	Children welcome, with minimum age where applicable	Enfants bienvenus	Kinder willkommen
	Dogs accommodated in rooms or kennels	Chiens autorisés	Hunde erlaubt
	At least one room has a tester/canopy bed	Lit à baldaquin dans au moins une chambre	Mindestens ein Zimmer mit Himmelbett
	At least one room has a fireplace	Cheminée dans au moins une chambre	Mindestens ein Zimmer mit Kamin
	Cable/satellite TV in all bedrooms	TV câblée/satellite dans les chambres	Satellit-und Kabelfernsehen in allen Zimmern
	Fax available in rooms	Fax dans votre chambre	Fax in Schlafzimmern
	No-smoking rooms (at least one no-smoking bedroom)	Chambres non-fumeur	Zimmer für Nichtraucher
	Elevator available for guests' use	Ascenseur	Fahrstuhl
	Air Conditioning	Climatisation	Klimatisiert
	Whirlpool / Jacuzzi in at least one room	Whirlpool / Jacuzzi dans au moins une chambre	Mindestens ein Zimmer mit Whirlpool / Jacuzzi
	Indoor swimming pool	Piscine couverte	Hallenbad
	Outdoor swimming pool	Piscine en plein air	Freibad
	Tennis court at hotel	Tennis à l'hôtel	Hoteleigener Tennisplatz
	Croquet lawn at hotel	Croquet à l'hôtel	Krocketrasen
	Fishing can be arranged	Pêche	Angeln
	Golf course on site or nearby, which has an arrangement with hotel allowing guests to play	Golf sur site ou à proximité	Golfplatz
	Shooting can be arranged	Chasse / Tir	Jagd
	Riding can be arranged	Équitation	Reitpferd
	Skiing	Ski	Schilaufen
H	Hotel has a helipad	Helipad	Hubschrauberlandplatz
	Licensed for wedding ceremonies	Cérémonies de mariages	Konzession für Eheschliessungen

TASTER'S CHOICE

Robin Davis

HILDON FROM

Britain Bubbles to Top

The fast-approaching holidays mean parties, and while Champagne is festive, a non-alcoholic choice for guests is a must. With its tiny bubbles, sparkling water makes a good substitute, but it can difficult to choose among the many brands.

Today's panel tasted 10 sparkling waters — seven imported from Europe and three domestic brands — but only one American-bottled water scored high enough to rate.

The panel found dramatic differences in taste. Several waters scored high and close together, then scores dropped off for the remaining products. Panelists said they could taste differences in the mineral content; the amount of carbonation also played a role in what they liked.

The top scorer was Great Britain's **Hildon** (750 milliters, $2.49 at Draeger's). One panelist thought it was "clean and pure-tasting;" two enjoyed its carbonation. All would buy it.

Vals (16.9 ounces, $1.69 at Draeger's) from France scored only one point lower. One panelist commented on its character, and three liked its strong mineral flavor. All would buy it.

California's **Calistoga** (one liter, 89-99 cents at many supermarkets) came in third. One panelist described it as "exciting." Two noted a salty taste. Four

would buy it; one might buy it.

Another British water, **Ty Nant** (750 milliliters, $2.19 at Andronico's) was only two points below Calistoga. One panelist thought the carbonation tasted fake, but another liked the "tingly" bubbles. Three would buy it, one might, and one would not.

The most expensive brand, **Acqua della Madonna** (750 milliliters, $3.19, at Draeger's) from Italy, came in fifth. One panelist thought the salty mineral taste "lingers unpleasantly," but another described it as "snappy." One would buy it, two might, and two would not.

Panelists were divided on **Perrier** (750 milliliters, $1.29 at many supermarkets) from France. One liked the salty, mineral flavor, and another liked the tiny bubbles. But two others thought it was nondescript. Two would buy it; three would not.

Apollinaris (from Germany), Crystal Geyser (from the U.S.), San Pellegrino (from Italy) and Arrowhead (from the U.S.) scored too low to rate.

Correction: The store listed as a source for Jolt and Virgin colas in the October 16 Taster's Choice column was incorrect. The colas can be purchased at Draeger's on the Peninsula.

Robin Davis is a Chronicle staff critic.

SPARKLING WATER

TASTERS	Hildon	Vals	Calistoga	Ty Nant	Acqua della Madonna	Perrier
Bowe	18	16	9	16	11	9
Carroll	16	16	16	18	10	16
Katzl	16	16	17	13	17	7
Passot	16	16	17	16	12	17
Webber	12	13	12	6	6	6
TOTALS	78	77	71	69	56	55

Panelists were Dan Bowe, associate culinary director, Center for Culinary Development; John P. Carroll, cookbook author; Donna Katzl, chef-owner Cafe For All Seasons, San Francisco; Roland Passot, chef-owner, La Folie in San Francisco and Left Bank in Larkspur and Menlo Park; and Kirk Webber, chef-owner, Cafe Kati, San Francisco. All products are tasted blind. A perfect score for any product would be 100.

and a deep burgundy color
— but some of the service st
parted when Serrano left.
nately, like a well-oiled mac
the new people fit into the se
cadence of service. The wait
there when you need them,
never hover. There's a prec

HONDA

First man, then machine

The Honda Accord has won critical acclaim from both the public and press alike.

What Car? Magazine voted it best in class in their 1999 Car of the Year Awards.

Now there's the choice of a 5 door model within the range, offering increased versatility.

Like all Accords, the 5 door is one of the quietest and most refined in its class.

It's powered by Honda's Formula One bred VTEC engine, which combines high power with high economy (147ps and 32.8mpg* from the 2.0i).

With multi-link double-wishbone suspension-which keeps the wheels as vertical as possible, thereby maximising road grip-plus ABS and air conditioning, it's a pleasure to drive.

Call 0345 159 159 or visit www.honda.co.uk

Same story, different ending.

The Honda Accord.

298 ACC

JOHANSENS AWARDS FOR EXCELLENCE
RECOMMENDED HOTELS – NORTH AMERICA, BERMUDA, THE CARIBBEAN

The 1999 Awards for Excellence winners at the Dorchester

The Johansens Awards for Excellence were presented at the Johansens Annual Dinner held at The Dorchester on November 2nd 1998.

The Special Award for Excellence – North America was given to **The Lodge at Moosehead Lake, Greenville, Maine.** We have been overwhelmed by the number of guest survey reports received, all of which have highlighted this inn as a truly exceptional property.

The award for the Most Excellent Inn – North America went to **Carter House, Eureka, California.** Renowned for its superb cuisine and wine cellar, a trip to the Californian coastline is not complete without a stay at the Carter House.

The award for The Most Excellent Hotel – North America was presented to **Monmouth Plantation, Natchez, Mississippi.** This former residence of General Quitman has been lovingly restored into one of the finest boutique hotels you will find. The hotel will charm you and is ideal for any special occasion.

Congratulations to these winners and thank you to everyone who sent in Guest Survey Report forms.

Each year we rely on appraisals made by Johansens guests in combination with the nominations from our team of Inspectors as a basis for making all our awards, not only to our Recommended Hotels – North America but also to our Hotels, Country Houses and Inns with Restaurants in Great Britain & Ireland and Recommended Hotels & Inns – Europe & The Mediterranean. In these categories, the award winners for 1999 were:

Johansens – The Most Excellent London Hotel Award:
The London Outpost of the Carnegie Club, London

Johansens – The Most Excellent City Hotel Award:
Channings, Edinburgh

Johansens – The Most Excellent Service Award:
Burpham Country Hotel, West Sussex

Johansens – The Most Excellent Country Hotel Award:
Summer Lodge, Dorset

Johansens Most Excellent Country House Award:
Caragh Lodge, Co. Kerry, Ireland

Johansens Most Excellent Traditional Inn Award:
The New Inn at Coln, Gloucestershire

Johansens Most Excellent Value for Money Award:
Beechwood Hotel, North Walsham, Norfolk

Johansens Most Excellent Restaurant Award:
Ynyshir Hall, Machynlleth, Wales

Johansens – Outstanding Excellence and Innovation Award:
Robin Hutson and Gerard Basset – Hotel du Vin Group of Hotels

Johansens – Europe: The Most Excellent Waterside Resort Hotel:
The Marbella Club, Marbella, Spain

Johansens – Europe: The Most Excellent Country Hotel:
Schlosshotel Igls, Igls, Austria

Johansens – Europe: The Most Excellent City Hotel:
La Tour Rose, Lyon, France

INTRODUCTION

From Carter House, Eureka, California
Winner of the 1999 Johansens Most Excellent Restaurant Award

It's been almost two decades since Christi and I first opened 3 rooms in The Carter House to overnight guests. From the beginning, we wanted our inn to provide an experience unique among accommodations and unique also to our location here in the amazing Redwood Region of Northern California. Setting a course for singularity meant more than creating comfortable rooms and tasty food, we had to create "a place apart" – a place of service, warmth and comfort which captures the unique flavour of our Redwood Coast region: a place for making memories.

Over the years, our inn has grown into what it is today – 32 luxurious rooms scattered among 4 gracious Victorian structures, a Grand-Award winning Restaurant, productive organic gardens supplying our kitchens with fresh produce and a wonderful wine shop, stocked with some of the world's finest vintages. Surely the greatest lesson we've learnt at Carter House though, is that the quality of a guest's lodging experience invariably transcends facilities, food and finery. What makes memories is the spirit of true hospitality at an inn – a gracious atmosphere of person-to-person caring service. Make no mistake, people are the heart and soul of our business.

On behalf of Christi and our entire staff at Carter House, I want to thank Johansens for this wonderful recognition and especially for gathering an illustrious group of inns and hotels, each of whom knows that the true pride of hospitality is in taking care of people and providing a setting in which golden memories are born.

Mark Carter

INTRODUCTION

From The Lodge at Moosehead Lake, Greenville, Maine
Winner of the 1999 Johansens Special Award for Excellence

We were overwhelmed and greatly honoured to receive the very first Special Award of Excellence given in the USA.

It was somewhat timely in that the fastest growing segment of the Tourism industry is "Adventure Travel" We are fortunate to be in an area that has more adventure activities than any other in New England.

There is excellent hiking, 1000's of miles of rivers, lakes and ponds for canoeing and kayaking, unbelievable mountain bike trails, Exciting white water rafting, great fly fishing in these streams and ponds and our piece de resistance – Go on a Moose Safari. In the winter there is downhill and cross country skiing, snowboarding, snowshoeing, snowmobiling and our winter piece de resistance – Dog sledding.

The Lodge has lots of public rooms with well padded chairs and sofas in front of log burning fireplaces. Here you can relax and enjoy phenomenal westerly views over Moosehead Lake and Squaw Mountain with its unbelievable sunsets.

This is why you should come "Rough it in Comfort" with us!

Roger & Jennifer Cauchi

Arizona and California

INN AT 410

410 NORTH LEROUX STREET, FLAGSTAFF, ARIZONA 86001
TEL: 1 520 774 0088 FAX: 1 520 774 6354 E-MAIL: info@inn410.com

Set in the mountain town of Flagstaff, The Inn at 410 offers fine accommodation and a superb location for those travelling to the Grand Canyon. The friendly owners offer advice to their guests on how to avoid crowds and enjoy the best views of this natural wonder. Situated at 7000ft, the Inn retains a delicately cool air throughout the seasons and is popular with sports enthusiasts wishing to tackle the alpine hiking and biking trails. The bedrooms are exquisite, colourful and highly detailed with thoughtful extras and traditional comforts. The true flavour of the West may be experienced in The Southwest with its Santa Fe décor, and the Dakota Suite, reminiscent of the Old West. The intimate setting of a perennial garden, which surrounds the patio and gazebo, is the perfect place to savour a quiet drink in the afternoon. The Inn is two blocks from historic downtown Flagstaff, an easy walk to shops and restaurants. Arizona's dramatic landscape may be admired during the one hour drive through the scenic Oak Creek Canyon to the red rocks of Sedona. Other attractions include the Hopi and Navajo villages and the ancient Indian ruins at Wupatki and Walnut Canon. **Directions:** From I-40, exit 195B north onto Milton. From I-17 continue north onto Milton. Follow Milton under the railroad overpass and curve to the right. Turn left at 1st stoplight onto Humphreys Street. At Dale turn right. Turn left onto N.Leroux. The Inn is on the right. Price guide: Rooms $125–$175.

MARICOPA MANOR

15 WEST PASADENA AVENUE, PHOENIX, ARIZONA 85013-2001
TEL: 1 602 274 6302 FAX: 1 602 266 3904 US TOLL FREE: 800 292 6403 E-MAIL: mmanor@getnet.com

Surrounded by palm trees and flowers, this Spanish-style Manor house, set in the heart of North Central Phoenix, is both intimate and elegant. Built in 1928, Maricopa Manor combines the refined atmosphere of a fine residence with the comforts and conveniences of home. The interior is beautifully furnished with cosy fireplaces and stylish paintings. The 6 suites in the Manor house and adjacent buildings are well-equipped offering every modern amenity. All are individually decorated, creating a sense of warmth and character. The rates include an extensive breakfast, featuring home-made breads and fresh fruit, which is served to guests in the comfort of their own suite. The Manor is only 5 miles from the busy centre of downtown Phoenix, which offers a plethora of restaurants and bistros. A variety of outdoor pursuits is available nearby such as hot-air ballooning, golf, horseback-riding and tennis. For the less adventurous, museums, theatres, art galleries and boutiques are within minutes of the manor. **Directions:** From Flagstaff, follow I-17 (south to Camelback Road). Turn left on Camelback to Third Avenue. Turn left on Third. Again one block turn right on to Pasadena Avenue and on to 15 West. Price guide: Rooms $99(summer)–$229(winter).

CANYON VILLA INN

125 CANYON CIRCLE DRIVE, SEDONA, ARIZONA 86351
TEL: 1 520 284 1226 FAX: 1 520 284 2114 US TOLL FREE: 1 800 453 1166

In 1992 Chuck and Marion Yadon opened this inspirational Spanish mission style inn at Sedona, gateway to the magnificent Oak Creek Canyon. Set at the foot of Coconino National Forest, against the green trees, red rocks and azure blue skies, this modern hotel maximises on the spectacular countryside. Most of the guest rooms (known as 'view rooms') have balconies or patios. Each has a different theme, with appropriate furnishings including lovely family antiques. All have Jacuzzis, a welcome luxury after clambering over rocks. Marion is responsible for the sumptuous breakfast that is served which includes home-made cinnamon rolls, enjoyed looking across to the mighty Bell Rock and Courthouse Butte. Afternoon hors d'oeuvres are an opportunity to mingle with the other guests. The Villa does not serve alcohol but there is an off-licence round the corner! The Yadons will arrange dinner reservations at recommended restaurants, Jeep tours, hot-air balloons and the Verde River Canyon Train Excursions to explore the area. Grand Canyon is a short two-hour scenic drive. Two golf courses are nearby and Sedona has intriguing galleries and shops. The Villa has a pool, sun terrace and peaceful reading garden. **Directions:** Interstate 17 north for 120 miles, exit 298, left onto Highway 179 for 8 miles then left onto Bell Rock Boulevard to Canyon Circle Drive, turning right. Price guide: Rooms $145–$225.

CASA SEDONA INN

55 HOZONI DRIVE, SEDONA, ARIZONA 86336
TEL: 1 520 282 2938 FAX: 1 520 282 2259 US TOLL FREE: 1 800 525 3756 E-MAIL: casa@sedona.net

High up, overlooking the majesty of canyon country with remarkable forest land surrounding the area, lies the Casa Sedona, a magnificent place in which to rest and take in the surrounding natural beauty. Designed by a Frank Lloyd Wright Architect, the Casa Sedona does not merely exist amidst its surrounds but incorporates the environment into its overall splendour. The exterior blends into the attractive and colourful landscaped grounds, whilst the interior is the height of elegance and comfort. Using natural materials where possible, the Casa Sedona invites its guests to repose in style, with a subtle colour scheme inspired by the earthy tones that are so abundantly visible in the area and simple and unobtrusive furniture that provides the utmost comfort. The rooms are equipped with a fireplace, spa tub and other modern features. Hearty Southwest style breakfasts are served under the Juniper trees and tasty appetisers may be enjoyed in the afternoons. There is a myriad of activities available to the guest, from hiking and horse-riding to organised tours in the Grand Canyon, or nature trails through the forest. If this all sounds a little too arduous, then why not simply relax in the hot tub and gaze at the clear night sky simply ablaze with stars. **Directions:** From Sedona, take Alt. 89A West, right on Tortilla Drive, straight over onto Hozoni Drive. Price guide (incl. breakfast): Rooms $130–$210.

TANQUE VERDE RANCH

14301 EAST SPEEDWAY, TUCSON, ARIZONA 85748
TEL: 1 520 296 6275 FAX: 1 520 721 9426 E-MAIL: lisa@tvgr.com

This is a unique and striking hotel in the Sonoran Desert. Its name means "Green Tank", for it is where the cavalry stopped to water their horses when fighting the Apache raiders. Tanque Verde has 640 acres bordered by the Coronado National Forest and the Saguaro National Park – the views are spectacular. The dude ranch's adobe buildings are traditional, with beamed ceilings and long verandahs. Accommodation is in cool casitas, with rustic and modern furniture; the bathrooms have attractive Mexican tiles. The various rooms are spacious, with big stone fireplaces, colourful Indian rugs, inviting sofas and fascinating memorabilia from the region. Stetsons are almost mandatory, indoors or out! Authentic cowboy breakfasts of chilli eggs and blueberry pancakes are prepared out on the range, then its time to 'Ride High' among the tall cacti. At dusk, drinks on the verandahs watching the sunset over the mountains are followed by superb dinners and good wine or a fantastic barbecue, then Country Western dancing. The ranch has pools, tennis courts, sun terraces, a children's programme and a boutique with cowboy gear. Golf is nearby. **Directions:** Interstate 10, Houghton Road exit north, turn east on Speedway Boulevard. Ranch driveway at dead end. Price guide: Rooms $260–$350 (double occupancy).

WHITE STALLION RANCH

9251 WEST TWIN PEAKS ROAD, TUCSON, ARIZONA 85743
TEL: 1 520 297 0252 FAX: 1 520 744 2786 E-MAIL: wsranch@flash.net

A friendly and welcoming atmosphere envelopes this old Southwestern ranch, surrounded by a 5 mile expanse of desert. The White Stallion Ranch combines the informal ambience of a working cattle ranch with the comforts and conveniences of a holiday resort. There are 35 bedrooms clustered around the ranch in separate buildings. All the rooms are air-conditioned with private bath whilst de luxe suites offer fireplaces, whirlpool tubs and king-size beds. The True family has created a most convivial environment throughout the ranch and this is clearly evident in the popular bar. Here, guests relax in casual attire and enjoy the hors d'oeuvres and drinks at 'Happy Hour'. A full selection of breakfast dishes is served in the attractive dining room. Inviting recipes may be savoured at the buffet at lunch or at dinner, which is also served family style. Outdoor pursuits such as hiking, tennis, basketball, horse-riding and swimming are available on site. Other pastimes include hay rides, playing with the animals at the petting zoo and enjoying the indoor redwood hot tub. Traditional cowboy entertainment is also offered at the ranch and includes moonlight bonfires, hearty barbecues, weekly rodeos and enjoying the native wildlife. Denim and stetsons are very welcome! **Directions:** The hotel is situated on West Twin Peaks road, adjacent to the Saguaro National Park. Price guide: Rooms $214–$288; suite $256–$350.

PINE INN

OCEAN AVENUE & MONTE VERDE, PO BOX 250, CARMEL, CALIFORNIA 93921
TEL: 1 831 624 3851 FAX: 1 831 624 3030 US TOLL FREE: 1 800 228 3851 E-MAIL: info@pine-inn.com

Set in the heart of the village of Carmel, this historic inn is surrounded by charming shops, a number of art galleries and lovely hidden courtyards. Built in 1889, the elegance and refined ambience of a bygone age has been carefully re-created throughout. A choice of standard, superior or de luxe bedrooms is available, as well as suites of varying sizes. Each room is tastefully decorated with European and Far Eastern nuances, while the restaurant, Il Fornaio, is furnished in a classically Italian style. Here, guests can enjoy the special traditions of Italy, choosing authentic food and wine from an imaginative menu and watching the cooks prepare the dishes in the open kitchen. As well as exquisite local pasta dishes, there is a good selection of entrées prepared on either a mesquite grill, in a wood-burning oven, or on a traditional rotisserie. Guests must indulge in the hearth-baked house breads, prepared from old Italian recipes. Popular activities include shopping and revisiting the past in the historic missions, while golf enthusiasts can take advantage of some of the world's most famous courses. Sun-worshippers must watch the beautiful sunsets from Carmel's sandy beach! **Directions:** The inn is only 7 miles from Monterey Airport. Take Highway 1 south to Ocean Avenue, Pine Inn lies between Lincoln and Monte Verde. Price guide: Rooms $105–$250; suites $250.

ELK COVE INN

6300 SOUTH HIGHWAY ONE, PO BOX 367, ELK, CALIFORNIA 95432
TEL: 1 707 877 3321 US TOLL FREE: 1 800 275 2967

If the pressures of everyday life are proving too much then escape to this secluded cove set in the scenic village of Elk, known as Greenwood by the locals who reminisce about its association with the lumber trade. The original house sits on the bluff overlooking a splendid beach. The atmosphere is the height of relaxation and the coastal location, with its freshwater creek running into the sea, is ideal for watching the most spectacular sunsets. Nature enthusiasts may marvel at the beautiful surrounds from either the gazebo, gardens, beach or rooftop deck. There is a wonderful path down the hillside and Asta, the resident dog, will guide visitors down to the Pacific ocean. For indoor relaxation, the comfortable sitting room is bedecked with interesting books and local artwork. The accommodation is delightfully varied. Four romantic cottages nestle on the edge of the cliff and a new building houses four luxury spa suites. All the bedrooms feature an array of modern comforts. The charming owner, Elaine Bryant, collects pottery from the 1940s and plays music from this period in the restaurant, where a gourmet breakfast comprising a multitude of courses may be sampled. The new outdoor hot tub is guaranteed to please and the sauna and massage room will be completed by the end of 1999. **Directions:** Elk Cove is north from San Francisco on HWY 101 West on HWY 128 south on HWY one to Elk. Price guide (incl. breakfast): Rooms $98–$278.

CARTER HOUSE

301 L STREET, EUREKA, CALIFORNIA 95501
TEL: 1 707 444 8062 US TOLL FREE: 1 800 404 1390 FAX: 1 707 444 8067 E-MAIL: 301wines.com/wines

The architectural charm of the old coastal city of Eureka has earned it the name "The Williamsburg of the West". The Carter House consists of four fine Victorian mansions that embellish the edge of Humboldt Bay at the entrance to historic Eureka's Victorian district: The original Carter House, the Hotel Carter, Carter House Cottage and the Bell Cottage. Each is generously appointed. The attractive interior décor and furnishings are the setting for hospitality of the highest class. Guests are welcomed by an aura of luxury and comfort. Beautiful fabrics, fresh fruit and flowers and a tasteful combination of modern and classical amenities enhance the restful and cheerful atmosphere. Guest rooms are delightfully equipped with every aid to relaxed enjoyment. Extra services are instantly at hand. Breakfasts and dinners are a gastronomic experience – fresh produce and culinary skills bring wide-spread renown to Restaurant 301. The award-winning wine list is selectively comprehensive. Gaps before and after evening meals are filled with hors d'oeuvres, cookies and other nourishments. Things to do and see locally include sailing, rowing, golf, tennis, riding, walking, going to the theatre, the concert, the Avenue of the Giants, the Redwood National Park and the Sequoia Park and Zoo. **Directions:** Off highway 101, a long drive north of San Francisco. Price guide: Rooms $105–$185;

GINGERBREAD MANSION INN

400 BERDING STREET, FERNDALE, CALIFORNIA 95536
TEL: 1 707 786 4000 FAX: 1 707 786 4381 US TOLL FREE: 800 952 4136

Built in 1899, the Gingerbread Mansion Inn retains many of its original features such as exquisite turrets and carvings. A unique combination of Queen Anne and Eastlake styles, the house is elaborately trimmed with ornate gingerbread decorations. The interior has been carefully restored and features plush carpets, rich Victorian wallpaper and cosy fireplaces. The eleven en suite bedrooms are furnished with an individual touch and are enhanced by lace comforters, claw foot bath tubs or tiled fireplaces. The warmth of the hospitality extended at the inn is shown in the small nuances such as the robes and bedside chocolate at turndown. Afternoon tea is served in the four Victorian parlours and comprises freshly baked cakes, biscuits, pastries and other delights. An extensive menu of home-made dishes is served in the elegant Dining Room at breakfast. There are excellent restaurants within easy walking distance. Guests may explore the Pacific coast and the Giant Redwoods; just a ½ hour drive away. Ferndale is a State historical landmark, with well-preserved Victorian homes, old-fashioned boutiques and grand English gardens. **Directions:** The hotel is 5 hours north of San Francisco, take the 101 Freeway. Then 5 miles to centre of town, turn left at bank. Take the Ferndale exit. Price guide: Rooms $140–$200; suite $230–$350.

LE PARC SUITE HOTEL

733 NORTH WEST KNOLL DRIVE, WEST HOLLYWOOD, CALIFORNIA 90069
TEL: 1 310 855 8888 FAX: 1 310 659 8508 E-MAIL: leparcres@aol.com

Le Parc Suite Hotel enjoys a tranquil location, despite being within a short drive of the fashionable shopping streets and nightclubs of the Beverly Hills area and downtown Hollywood. The beach lies just 30 minutes' away. All of the 152 suites are tastefully decorated with fine art prints and offer an impressive range of facilities including a kitchenette with fridge and microwave, minibar, multi-line data phones and a television with a choice of movies and video games. A twice-daily maid service ensures the highest standards are maintained. On the third floor there is a charming breakfast area where guests can choose from an extensive menu of continental and typical American fayre, while in the café, there is a choice of meat or fish entrées and delicious desserts. A marvellous range of recreation and fitness facilities includes roof-top heated pool and cabanas, whirlpool spa, floodlit tennis court, a fitness centre with sauna and circuit training equipment. To take maximum advantage of these, a private tennis instructor, athletics trainer and masseurs are also available. Pastimes include shopping in Hollywood and visiting the nearby restaurants, museums and Beverly Hills. **Directions:** 1 block west of La Cienega Boulevard between Santa Monica Boulevard and Melrose Avenue. Price guide: Suites $300–$400. Corporate rates starting at $195.

THE BED & BREAKFAST INN AT LA JOLLA

7753 DRAPER AVENUE, LA JOLLA, CALIFORNIA 92037
TEL: 1 858 456 2066 FAX: 1 858 456 1510

This lovely inn stands in the cultural centre of the seaside community of La Jolla in northern San Diego. The beach, with its multitude of watersports, is just a block away, the Museum of Contemporary Art is across the street and close by are the Scripps Institute of Oceanography and U.C San Diego. Built in 1913, the inn is one of the finest examples of Irving Gill's Cubist style architecture and is listed as Historical Site 179 on the San Diego Registry. The original gardens were planned by renowned horticulturist Kate Sessions and enjoyed by John Philip Sousa and his family when they lived here in the 1920s. The gardens are still magnificent and feature a shady patio where guests can enjoy the tranquillity over late afternoon wine and cheese. Many of the bedrooms and suites overlook the gardens and some open onto them. All the rooms are individually and beautifully decorated in elegant cottage style and offer every modern facility. Superb breakfasts are served in the intimate dining room or in the garden. The inn is only a short stroll away from a variety of restaurants and shops and within easy reach of Old Town San Diego. **Directions:** West of Highway 5 between San Diego and Los Angeles. Exit onto Jolla Village Drive. Price guide: Rooms $129–$240; suite $279–$329.

TWO ANGELS INN

78–120 CALEO BAY, LA QUINTA, CALIFORNIA 92253
TEL: 1 760 564 7332 FAX: 1 760 564 6356 E-MAIL: deuxanges@aol.com

Situated in the desert city of La Quinta, The Two Angels Inn is a newly built bed and breakfast hideaway designed in the manner of a European chateau. As the inn is the private home of owners Hap and Holly Harris, the emphasis is on personal and warm service in hospitable and comfortable surroundings. The inn offers 11 individually designed rooms, each with their own name reflecting their unique character and atmosphere. All are equipped with a king or queen-size bed and have a balcony or patio with breathtaking views of Lake La Quinta and the Coachella Valley. Two of the rooms are tucked away in the boathouse and benefit from their own outdoor hot-tub. Visitors can relax in the landscaped gardens, or take meditation and yoga lessons in the meditation library. A full gourmet breakfast is served in the elegant dining room, while hors-d'oeuvres and fine wines are offered in the late afternoon. The surrounding area is famed for its golf, cycling, tennis and polo, with trips to the nearby theatres, museums and casinos also available. Palm Springs, with its shops and museums, is only a half hours drive away. **Directions:** From Los Angeles, take Interstate 10 towards Indio exiting right onto Washington Street. Cross highway 111 and turn left onto Avenue 47. Go one block to Caleo Bay, and follow to the inn. Price guide: Rooms $150–$350.

JOSHUA GRINDLE INN

**44800 LITTLE LAKE ROAD, PO BOX 647, MENDOCINO, CALIFORNIA 95460
TEL: 1 707 937 4143 US/CANADA TOLL FREE: 1 800 474 6353 E-MAIL: stay@joshgrin.com**

A local banker from the East Coast, Joshua Grindle built this house for his bride at the close of the 19th century. Constructed across two acres of land within walking distance of the ocean, The Joshua Grindle Inn is a tribute to New England-style architecture and décor. The welcoming owners, Jim and Arlene Moorehead, possess a keen eye for detail and this is evident throughout the inn. Beautiful original Victorian fireplaces feature in the main house whilst the water tower and cottage display woodburning stoves. The ten en suite bedrooms are furnished in an eclectic manner with views of either the ocean or the English-style garden with its herbaceous borders and attractive verandah.

Breakfast is served on the centrepiece of the dining room: a large, pine harvest table dating back to the 1830s. Wine and appetisers or tea and coffee may be enjoyed each afternoon beside the fireplace of the enchanting parlour. Cookery books, local artwork, ceramics and clothing may be bought in the shop on site. A number of convivial bars, cafés and restaurants are only a short walk away in town whilst sports enthusiasts may enjoy hiking, fishing, golf and watersports by the beach. **Directions:** From San Francisco take Highway 101 north to highway 128 west. Then highway 1 north to Mendocino, turn west on little lake. Price guide (incl. breakfast): Rooms $110–$215.

MARTINE INN

255 OCEANVIEW BOULEVARD, PACIFIC GROVE, CALIFORNIA 93950
TEL: 1 831 373 3388 FAX: 1 831 373 3896 US TOLL FREE: 1 800 852 5588

The Martine Inn, built in 1899, is a unique hotel in a superb setting, overlooking Monterey Bay. Its proprietors have ensured that its past is its present – it has a quintessential Victorian era ambience, yet rose walls add the Mediterranean influence favoured by a past owner. Guests are instantly impressed by the courtesy of the staff, reminiscent of bygone days, as they are taken to their elegant bedrooms, with delicate wall coverings and drapes, the finest period furnishings. The bathrooms are joyous – claw feet tubs and brass fittings. Downstairs handsome antiques are in evidence, a traditional library – and every evening guests assemble in the parlour for wine and hors d'oeuvres (there is no spirits licence) reminiscent of a fin-de-siècle houseparty. The table settings are enhanced by exquisite china, the finest crystal and handsome old silver. The Martines have an enviable collection of vintage autos, the games room has a 1917 nickelodeon and pool table. Nearby are golf, every water sport, tennis and fascinating places to explore (splendid well-filled picnic hampers can be ordered). Directions: Highway 1 to Pebble Beach turnoff, Highway 68 to Pacific Grove, Righthand lane to ocean (Forest Avenue), then right into Oceanview Boulevard. Price guide: Rooms $165–$300.

PELICAN INN

HIGHWAY 1, MUIR BEACH, CALIFORNIA 94965
TEL: 1 415 383 6000 FAX: 1 415 383 3424

English visitors arriving at this enchanting inn follow in the footsteps of Francis Drake, who landed here some 400 years ago in his ship 'The Pelican' – hence its name. Just 20 minutes from the Golden Gate Bridge, yet it stands in a traditional flower-filled cottage garden, with honeysuckle climbing up the walls. A slate roof and mullioned windows add to The Pelican's 16th century ambience. The interior maintains this historic theme – a magnificent collection of antiques and memorabilia from that era, big fireplaces, oak beams, white walls and a charming 'Snug' for residents. The bedrooms are also reminiscent of the period – guests may sleep in a half-tester canopy bed, with colourful rugs on the floor, a decanter of sherry by the bed and start the day with a true English breakfast. All rooms have an en suite bathroom. The convivial bar, its panelled walls decorated with brasses and a dartboard, serves ales, sherries, wine and port. A wide range of traditional British pub food is offered. Dining at authentic refectory tables in the attractive restaurant, guests appreciate a more sophisticated menu. Muir Beach is sheltered by trees and encompassed by the woods, scented with pine trees – the essence of relaxation. **Directions:** Leave Golden Gate on Highway 101, taking Highway 1, Stinson Beach exit. Price guide: Rooms $175–$210 (includes full English breakfast).

THE INK HOUSE

1575 HELENA HIGHWAY AT WHITEHALL LANE, ST HELENA, CALIFORNIA 94574-9775
TEL: 1 707 963 3890 FAX: 1 707 968 0739 E-MAIL: inkhousebb@aol.com

Named after its original 19th century owner, the Ink House is an historic Victorian hotel at the heart of the world famous Napa Valley. Surrounded by beautiful gardens, the hotel is a wine lover's dream. An observatory at roof level provides panoramic views of the vines stretching in each direction up to the Napa Valley hills. Seeing the grapes in their natural splendour is certain to work up a thirst and the hotel offers a wine tasting every evening, as well as trips to local vineyards where some of the finest wines on the continent can be tasted at source. The Ink House is a throwback to colonial times. The dining room is brimming with Victorian furniture, silver ornaments and bone china, while four magnificent stained glass windows adorn the entrance. The walls are adorned with sepia photos of the De Filipi family, oils and pastels of equestrian scenes painted over 100 years ago. There are also original pieces by owner Diane De Filipi's uncle. Needless to say, vintages of exceptional quality accompany the sumptuous meals, which are served by attentive and friendly staff. Historic St. Helena is only five minutes away with its museums and unique shops, teeming with curio. **Directions:** From San Francisco, take freeway 101 north to highway 37, and continue until highway 121. Take highway 29 north to Napa Valley and St. Helena. Price guide (incl. breakfast): Rooms $100–$205.

RED CASTLE INN HISTORIC LODGING

109 PROSPECT STREET, NEVADA CITY, CALIFORNIA 95959
TEL: 1 530 265 5135 FAX: 1 530 265 3560 USA: 800 761 4766

The intriguing name of this legendary hotel in Nevada City – known as the Queen City of the Northern Mines – is indicative that the ambiance is that of nostalgia for the gold rush '49ers. The house is exquisite, red brick and ornate white filigree paintwork, set against cedar trees. The interior reflects its fascinating past, the decor and furniture authentic to the era, and delightful memorabilia, paintings and books have been carefully researched and chosen. The gardens are terraced with fountains playing, and planted with traditional roses and honeysuckle. There are no televisions, old time traditions prevail and there are storytellers, sometimes music, and the art of conversation is cherished. The guest rooms are wonderfully romantic, with exquisite chintz and wallhangings, and open onto verandahs or the garden. The Red Castle is a 'B&B', it has no restaurant nor bar. Breakfast is a feast of old-fashioned dishes and homemade breads which guests enjoy in the 'grand parlour', garden or their rooms. A full Victorian afternoon tea is another delight. For those requiring something stronger, the local supplier will deliver. Picnics can be arranged by the creek and historic Nevada City is down the garden path. There is good skiing close by. **Directions:** Leave Highway 80 for 49 or 20. The Red Castle is two blocks from the town centre. Price guide: Rooms $115–$155; suite $110–$150; exclusive use $920.

THE WILLOWS

412 WEST TAHQUITZ CANYON WAY, PALM SPRINGS, CALIFORNIA 92262
TEL: 1 760 320 0771 FAX: 1 760 320 0780 TOLL FREE: 1 800 966 9597 E-MAIL: innkeeper@thewillowspalmsprings.com

The Willows is a delightful ochre stucco and red roofed, very private villa shaded by tall palm trees and overlooked by the heights of Mount San Jacinto from where a waterfall tumbles into a pool just outside the stone-floored dining room. Built in 1927 in the Old Palm Springs Village, The Willows has been meticulously restored to its former Mediterranean-style grandeur, refinement and elegance. The architecture is striking, with beautiful mahogany beams enhancing the great hall and frescoed ceilings on the cool veranda. Honeymooning film stars Clark Gable and Carole Lombard and the scientist Albert Einstein are amongst the many distinguished guests who have enjoyed the villa's luxurious ambience. The eight bedrooms are excellently furnished with antiques and sumptuous linens and have private baths, stone fireplaces, hardwood floors, garden patios and mountain views. Guests enjoy a full gourmet breakfast and afternoon hors d'oeuvres in the restful dining room. Excellent lunches and dinners prepared in a French restaurant opposite can be served in the villa. Energetic guests can walk an original stone path through a hillside garden to secluded lookouts to contemplate and view the sun-blanched surrounds. Others may want to just relax around the shaded swimming pool or take advantage of nearby tennis and golf facilities. **Directions:** From Los Angeles take Freeway 10 to 111, close by airport. Price guide: Rooms $250–$500; Summer rate $175–$375.

San Francisco

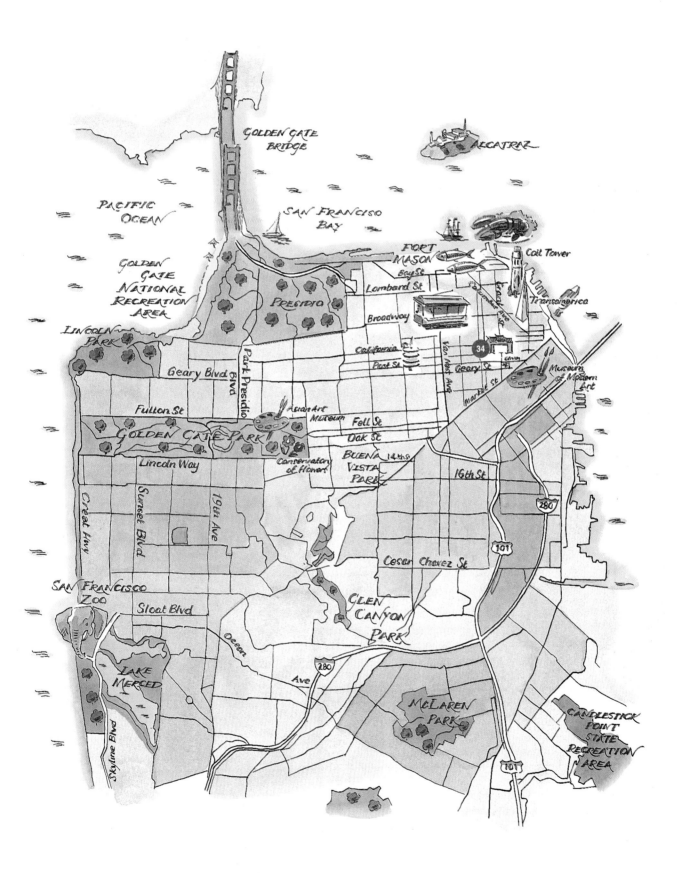

NOB HILL LAMBOURNE

725 PINE STREET, SAN FRANCISCO, CALIFORNIA 94108
TEL: 1 415 433 2287 FAX: 1 415 433 0975 US TOLL FREE: 1 800 274–8466 E-MAIL: nhl@jdv.com

Connoisseurs of hotel life call the downtown Nob Hill Lambourne "San Francisco's Healthiest Hotel" because of its collection of rejuvenating spa services and amenities which have left them feeling healthier than when they arrived. Its 20 luxurious and tastefully appointed bedrooms embody an innovative concept for both the leisure and business traveller. Each guest room and suite is designed to function as an office as well as an elegant place to spend the night. Each has a mini-kitchen and exotic bath bar, fax machine, voice mail, a complete library of San Francisco-based movies – and luxurious fluffy mattresses and down pillows which many guests insist on purchasing when checking out. Exercise equipment is in every suite, there is an Oriental-inspired spa treatment room, a variety of spa packages, aromatherapy bath amenities and a natural remedy bar for the ailing traveller. For all its executive and healthy living trimmings the Lambourne is far from computer driven. It has quiet, efficient service and stylish comfort. There is a relaxing lounge and breakfast room and although there is no restaurant, there are many dining areas close by. Valet car parking service. **Directions:** In downtown San Francisco within easy reach of the Powell Street and California St cable car routes. Price guide: Rooms $210–$220; suites $250–350.

GERSTLE PARK INN

34 GROVE STREET, SAN RAFAEL, CALIFORNIA 94901
TEL: 1 415 721 7611 FAX: 1 415 721 7600 US TOLL FREE: 1 800 726 7611 E-MAIL: innkeeper@gerstleparkinn.com

Set in the heart of Marin County, just 11 miles north of San Francisco, the Gerstle Park Inn is a truly breathtaking example of elegance and refinement nestled in a park-like setting amidst giant Redwoods. The historic San Rafael estate, over a hundred years old, continues to provide a beautiful location for those wishing to escape city life. The interior is a testament to exquisite taste, furnished luxuriously throughout with antiques and fine examples of both Oriental and Western art. The rooms are no less stunning, both in terms of spacious comfort and the numerous conveniences and amenities offered. Each room is en suite with its own private balcony; King suites have Jacuzzi tubs. Full gourmet breakfast is served in the dining room which overlooks the gardens through the arched windows. Guests may help themselves to various snacks throughout the day and are invited to mingle on the verandah with a glass of wine, served daily at 5.30pm. The croquet court, fruit orchard and superbly manicured gardens invite simple relaxation; other activities include to hiking, biking, a ferry trip on the Bay or Wine Country excursion. Downtown San Rafael is a only a short drive or leisurely stroll to shops, restaurants and theatres. **Directions:** From Highway 101, exit at Central San Rafael, go west on 4th Street, left on D Street, right on San Rafael Avenue, left onto Grove Street. Price guide (incl. breakfast): Suites $159–$220; cottages $179–$250.

WOOLLEY'S PETITE SUITES

2721 HOTEL TERRACE ROAD, SANTA ANA, CALIFORNIA 92705
TEL: 1 714 540 1111 FAX: 1 714 662 1643 E-MAIL: wps@petitesuites.com

Known locally as 'Orange County's best-kept secret', Woolley's Petite Suites is a well-situated hotel offering comfortable accommodation and value for money. Ideal for those wishing to explore the delights of California, many major tourist attractions are within the locality of this pleasant hotel. The accommodation comprises 183 junior suites, beautifully appointed with king-size beds, fold-out sofas and a thoughtful range of additional comforts. Cable television, a wet bar and a micro-kitchen all add to the home-away-from-home atmosphere. Children under twelve may stay in their parents room for free. A cooked breakfast is served in the bright, sunlit patio. Each evening over two hours, guests may gather and converse, sipping complimentary cocktails. Outdoor pursuits include fishing and sailing at Newport Beach harbour, golf and horse-riding nearby. A number of major attractions lie within easy driving distance such as Disneyland California, Knotts Berry Farm, South Coast Shopping Center and Newport Beach. **Directions:** Woolley's Petite Suites is conveniently located to the Orange County/John Wayne airport, just off the Newport Freeway 55. Price guide (incl. breakfast): Suite $89–$99.

BRIGADOON CASTLE

9036 ZOGG MINE ROAD, PO BOX 324, IGO, CALIFORNIA 96047
TEL: 1 530 396 2785 FAX: 1 530 396 2784 US TOLL FREE: 1 888 343 2836

Located in Shasta County in the northern reaches of California, Brigadoon Castle is at the centre of the region's most beautiful scenery. Voted one of the top 10 Inns of America 1998, this Elizabethan-style manor house is set amid 86 acres of mountain forest and meadow, making it a perfect choice for those seeking a quiet escape from modern day living. There are 5 rooms, each of them unique in its design and offering every imaginable comfort. In the two-level Tyler's Tree Top Room, for example, there is a spacious sitting room on the lower level, with a circular staircase leading up to a bedroom with ivy-covered arrow port windows and murals on the walls. The private bathroom features an Italian slab marble vanity and shower. The Bonny Jean Room provides exquisite accommodation with its Queen-sized, cast-iron bed and marble bath. French doors open on to a balcony with a gothic wrought-iron rail overlooking the gardens and forest. Offering the ultimate experience of seclusion is "The Cottage" guest house, which lies very close to the castle and looks out over mountain creek. A generous breakfast is provided, while weekend rates include a delicious dinner. **Directions:** From Sacramento and San Franciso take I-5 north. Take 299 west to Placer Road and go south to Igo. Straight at T-junction into Zogg Mine Road and proceed to castle gates. Price guide: Rooms $150–180; cottage suites $210–$285.

THE ALISAL GUEST RANCH & RESORT

1054 ALISAL ROAD, SOLVANG, CALIFORNIA 93463
TEL: 1 805 688 6411 FAX: 1 805 688 2510 US TOLL FREE: 1 800 425 4725 E-MAIL: sales@alisal.com

The Alisal Guest Ranch and Resort, operational since 1946, continues to run 2000 head of cattle on 10,000 acres of prime Californian land. This extraordinarily beautiful ranch, hidden in the Santa Ynez Valley with sycamores and oaks dotted around, is a paradise for any equestrian aficionado. The cottages are elegantly rustic, catering to the individual guest's every need. Designed in the traditional Californian ranch style, they include fine examples of Western art. All the cottages look out over impressive gardens and guests can simply lounge on the covered porches taking in the surroundings. Dinner is served in a spacious dining room, offering hearty meals prepared with the freshest ingredients. The generous portions are sure to satisfy the most voracious eater. If riding does not appeal, why not try a spot of fishing on the vast lake or enjoy a game of tennis and golf which are available with workshops open to people of all ages. The Alisal is truly a place worth visiting: the panoramic views, the exciting activities and the wholesome atmosphere combine to produce an experience one would find hard to forget. **Directions:** US Highway 101 from Los Angeles or San Francisco to Buellton and exit at Highway 246. Coming from north turn left from off ramp; from south turn right. Follow signs to Solvang, turn right on Alisal Road. Price guide (including breakfast & dinner): Rooms $355–$400; suite $410–$450.

THE FOXES BED & BREAKFAST

77 MAIN STREET, PO BOX 159, SUTTER CREEK, CALIFORNIA 95685
TEL: 1 209 267 5882 FAX: 1 209 267 0712 US TOLL FREE: 1 800 987 3344

Situated in the middle of historic Sutter Creek, one of California's most celebrated goldrush towns, The Foxes Inn is a Victorian edifice dating from the mid nineteenth century. Owners Pete and Min Fox, who have run the inn for nearly 20 years, offer visitors a unique blend of graceful hospitality in idyllic surroundings. The bedrooms are nothing short of sumptuous. Each spacious room has been individually designed and adorned with soft furnishings in rich warm colours and luxuriant bathtubs and/or showers. The Foxes Inn prides itself on the quality of its cooked-to-order breakfasts, which can be taken in the bedrooms or outside in the garden. Within walking distance of the inn is the heart of Sutter Creek whose bustling antique shops and boutiques reflect its origins as a trading post. It also boasts some of the finest museums and art galleries of the region, along with a vibrant theatrical community. Wine-lovers can visit the many family-owned vineyards dotted around the area. In nearby Jackson, the Amador County Museum recreates an era when adventurers came from far and wide to seek their fortune in the mines. Within easy driving distance is the Chaw'se Indian Grinding Rock Park, brimming with native American lore and artefacts. **Directions:** From Sacramento, take highway 16 to highway 49 and turn south. Price guide: Rooms $125–$165; suite $150–$195.

TALISKER.
A PLACE WHERE THE THUNDER ROLLS OVER YOUR TONGUE.

Of all the islands that defend Scotland's west coast from the Atlantic, Skye is the most dramatic. How fitting then that this is the home of the fiery Talisker. Standing on Skye's western shore, the distillery lies in the shadow of The Cuillins. Jagged mountains that rise out of the sea to skewer the clouds for a thunderous retort. In the shadow of these peaks, next to a fearsome sea, Talisker takes its first breath and draws it all in. Skye's explosive fervour captured forever in its only single malt. That Talisker is not a whisky for the faint-hearted is beyond dispute. Indeed even when one seasoned whisky taster once went as far as calling it "The lava of The Cuillins", no one disagreed.

Hawaii

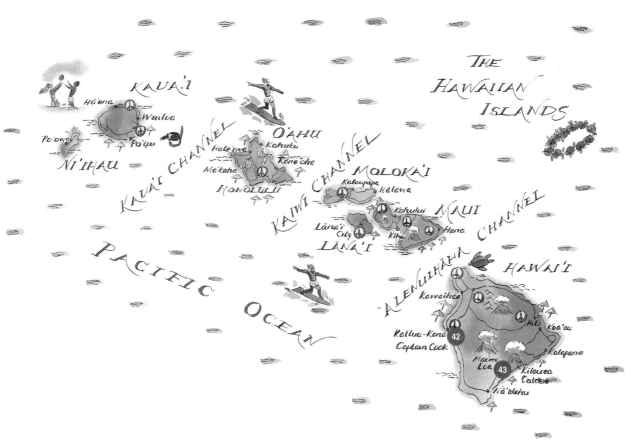

KAILUA PLANTATION HOUSE

75-5948 ALII DRIVE, KAILUA-KONA, HAWAII 96740
TEL: 1 808 329 3727 FAX: 1 808 326 7323

Set on the Pacific Coast and surrounded by all the wondrous beauty that Hawaii has to offer; the Kailua Plantation House is a friendly, intimate house providing quality service and luxuriant comfort to every guest. Set against the stunning backdrop of the ocean, where guests can watch whales basking in the waters, the house is spacious and inviting, tiled floors and simple colour schemes combining with plush furnishings to provide an atmosphere of complete relaxation. The rooms are each individually designed, and are as accommodating as they are convenient. Each has its own private balcony (known locally as 'lanai') offering superb views of the surrounding area. Each afternoon, visitors can sit back and relax whilst sipping on some refreshing wine, or reading one of the vast selection of books available and absorb the ambience of the unique surroundings. The hosts, John and Donna Strach will make each stay as care-free as possible and will advise on any matter, from what to do and where to do it, to the best place to sample the island's fine cuisine. At Kailua, fishing, sailing, diving or playing a round of golf may all be enjoyed nearby. Those wishing to explore can visit the volcanoes or wander around the exotic gardens. **Directions:** South on main coast highway from Kona Airport. Price guide (incl. breakfast): Rooms $160–$235.

CHALET KILAUEA – THE INN AT VOLCANO

BOX 998, WRIGHT ROAD, VOLCANO VILLAGE, HAWAI'I ISLAND 96785, HAWAII
TEL: 1 808 9677786 (OFF ISLAND TOLL FREE: 800 9377736) TOLL FREE FAX: 1 800 577 1849

Tucked away in the fern forest of Volcano Village – just a mile from the main entrance to Volcanoes National Park – stands Chalet Kilauea - The Inn at Volcano. This stylish cedar-shingled inn is set in lush landscaped gardens and offers the standard of amenities and hospitality only found in the world's most exclusive resorts. A multitude of treasures from around the globe are scattered throughout the spacious living areas and bedrooms. The latter are themed – 'Out of Africa' and 'Oriental Jade' feature marble bathrooms with Jacuzzi and indigenous artworks, while 'Continental Lace' has been decorated and furnished with honeymooners in mind. Original Turner and other examples of fine art adorn the 'Owner's Suite', while the 'Treehouse

Suite' is dominated by a spiral staircase. 'Hapu'u Forest Suite' is a separate, elegant, mountain cabin. All the bedrooms contain personal extra touches, including tropical flower arrangements and chocolates on the bed. Luxury is a byword, with the day starting off with a three-course candlelit gourmet breakfast and ending with star-gazing from the Jacuzzi, overlooking the gardens. A selection of 6 one or two bedroomed cottages and vacation homes are available for families, groups or those seeking a more private retreat. Activities include lava-viewing, biking, swimming and bird-watching. **Directions:** From Hilo Airport take highway to Hawaii Volcanoes National Park. Price guide: Homes $125–$225; rooms $135–$155; suites $175–$395.

PREFERRED PARTNERS

Preferred partners are those organisations specifically chosen and exclusively recommended by Johansens for the quality and excellence of their products and services for the mutual benefit of Johansens members, readers and independent travellers.

 Barrels & Bottles

 Classic Malts of Scotland

 Conqueror

 Dorlux

 Ercol Furniture Ltd

 Hildon Ltd

 Marsh UK Ltd

 Knight Frank International

 Honda (UK)

 Moët Hennessy

 Pacific Direct

Washington and Oregon

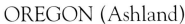

THE WINCHESTER COUNTRY INN

35 SOUTH SECOND STREET, ASHLAND, OREGON 97520
TEL: 1 541 488 1113 FAX: 1 541 488 4604 US TOLL FREE: 1 800 972 4991 E-MAIL: ashlandinn@aol.com

Tradition and elegance combine in the beauty of Oregon's stunning environment to produce a classic example of refinement and chic style; the Winchester Country Inn. This traditional Victorian stately home is in perfect harmony with its surroundings, situated in the midst of an English country garden in the heart of the USA. As guests approach the main building pansies line the path that leads to the front entrance, the gardens are encompassed by a herbaceous border whilst colourful tulips are scattered throughout the grounds. The interior is no less stunning, the rooms are a tribute to comfort and subtlety, with soft, warm shades and opulent furniture. Dinner may be taken in the popular restaurant, whilst in the summer, food is served outdoors. Wherever guests dine, the sumptuous flavours and textures are of the highest standards. The quaint gazebo is a perfect site for small weddings and receptions. Sporting activities available nearby include fishing, golf, ballooning or skiing while the more artistic guest may wish to visit the Ashland Shakespeare Festival or the Britt Music Festival, information on which may be obtained from the inn. **Directions:** Approx. 5 hours South from Portland, 6 hours North from San Francisco, 3 miles from I-5 East. Price guide (incl. breakfast): Rooms $105–$145; suite $145–$210.

THE CAMPBELL HOUSE – A CITY INN

252 PEARL STREET, EUGENE, OREGON 97401
TEL: 1 541 343 1119 FAX: 1 541 343 2258 US TOLL FREE: 1 800 264 2519

This is a large and gracious Victorian inn standing serenely in the heart of historic Eugene, midway between the majestic Cascade Mountain Range and the Pacific Ocean. Built in 1892, the property has been sympathetically restored in the tradition of a fine European hotel. The Campbell House has all the amenities the discerning traveller seeks: timeless elegance, tasteful décor and excellent service. The well-equipped bedrooms are all en suite, some offering a gas fireplace, four-poster bed, air conditioning and Jacuzzi. Complimentary coffee can be enjoyed in the guest rooms and wine is served in the hotel during the evenings. The hotel has a no-smoking policy. The Campbell House is within easy walking distance of a variety of excellent restaurants, antique shops and boutiques, the Hult Center for the Performing Arts and the bustling, 5th Street Public Market. For the more active, the renowned "Pre's Trail" jogging path is just half a mile away and there are many riverside paths for cyclists. Challenging whitewater rafting and several public golf courses are within easy reach. **Directions:** From I-5, exit at 194B. Follow Coburg Road-Downtown (Exit 2) City Center Mall signs to East 3rd Street to Pearl Street. Price guide: Rooms $80–$185; suites $159–$350.

COLUMBIA GORGE HOTEL

4000 WESTCLIFF DRIVE, HOOD RIVER, OREGON 97031-9970
TEL: 1 541 386 5566/1 800 345 1921 FAX: 1 541 387 5414 E-MAIL: cghotel@gorge.net

The mighty, snow-white craggy heights of Mount Hood soar majestically over this opulent hotel which is situated atop an ice cold waterfall tumbling 210 feet to the swirling Columbia River below. Huge firs enclose acres of landscaped gardens and grounds. It is a setting of unsurpassed beauty that has drawn thousands of visitors looking for a unique experience to the hotel: among them US Presidents Roosevelt and Coolidge and film star legends such as Myrna Loy, Jane Powell, Shirley Temple and Rudolph Valentino, after whom one of the elegant lounges is named. Opened in 1921 on the site of a former Indian meeting ground, the Columbia Gorge is a gracious, secluded and memorable retreat. All 40 en suite guest rooms are distinctive, featuring beautiful antique furniture and offering fine views. The speciality rooms have polished brass or canopy beds and some of the larger suites have open fireplaces. Dining is an impeccably serviced experience. Meals are a gastronomic delight and the restaurant has won many accolades including best breakfast and best restaurant in Oregon. Columbia Gorge has every sporting and leisure activity available. For the adventurous, there is mountain biking, windsurfing, fishing, rafting, skiing on Mount Hood, viewing the stars at Goldendale Observatory or touring Bonneville Dam. **Directions**: Take exit 62 off the I 84. Turn left and left again. The hotel is on the right. Price guide: Rooms $159–$279; speciality rooms $295–$365.

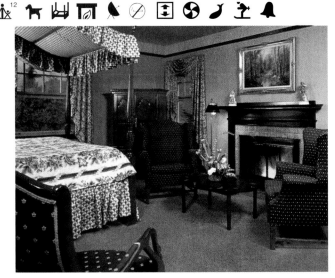

TURTLEBACK FARM INN

1981 CROW VALLEY ROAD, EASTSOUND, WASHINGTON 98245
TEL: 1 360 376 4914 FAX: 1 360 376 5329

Turtleback Farm stands in 80 acres of forest and farmland within the shadow of Turtleback Mountain on the island of Orcas, considered one of the loveliest of a chain dotting the sparkling waters of Washington State's San Juan archipelago. Fir trees frame open fields which produce hay for the resident sheep whose wool is made into guest-room comforters. Built in the late 1800s, this historic inn has been sympathetically renovated. While preserving the integrity and character of the original "Folk National" farmhouse, it has been enhanced by the addition of warm woods, a fresh, uncluttered décor and the 20th century amenities discerning guests expect. The living room has a

beautiful Rumford fireplace, comfortable seating and a games table. The large dining room has a convenient bar. Each bedroom has a private bath and is furnished with a blend of fine antiques and contemporary pieces. Breakfast is served in the polished wood floor dining room or on the expansive deck overlooking the picturesque valley below. New last year is the Orchard House, a separate barn-style building with four king-bedded rooms, complete with sitting and dining areas. **Directions:** Six miles from the ferry landing and four miles from Eastbound, the island's principal village. Price guide: Double from $70–$160; Single $10 less; The Orchard House $210.

ANN STARRETT MANSION

744 CLAY STREET, PORT TOWNSEND, WASHINGTON 98368
TEL: 1 360 385 3205 FAX: 1 360 385 2976 E-MAIL: edel@starrettmansion.com

The Ann Starrett Mansion is a wonderful place to stay for two special reasons; firstly it is a genuine old inn and secondly it houses an amazing accumulation of curios and objects of virtue. The building was erected in 1889 by George Starrett who gave it, as a wedding present, to his new bride Ann. On the outside she added gables, porches and an octagonal turret. She adorned the interior with the best and the latest features of the era. Today, the mansion is a beautifully preserved tribute to the gentle and cultured style of living at the turn of the last century. The intrinsic character of the bedrooms and suites is ornate and welcoming, the common rooms embellished with pictures and furnishings from an earlier golden age. Breakfast is a delight. On a rainy day you need never leave the mansion, as there is a fascinating collection of memorabilia to discover and to study. Port Townsend, with its host of excellent galleries, shops, museums, restaurants and after sundown night spots must be explored. Outside, there are challenges on the tennis court, on the golf course and at sea where you can go canoeing or even watch the whales in Puget Sound. **Directions:** 1½ hours from Seattle. Take Bainbridge Island ferry to the Olympic Peninsula, then SR305, SR3 and SR104 into Port Townsend. Price guide: Rooms $90–$225.

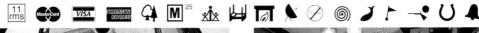

Seattle

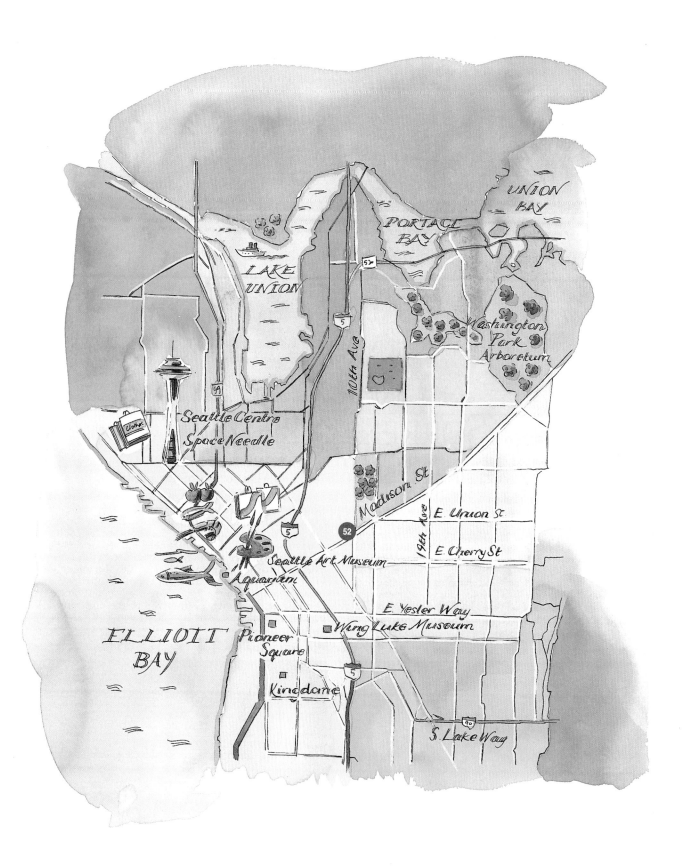

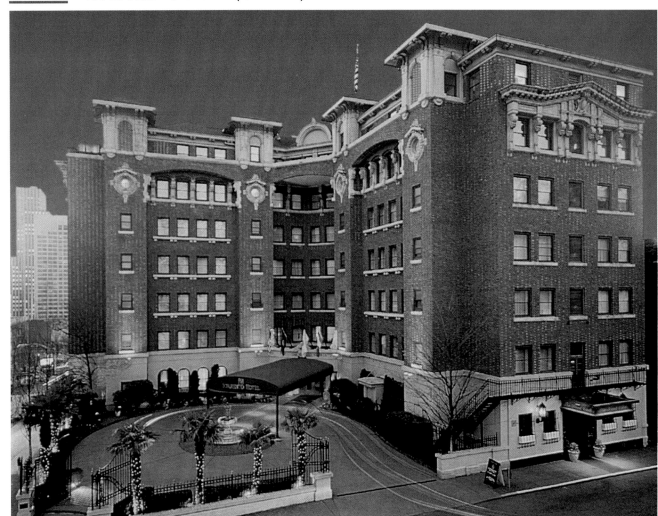

SORRENTO HOTEL

900 MADISON STREET, SEATTLE, WASHINGTON 98104–9742
TEL: 1 206 622 6400 FAX: 1 206 343 6155 E-MAIL: sorrento@earthlink.net

The name Sorrento conjures up elegant Italy and this elite hotel in the centre of Seattle meets such expectations. New arrivals enter through wrought iron gates flanked by palm trees and drive past a decorative fountain to reach the grand portico of this graceful curved establishment with its fin de siècle embellishments. This hotel, renowned for its courteous staff and impeccable style, has a subtle European influence – the tiled murals over a fireplace, flowers in the niche of a brick wall, the charming patio at the back of the building, a "je ne sais quoi" which adds to its charm. The guest rooms are luxurious, traditional mahogany furniture and gorgeous fabrics side by side with high technology – with oversized bath towels and bed-warmers among the many lavish comforts! Peaceful afternoon tea in the attractive Fireside Room or sophisticated cocktails in the fashionable Bar end the day before dining superbly in the Hunt Club Restaurant, delightfully evocative of Tuscany. Special celebrations or distinguished corporate events are held in the exciting Top of the Town Room. The hotel has complimentary town cars to the waterfront, Pike Place Market and the convention centre. Boat trips round the harbour are fun – in the hotel there is a Nautilus fitness centre. **Directions:** Interstate 5 brings you to the city centre. Valet parking. Price guide: Rooms $195–$240; suite $240–$1600.

Colorado, Wyoming and Utah

CASTLE MARNE

1572 RACE STREET, DENVER, COLORADO 80206
TEL: 1 303 331 0621 FAX: 1 303 331 0623 US TOLL FREE: 1 800 926 2763 E-MAIL: info@castlemarne.com

Historic Castle Marne, a Victorian property transformed into a bed and breakfast inn, is both charming and elegant with a unique atmosphere. Many vestiges of the castle's past are scattered throughout the rooms such as hand-rubbed woods, family heirlooms and ornate fireplaces. Following a careful restoration, original features dominate the interior, which is enhanced by rococo gilt mirrors and fine antiques. The individually decorated bedrooms are stylish and display nuances of the period. Guests are made to feel extremely welcome by the friendly and hospitable owners. The comfortable parlour is ideal for reclining and reading a book beside the beautifully carved fireplace. Special private six-course candlelight dinners can be arranged. Guests may indulge in scrumptious breakfasts and afternoon tea. House specialities include stuffed tomato with egg and spinach purée topped with parmesan and Jack cheeses and the home-baked cakes and biscuits at teatime are a delight to the palate. There are several museums and historic sites clustered around the area. Other attractions include the zoo, botanical gardens or perusing the shops at 'Cherry Creek'. **Directions:** From DIA, Pena Boulevard head to I–70 west, exit Quebec Street. Travel south (left) to 17th Avenue, turning right to York Street. Turn left into 16th Avenue and then right into Race Street. Price guide: Rooms $90–$195; suite $235.

TALL TIMBER

1 SILVERTON STAR, DURANGO, COLORADO 81301
TEL: 1 970 259 4813

Before reaching Tall Timber, which can only be accessed by a narrow gauge train, visitors must pass through some of the most rugged countryside in the United States. Passing through the Canyon del Rio Las Animas Perdidos is an experience that reanimates the soul, as verdant forest and stark granite canyons crowd the eye's view. Surrounded by the dense San Juan National Forest, Tall Timber is comprised of a series of luxurious two-storey apartments, each with their own living room featuring a stone fireplace and balcony. International cuisine is served in truly sublime surroundings. Silverware, fine china and cut crystal adorn the tables, each of which has a breathtaking view of the forest sweeping out into the distance. With no telephones, radios or televisions in this idyllic hideaway, visitors can truly regain their oneness with nature. The air at Tall Timber, which is 7,500 feet above sea level, is almost as intoxicating as the natural beauty of the surroundings. Visitors can pass the day hiking along mountain trails or horse riding through the luscious forest. Tall Timber also offers exceptional trout fishing, as well as white water rafting. Visitors of a less active persuasion can bathe in the heated pool, or at the base of a nearby waterfall. Hot therapeutic spas and professional massages are also available. **Directions:** The hotel can only be accessed by the train or helicopter. Price guide: Rooms $1550–$3200; suite $1950–$4400.

THE INN ON CAPITOL HILL

225 NORTH STATE STREET, SALT LAKE CITY, UTAH 84103
TEL: 1 801 575 1112 FAX: 1 801 933 4957 US TOLL FREE: 1 888 843466 E-MAIL: reservations@utahinn.com

Situated in Utah's famous Salt Lake City, this guest house is an exquisite example of the pioneer era and has been lovingly restored by the owners, Marla and Dan Oredson to reflect the early part of the century when Utah was known as Deseret. The antique furnishings, hand-rubbed wood panels, rich jewel-toned Oriental carpets and lace window coverings are reminiscent of a time when gracious hospitality reigned. Elegance and comfort are the key notes. Displayed throughout the house are 41 framed historic photographs, reminding visitors of a bygone era. Guests relax in the music room with hand-painted wallpaper and two antique pianos or in the parlour with its intricate tapestry sofas. Each bedroom has been individually decorated representing a period in Utah history. The Ute room is furnished in the style of a Native American tribute and the Pioneer room features a carved pine headboard and wagon wheel chandelier. Many of the rooms feature fireplaces, balconies and patios. All rooms are fully equipped with private bathrooms, jetted tubs and queen or king beds. The Inn is the perfect place for weddings, family or business meetings, newlyweds, anniversaries or anyone with a penchant for early 1900s elegance. Downtown, State Capitol, Temple Square and an array of shops are only two blocks away. **Directions:** From Airport take North Temple to State Street, then turn left on State one block up on the left. Price guide (incl. breakfast): Rooms $119–$229.

LA EUROPA ROYALE

1135 EAST VINE STREET, SALT LAKE CITY, UTAH 84121
TEL: 1 801 263 7999 FAX: 1 801 263 8090 US TOLL FREE: 1 800 5238767 E-MAIL: tflynn@laeuropa.com

This recently opened small hotel in the heart of the Salt Lake Valley is as exquisite a hotel as one could hope to find. Set amidst two acres of superbly managed land, the hotel is nestled amongst landscaped gardens, ponds, flowers, trees and fountains, all combining to provide a veritable feast for the senses. Once inside, the hotel continues to impress with huge open rooms and comfortable yet elegant furniture. Subtle and refreshing colours are omnipresent. The public rooms are bedecked with artwork collectables from Europe and South America. The guest rooms offer comfort amidst style and are enhanced by gorgeous fireplaces, whilst the bathrooms feature whirlpool tubs and separate showers. The dining room is a delectable arena in which to enjoy food that is as tasty as one would expect from a hotel of this standard. There is a veritable plethora of activities at La Europa Royale from walking around the exquisite grounds to indulging in a spot of skiing on any of the numerous slopes that are only a half an hour's drive away. For those who would rather take a look around the city, the hotel is only 15 minutes from the city centre where one can visit Temple Square or enjoy the theatre or any of the concerts that regularly take place. **Directions:** From airport take I-215 Freeway south, Exit 9 to 6600 South, right to 1300 East, left to Vine Street 6090 South, left to 1135. Price guide (incl. breakfast): Rooms $155–$235.

NAGLE WARREN MANSION

222 EAST 17TH STREET, CHEYENNE, WYOMING 82001
TEL: 1 307 637 3333 FAX: 1 307 638 6879 US TOLL FREE: 1 800 811 2610

One of Cheyenne's most stylish residences, the Nagle Warren Mansion is steeped in a rich and interesting history. Built in 1888 by Erasmus Nagle, the mansion was home to Francis E. Warren, Governor and Wyoming Senator. Set on the edge of downtown Cheyenne, the elegant Victorian décor is complemented by the fine craftsmanship of a bygone era. Vestiges of the past are evident as guests walk up the ornate wooden staircases admiring the authentic period touches. Antique furnishings abound throughout the mansion. In the 12 bedrooms, the contemporary guests' needs have been met with each room offering air conditioning, telephone and colour television. The delicious breakfast includes freshly baked muffins and special recipes by the cook are a daily treat. Guests can spend the day hiking through mountains after which the outdoor hot tub is most inviting! Set in an enclosed gazebo, it will delight guests regardless of the season. Less strenuous pastimes include shopping or exploring historic Cheyenne. **Directions:** From I-25 proceed to I-80 east, leave at Exit 362. If you are eastbound turn left on Central, if westbound turn right. Price guide (incl. breakfast): Rooms $95–$125; suite $125–$150.

THE ALPENHOF LODGE

TETON VILLAGE, JACKSON HOLE, WYOMING 83025
TEL: 1 307 733 3242 FAX: 1 307 739 1516 US TOLL FREE: 1 800 732 3244 E-MAIL: alpenhof@rmisp.com

It is delightful to find this Four Diamond Bavarian hotel at the foot of the Teton mountains, adjacent to the ski-lifts in the heart of Jackson Hole, the popular Wyoming ski resort – close to the small town of Jackson in an area busy throughout the year with visitors to Yellowstone National Park and the scene of Wild West rodeos and shoot-outs in summer. The Alpenhof Lodge is a traditional chalet, with its wooden façade, window boxes and shutters. The elegant interior displays many fine examples of Bavarian wood-carving. The welcoming reception area is filled with flowers; the staff are friendly and helpful. Hand-built furniture from Europe features in many of the spacious, light and airy bedrooms – some with balconies. Efficient bathrooms ensure that plenty of hot water is available after a hard day's skiing or hiking. Expansive windows, sun terrace and warm fireplace are dominant upstairs in the Alpenhof Bistro serving the best lunches, après-ski snacks and drinks and creative dinners. Downstairs, the elegant Alpenhof Dining Room, Jackson Hole's only 4 star restaurant, is renowned for its gourmet menu, including wild game and award-winning wine list. In winter, alternatives to skiing are snow mobiles into Yellowstone and sleigh rides through the Elk Refuge. In summer, ballooning, golf, hiking, fishing, river rafting, climbing, riding and swimming. **Directions:** Jackson Hole is signed from Highway 22. Price guide: Room $128 suite $488.

As recommended

Michigan and Wisconsin

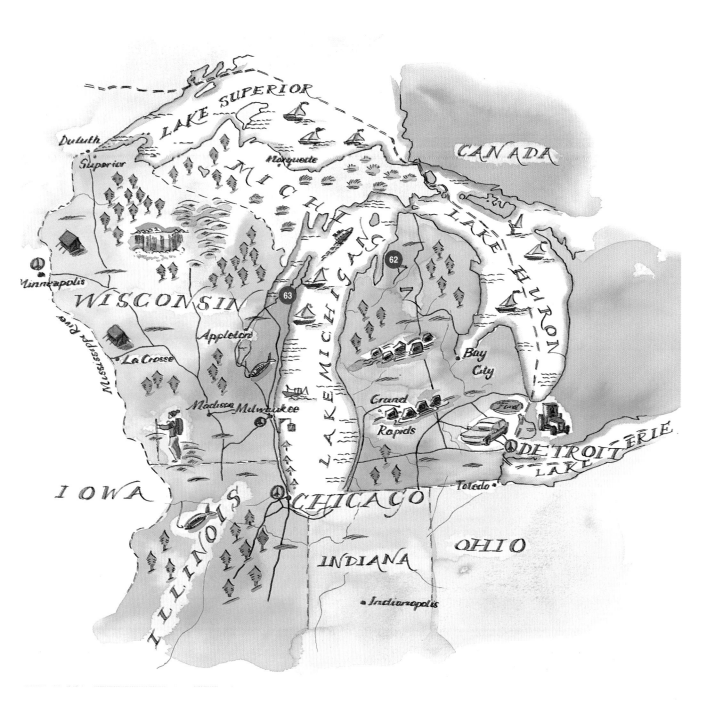

STAFFORDS PERRY HOTEL

BAY AT LEWIS STREET, PETOSKEY, MICHIGAN 49770
TEL: 1 231 347 4000 FAX: 1 231 347 0636 US TOLL FREE: 1 800 737 1899 E-MAIL: perry@northlink.net

Petoskey is a small city on Lake Michigan's Little Traverse Bay. It has a fin de siècle appeal, with its Victorian street lamps and elaborate summer homes built by the Midwestern tycoons of that era. Particularly fascinating is the Gaslight District, – the artists' quarter, abounding with galleries, boutiques and home to The Perry Hotel. This attractive residence has a graceful facade, with a grand entrance, a verandah, a Rose Garden and spectacular views over the Bay. The charming guest rooms – some with balconies – are decorated with floral drapes and wallpapers, the furniture blending perfectly. The bathrooms are modern. Guests rendezvous in the elegant Victorian Salon for evening drinks, enjoyed on the verandah in clement weather. Meals are served in the uniquely named H.O. Rose Room, a sophisticated restaurant facing the Lake, where a pianist plays at weekends. The imaginative cosmopolitan menu includes American 'comfort foods'. Over 100 excellent wines are listed. Informal meals, beer and good jazz or folk music can be found in the basement Noggin Room Pub. This is a golfer's paradise, with 8 challenging courses nearby. Excursions to Mackinac Island and Tahquamenon Falls are entertaining. Visitors enjoy the beaches in summer and ski in winter. **Directions:** Leave the US31 at Lewis Street. Ample parking. Price guide: Rooms $75–$185.

INN AT CEDAR CROSSING

336 LOUISIANA STREET, STURGEON BAY, WISCONSIN 54235
TEL: 1 920 743 4200 FAX: 1 920 743 4422 E-MAIL: innkeeper@innatcedarcrossing.com

Built in 1884, the Inn at Cedar Crossing is the result of careful restoration, carried out with sensitivity and enthusiasm. Listed on the National Historic Register, this charming inn reveals its past in the open banister staircase, pressed tin ceilings and a majestic fireplace. Despite its age, however, the inn offers every modern comfort and amenity. Each of the nine bedrooms is furnished with interesting antiques and ornaments and many offer a fireplace, double whirlpool tub or both. The exquisite taste of the inn's owners is much in evidence in the choice of beautiful décor, fabrics and wallpapers. Hearty breakfasts, generous lunches, and dinners featuring imaginative local cuisine, are all served in the elegant dining rooms, reminiscent of the Victoria era. Specialising in fresh fish and seafood, the dinner menu includes roast duck confit cassonlet, chile pepper ravioli, rock shrimp with linguine, and nightly fresh catch. Muffins, scones and coffee cakes, served straight from the oven, and some of the many luscious desserts are designed to please those with a sweet tooth. An impressive wine list features both New World and Continental vintages. While Sturgeon Bay has plenty to offer, including interesting boutiques, galleries and museums, further afield lies the enthralling beauty of Door County with its superb and varied landscape. **Directions**: From Milwaukee north on I43 rte 57N to Sturgeon Bay. Price guide: Rooms $99–$169.

MARSH
An **MMC** Company

Marsh, the world's leading insurance broker, is proud to be the appointed Preferred Insurance Provider to Johansens Members Worldwide

ARE YOU A HOTELIER?

There is never a spare moment when you're running a Hotel, Inn, Restaurant or Country House. If you're not with a customer, your mind is on stocktaking. Sound familiar?

At Marsh, we realise you have little time to worry about your insurance policy, instead, you require peace of mind that you are covered.

That is why for over 20 years Marsh have been providing better cover for businesses like yours.

Our unique services are developed specifically for establishments meeting the high standards required for entry in a Johansens guide.

CONTACT US NOW FOR DETAILS OF THE INSURANCE POLICY FOR JOHANSENS

01892 553160 (UK)

Insurance Policy for Johansens members arranged by:
Marsh UK Ltd.
Mount Pleasant House,
Lonsdale Gardens,
Tunbridge Wells, Kent TN1 1NY

ARE YOU AN INDEPENDENT TRAVELLER?

Insurance is probably the last thing on your mind. Especially when you are going on holiday or on a business trip. But are you protected when travelling? Is your home protected while you are away?

Marsh offer a wide range of insurances that gives you peace of mind when travelling.

FOR DETAILS ON THESE SERVICES RING (UK):

TRAVEL	**01462 428041**
PENSIONS & FINANCIAL SERVICES	**0171 357 3307**
HOUSEHOLD	**01462 428200**
MOTOR	**01462 428100**
HEALTHCARE	**01462 428000**

Louisiana and Mississippi

MADEWOOD PLANTATION HOUSE

4250 HIGHWAY 308, NAPOLEONVILLE, LOUISIANA 70390
TEL: 1 504 369 7151 FAX: 1 504 369 9848 E-MAIL: madewoodpl@aol.com

Madewood, a great plantation house in Louisiana, has been so authentically restored that several films have been made with the mansion in the star role. A National Historic Landmark, its beauty is accentuated by its setting – extensive parkland encompasses the original slave quarters, kitchen and family graveyard. The classic façade, with its pillars, is magnificent and the interior has the same aristocratic grace. Guests stay in one of the original bedchambers in the main house, where modern facilities blend harmoniously with period antiques whilst retaining the character of the house. Here you will experience a refreshing return to the art of conversation, as there are no televisions or telephones in the bedrooms. Non-smoking prevails throughout. Original artworks from the owner's collection are omnipresent, particularly in the drawing room with its exquisite pieces. Residents gather in the handsome Library at 6.00pm for a preprandial wine and cheese, before a Southern-style dinner, round the immense oak table. Coffee and brandy are served in the Parlour, where guests mingle and converse. Exploring the Bayou country, boat trips down the Mississippi and antique-hunting in shops along the Bayou are popular pastimes. **Directions:** I–10 West, exit 182, cross Sunshine Bridge, then Highway 70 to Spur 70, signed Bayou Plantations. Left for 1 mile then left onto Highway 308. The house is 2.2 miles south of Napoleonville. Price guide (2 persons incl dinner): Rooms $225.

New Orleans

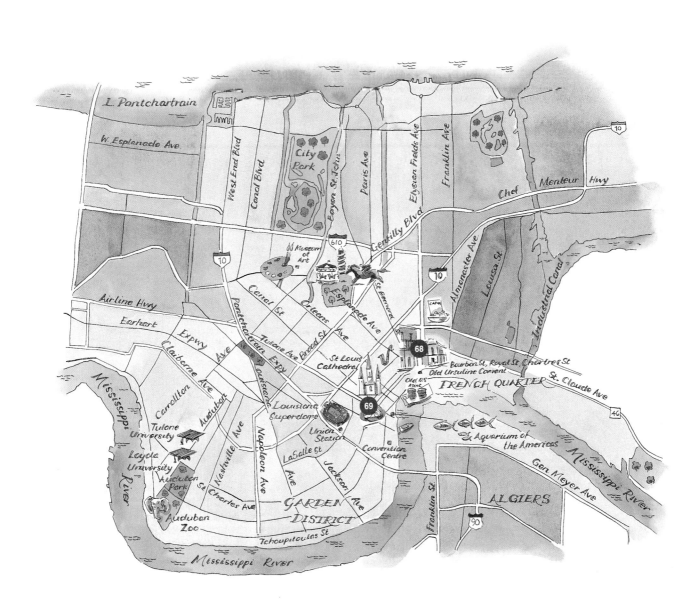

THE CLAIBORNE MANSION

2111 DAUPHINE STREET, NEW ORLEANS, LOUISIANA 70116
TEL: 1 504 949 7327 FAX 1 504 949 0388

This historic, cream and white hotel with its attractive ironwork is situated overlooking the greenery of Washington Square Park in the popular and vibrant French Quarter of New Orleans. Surrounded by art galleries, jazz clubs and restaurants, it has been tastefully restored to its original 1850's Greek Revival style and is listed in the national historic register as an outstanding example of the American-plan house in an urban setting. Its rooms are high and spacious and the décor and furnishings exquisite. Ambience is old world yet upbeat like a jazz ensemble, echoing all that is unique in New Orleans, offering visitors 19th century elegance and style with 20th century comforts and amenities. Soft, comfortable sofas and armchairs, highly polished wooden floors, richly patterned curtains and gentle colourings contribute to a homely, friendly and sophisticated atmosphere. Owner Cleo Pelleteri's attitude is free and easy. Guests may come and go as they please and are even encouraged to tell her when they feel like having their breakfast served. The five spacious en suite bedrooms and two suites are beautifully furnished and have large tester beds. All the facilities are individually controlled including the air conditioning. Guests can relax and enjoy the sunshine in a little garden which surrounds a secluded pool. There is also an adjoining small cottage for those seeking extra privacy. **Directions**: The inn is just off Elysian Field, facing Washington Square. Price guide: Rooms $150–$300.

WINDSOR COURT HOTEL

300 GRAVIER STREET, NEW ORLEANS, LOUISIANA 70130
TEL: 1 504 523 6000 FAX: 1 504 596 4513

This award winning hotel offers the most impeccable service you could hope to receive. The hotel has a British theme, hence its name, and the reception rooms are adorned with magnificent works of art. The majority of guest rooms are suites and are stylishly furnished with thick carpets, subtle fabrics and every possible amenity. The marble bathrooms are spacious and feature an array of toiletries and fluffy towels. The stunning open air pool on the fourth floor is ideal for relaxing after a long day whilst the more energetic may wish to make use of the well-equipped fitness centre. The Grill Room is presided over by a French chef who prepares exciting dishes which fuse the finest European flavours with the regional produce of the South. The hotel is beside the French Quarter, with its attractive architecture and maze of interesting streets which are filled with antique shops, galleries, boutiques and curio. New Orleans is a wonderful area with a great variety of attractions. The lively nightlife may be experienced in the many jazz clubs, bars and restaurants. For those who wish to explore further afield there is the Bayou region and a fine array of plantation houses, for which the South is famous. **Directions:** Take I–10, east to downtown, Superdome exit (234B exit), right on Poydras Street, down 1 mile, left on South Peters (2nd to last traffic light before Mississippi River), 1 block down, take left onto Gravier Street and left into the hotel courtyard. Price guide: Rooms $250; suite $340–$675.

FATHER RYAN HOUSE INN

1196 BEACH BOULEVARD, BILOXI, MISSISSIPPI 39530
TEL: 1 228 435 1189 FAX: 1 228 436 3063 E-MAIL: fryan@fryan.wm

Overlooking the brilliant white sand of the Mississippi Gulf Coast, the Father Ryan House is a luxurious inn dating from the 19th century, that simply exudes history. Named after former resident Father Abraham Ryan, Poet Laureate of the Confederacy, the inn has an appropriately magical feel reflecting its imperious past. Assiduously restored to its former splendour, it offers fifteen individually decorated rooms bedecked with antiques and paraphernalia of historical note. From the balconies of the suites visitors enjoy magnificent views of Gulf of Mexico or relax in their own individual whirpool. Some of the most impressive features of the rooms and suites at the House include hand-crafted beds, handmade needlework carpets and antiques dating from the 1800s. Father Ryan House provides quiet and contemplative surroundings. Visitors can swim in the pool, stroll on the beach or relax in the lush landscaped gardens. The more active will want to avail of the historic home of Jefferson Davis in nearby Beauvoir, or take a trip to Fort Massachusetts. There is also excellent shrimp fishing off the Gulf Coast, which has 18 championship standard golf courses. **Directions:** From New Orleans, take exit 46-A off the Interstate-10. Turn left onto highway 90. Father Ryan House is six blocks west. Price guide: Double $100–$175, suites from $165.

FAIRVIEW INN

734 FAIRVIEW STREET, JACKSON, MISSISSIPPI 39202
TEL: 601 948 3429 FAX: 601 948 1203 TOLL FREE: 888 948 1908

This gracious pillared white house with its sweeping driveway and beautifully landscaped gardens is reminiscent of George Washington's Mount Vernon residence. Situated in the exclusive Belhaven District of Jackson, it is a grand Colonial Revival house listed in the National Register of Historic Places. From the moment guests step into the traditional hallway, the charm and luxurious atmosphere of this property is apparent, with reception rooms to left and right, sparkling chandeliers and polished wooden floors scattered with antique rugs. The Simmons family has owned the house since 1930: there are old family portraits, photographs and crests tracing the history of the family name. The house has two luxurious bedrooms and six opulent suites. All incorporate the original characteristics of 1908 when the house was built combined with every accessory and comfort that today's visitor expects. Two of the suites are very private and have their own entrances and car parking. There is a large, elegant dining room where co-owner Carol Simmons and her French chef serve excellent gourmet meals. The hotel is close to the centre of Jackson and its historical attractions, art galleries, museums and theatres. **Directions:** From I-55 exit at 98A into Woodrow Wilson Drive. Turn left at the second traffic lights into North State Street and Fairview Street is first left after the second traffic lights. Price guide: Rooms $115; suite $165.

THE DUFF GREEN MANSION

1114 FIRST EAST STREET, VICKSBURG, MISSISSIPPI 39180
TEL: 1 601 636 6968 FAX: 1 601 661 0079

A long, wide stairway leads onto the wrought-iron fenced porch fronting the white doorway of this magnificent mansion situated in the historic district of Vicksburg. Considered to be one of the finest examples of Palladian architecture in the State, it escaped destruction during and after the Civil War's siege by serving as a hospital for Confederate and Union soldiers. Beneath its high ceilings and richly decorated walls of cardinal reds, deep blues and rich greens the polished floors carry bloodstained marks from wounds. In one room, the ceiling beams show where a cannon-ball struck. Original works of art hang throughout and most of the furniture is antique. Duff Green contains four luxurious bedrooms with amenities to satisfy the expectations of the most discerning visitor. All have an individual character, open fireplaces and porches where guests can relax in the evening air. Guests may also enjoy the free bar in one of the charming reception rooms and during the day can sunbathe on the secluded patio surrounds of a swimming pool. Vicksburg is famous for its battlefield where Civil War skirmishes are re-enacted. **Directions:** From Jackson, take I-20 west and exit at 4B into Clay Street. After approximately 2½ miles turn into Cherry Street. First East Street is on the right. Price guide: Rooms $85–$125.

Florida, Georgia and South Carolina

CHATTANOOGA

Charlotte

Blue Ridge Mountains

SOUTH

CAROLINA

ATLANTA

Dance

94

93 Charleston

91

89

87 86

88 Savannah

GEORGIA

84

83

82

Pensacola

90

JACKSONVILLE

Tallahassee

Lake City

Apalachee Bay

F L O R I D A

Disney World

ORLANDO

Cape Canaveral

79

TAMPA

76

Everglades

75 Fort Lauderdale

80 MIAMI

81

Key West

77

78

Florida Keys

74

HAWK'S CAY RESORT

61, HAWK'S CAY BOULEVARD, DUCK KEY, FLORIDA 33050–3756
TEL: 1 305 743 7000 FAX: 1 305 743 2805 E-MAIL: reservations@hawkscay.com

Watch the sun go down across the marina and absorb the panoramic views of the resort's magnificent surroundings. Hawk's Cay Resort is situated on Duck Key, which provides guests with relaxing scenery and a tranquil ambience. Accommodation comprises quaint cottages in a delicate shade of rose pink or island-style inn. There is a wide array of activities, both on or off site and entertainment includes sports such as tennis, fishing and golf. Water sports include snorkelling, glass-bottom boating and kayaking excursions. Young ones can join the Kids Island Adventure Club and have fun whilst being educated about marine life and the environment. They can participate in interactive dolphins programs, play in the sand, paint and sail, leaving their parents to relax with the knowledge that their children are being supervised within the safety of the site. The breakfast buffet at Palm Terrace is guaranteed to satisfy the largest appetite whilst taste buds are treated to a gourmet experience at the resort's excellent restaurants, offering Italian, Mexican and seafood. **Directions:** Hawk's Cay Resort is 90 miles south of Miami and 60 miles (98 km) north of Key West. Accessible from the Overseas Highway, the island of Duck Key is situated between Islamorada and Marathorn. Price guide: Rooms $180–$375; suite $325–$850; villas $275–$475.

LAGO MAR

1700 SOUTH OCEAN LANE, FORT LAUDERDALE, FLORIDA 33316
TEL: 1 954 523 6511 FAX: 1 954 524 6627 E-MAIL: reservations@lagomar.com

The traditional legacy of warmth and hospitality combined with excellent service has continued through three generations of the Banks family, resulting in a most charming property. The gardens are enchanting with palm trees, a lagoon pool with arched footbridge and beautiful colours emanating from the hibiscus, alamanda and bougainvillaea. The spacious bedrooms are the essence of luxury, affording views over the ocean, lake or gardens. Comfortable furnishings and dining areas are complemented by the vast range of modern amenities. The attractive Lounge is enhanced by hand-painted table tops and an elegant grand piano and is often frequented by those seeking a pre-dinner drink. Continental and American cuisine with a hint of Caribbean flavours can be savoured in the formal restaurant or enjoyed in the coffee shop, grill or terrace. Sports enthusiasts will enjoy the two swimming pools, miniature golf course and two tennis courts, overlooking the ocean. Water-taxis are available to take guests to the many nearby attractions. The cruise ships at Port Everglades, the Convention Center and many major sports venues are within easy reach. South Florida is surrounded by several fine restaurants, amusement parks and exquisite shops. **Directions:** The hotel is just 10 minutes away from Fort Lauderdale's International Airport. Price guide: Rooms $110–$235; suite $145–$675.

HARRINGTON HOUSE BEACHFRONT BED & BREAKFAST

5626 GULF DRIVE, HOLMES BEACH, FLORIDA 34217
TEL: 1 941 778 5444 FAX: 1 941 778 0527 US TOLL FREE: 1 888 828 5566 E-MAIL: harhousebb@mail.pcsonline.com

This paradisiacal island, known as Anna Maria, is renowned for its glorious sunsets, pure sands and is surrounded by the warm waters of the Gulf of Mexico. Harrington House is a charming beachfront property built in the 1925 Coquina style with good accommodation and a fine standard of service. The 13 air conditioned bedrooms have been lovingly restored and feature private baths, cable television and many thoughtful extras. Most of the rooms are enhanced by French doors opening onto balconies from where guests may bask in the sun and admire the views. A full island breakfast comprises delights such as strawberry pancakes and fresh fruit platters. There is an intimate gazebo nestling on the beach where sun-gazers recline with a basket of popcorn or some home-baked cookies and enjoy the ambience of this tropical hideaway. Guests may saunter along the sandy white beaches, enjoy free use of kayaks and bicycles and frolic in the waters with the dolphins. The nearby towns of Sarasota and Bradenton have many places of interest including Ringling Museum of Art, Selby Botanical Gardens and Bishop Planetarium. Major tourist attractions such as Walt Disney World, Epcot Centre and Sea World are within a two hour drive of the house. **Directions:** Take route 64 to route 789 Holmes Beach. Price guide (incl. breakfast): Rooms $129–$239.

ISLAND CITY HOUSE

411 WILLIAM STREET, KEY WEST, FLORIDA 33040
TEL: 1 800 634 8230/305 294 5702 FAX: 1 305 294 1289

150 miles south of Miami in Old Town Key West you will find one of the oldest operating guest houses on the island; the Island City House Hotel. Adorned with coconut palms and steeped in history, the hotel consists of three historic buildings; the Island City House mansion, the Arch House and the Cigar House, joined by lush tropical gardens with winding brick walkways throughout. The large pool with tile alligator and the Jacuzzi provide ideal places to laze in the sun and relax. The hotel offers 24 one and two bedroom parlour suites featuring beautiful antiques, wood floors and ceiling fans. A complimentary Continental island buffet is served in the garden daily. The friendly and attentive staff will be happy to recommend restaurants, places of interest and shops on Duval Street or arrange snorkelling trips to the island's reef, sunset sails, kayak eco-tours and many other activities. Those who wish to explore the island on their own may hire bikes from the property itself. **Directions:** Arrive at Key West on US1, right onto Roosevelt Blvd, right onto Palm Avenue and continue until the road becomes Eaton Street, left on William Street. Price guide: Suites $115–$240. Children under 12 stay free.

SIMONTON COURT HISTORIC INN & COTTAGES

320 SIMONTON STREET, KEY WEST, FLORIDA 33040
TEL: 1 305 294 6386 FAX: 1 305 293 8446 US TOLL FREE: 1 800 944 2687

Two acres of landscaped private grounds and the fragrant scent of tropical flowers blooming beneath gently swaying palms greet visitors to serene and secluded Simonton Court. Situated in the heart of Old Town it was formerly a cigar factory. Now it is the personification of elegance, charm and service, a welcoming haven of relaxation. The Court consists of a two-storey inn, manor house, mansion, townhouse suites and six beautifully restored and furnished cottages built in 1880 as homes for the factory workers. The cottages retain their original charm but have all modern amenities. A brick walkway connects the cottages as it runs through the colourful, flower-filled gardens which feature four pools, a hot tub and twinkling lattern illumination at night. The variety of accommodation comprises luxurious suites and guest rooms, each with every comfort from a queen or king-size bed to air-conditioning and microwave. Many have a Jacuzzi, private porch or sun deck. Simonton Court is only one block from Duval Street with its popular boutiques, galleries, restaurants, clubs and pubs. The beach and harbour are within a short walk. Adults only, over the age of 18. **Directions:** Take US Highway 1 to Key West and then follow Roosevelt Boulevard to Truman Avenue. Turn right on Simonton Street and continue to Eaton Street. Simonton Court is on the left just past the Eaton Street intersection. Price guide: Rooms $125–$435; cottages $235–$435.

CHALET SUZANNE

3800 CHALET SUZANNE DRIVE, LAKE WALES, FLORIDA 33853–7060
TEL: 1 941 676 6011 FAX: 1 941 676 1814 E-MAIL: info@chaletsuzanne.com

This is a small part of heaven in Central Florida – a Swiss oasis! This enchanting small hotel stands in 70 acres of parkland and tropical trees. It has been brilliantly designed, a series of chalets round a paved courtyard ensure that each guest room has its own private entrance and balcony or patio. The rooms are beautifully decorated in joyous colours, each different from the next, air-conditioned and with many luxurious amenities. The bathrooms are mostly vast and several have jet tubs. Splendid hospitality trays await new arrivals! The Hinshaws have been superb hosts for many years and welcomed many prestigious guests. The Little Swedish Lounge (the bar) has an inviting ambience and the Wine Cellar is fascinating. The pièce de résistance is the acclaimed restaurant, with its Art Deco stained glass windows and lovely table settings complementing the absolutely brilliant cooking, always exquisitely presented. Strolling in the park by the lake or a gentle game of croquet is therapeutic. The pool is close to the chalets. The hotel has a boutique, ceramic studio and chapel antiques. Tours of Chalet Suzanne Soup Cannery can be arranged! Florida high life and Disney World are nearby. Good golf is accessible. **Directions:** The Chalet has its own small airstrip. From Interstate 4, take exit 23, go south on US27 for 18.5 miles. Turn left onto Chalet Suzanne Road. Price guide: Rooms $159–$229; suite $229.

HOTEL OCEAN

123038 OCEAN DRIVE, MIAMI BEACH, FLORIDA 33139
TEL: 1 305 672 2579 FAX: 1 305 672 7665 E-MAIL: ocean1230@aol.com

Nestling on the foot of the beach and ocean, this charming hotel boasts a Mediterranean façade and an interior enhanced by Art Deco original pieces, typical of properties in the Miami Beach area. Service is an important criterion and the friendly and enthusiastic staff aim for excellence. French and English antiques adorn the public rooms whilst authentic 1930's furniture may be found throughout the house. The 27 bedrooms, all with en suite facilities, contain many thoughtful additions such as a safe, colour television and video, a mini-bar and soft bathrobes. Whirlpools, balconies and private elevators are displayed in the penthouse suites, affording glorious views of the ocean. The convivial restaurant and café, Les Deux Fontaines, offers a creative menu complemented by stylish presentation. Specialising in seafood, popular dishes include local produce and tropical fish such as Mahi-Mahi, lobster and yellowtail. The restaurant is ideal for private dining or banquets, seating up to 400 people. The hotel is just steps away from the beach and sea, perfect for strolls along the warm white sands or a dip in the ocean. Other nearby outdoor pursuits include tennis, water-skiing, golf, fishing or shooting. **Directions:** From Miami airport, take the MacArthur Causeway. Follow the signs to Miami Beach and then on to Ocean Drive. Turn left, proceed 7 blocks and the hotel is between 12th and 13th Street. Price guide: Rooms $179–$215; suite $275–$325; penthouse $515.

THE RICHMOND

1757 COLLINS AVE, MIAMI BEACH, FLORIDA 33139
TEL: 1 305 538 2331 FAX: 1 305 531 9021 E-MAIL: reservations@richmondhotel.com

"The Richmond is a modern Art Deco masterpiece". Located directly on the ocean front, the dazzling swimming pool and huge half-moon heated Jacuzzi are surrounded by a nationally honoured tropical garden of indigenous coconut palms, blooming bougainvillaea and a myriad of other exotic foliage. It is idyllic and joyful by day and wonderfully romantic at night. The Verandah Café is beautifully situated overlooking the pools and features a bountiful choice of favourite dishes. There is also a fully-equipped fitness centre. The bedrooms are charming and restful; many with glorious views. Everything is appointed with top line cotton linens. The Richmond is a short walking distance from the Miami Beach Convention Center, Lincoln Road, Ocean Drive, restaurants, clubs and shops. The Richmond considers itself to be more than a hotel; it is the three generations of the family that built the Richmond and continue to personally welcome visitors from around the world. **Directions:** Take Airport Expressway 112 East (direction Miami Beach) to the Toll Plaza. Continue East to I–195 (Miami Beach). Exit on Alton Road South to 17th Street. Left on 17th Street to Collins Avenue (AIA). Left on Collins Avenue. The Richmond is located 3/4 block north on the East Side (Oceanside) Collins Avenue. Valet parking. Price guide: Rooms $170–$275; suite $325–$400.

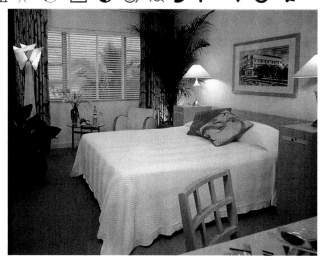

GREYFIELD INN

CUMBERLAND ISLAND, PO BOX 900, FERNANDINA BEACH, FLORIDA 32035-0900
TEL: 1 904 261 6408 FAX: 1 904 321 0666 E-MAIL: seashore@net-magic.net

This lovely mansion is located on Georgia's largest and most southerly barrier island, Cumberland Island. Much of the island has been designated as a National Seashore, protecting it from development. The limited number of visitors allowed daily ensures a peaceful environment for the wild horses, deer, armadillos and numerous species of birds that make their home here. Greyfield's private area includes more than 1,300 acres and guests can spend their days swimming, hiking, beach combing, clam-digging and hunting for sharks' teeth. A memorable breakfast includes orange juice, muffins, fruit pancakes and smoothies. A picnic lunch in a basket is prepared for enjoying at your leisure. In the evening, the gourmet dinner is a more formal affair. It is served in the candlelit dining room, which is decorated with flowers and offers a stunning view of the island's sunsets. The nightly entrée comprises seafood, game hen, lamb or beef tenderloin, home-made breads, fresh vegetables and delicious desserts. An excellent wine list accompanies the menu. Greyfield maintains a well-stocked bar, located in the gun room. The well-appointed bedrooms are air-conditioned. This is the former home of the Carnegies and many original photographs and pieces still adorn this welcoming inn. **Directions:** Leave I–95 to exit 129 in Florida, then A1A to Amelia Island to the ferry terminal. Price guide: Rooms £275–£395.

THE LODGE ON LITTLE ST. SIMONS ISLAND

PO BOX 21078, LITTLE ST. SIMONS ISLAND, GEORGIA 31522 – 0578
TEL: 1 912 638 7472 FAX: 1 912 634 1811 E-MAIL: lssi@mindspring.com

Robinson Crusoe might have loved this perfect place. The Lodge on Little St. Simons Island refreshes and invigorates the soul, placing the visitor firmly and comfortably in touch with nature. The island is one of many that cluster off the coast of Georgia between Savannah and Jacksonville can be reached by private boat through the salt marshes. Nature lovers feel wonderful when they stay at The Lodge, a unique inn on this wildlife sanctuary, a haven of peace and outstanding beauty. Accommodation is in five cabins, with rustic furnishings, nothing elaborate but extremely comfortable, with plenty of hot water for showers after a day's activities. Breakfast is at 9 o'clock and those not wishing to lunch may request picnic lunches. Guests meet for

cocktails and canapés early evening and dine together, enjoying traditional regional dishes; the wine flows. No smoking indoors! Preservation of the creatures in this environment – and protection of the Lodge residents – are paramount and codes of behaviour have been established. There is so much to do – Interpretive Naturalist programmes, riding, canoeing, swimming, fishing, cycling and there is transport down to the 7-mile beach. Ornithologists have an opportunity to see the rarest species. **Directions:** Arrive by boat from Hampton Club Marina on St Simons Island (not far from Brunswick). Price guide: Rooms $325–$550; suite $550–$900; full house $600–$1900; Full Island $4400–$6200.

HENDERSON VILLAGE

125 SOUTH LANGSTON CIRCLE, PERRY, GEORGIA 31069
TEL: 1 912 988 8696 FAX: 1 912 988 9009

A collection of charming cottages in the style of 19th century Southern plantation houses, graced with wide shady porches, nestle in the village which is situated in the historic heartland of Georgia. The 24 spacious guest rooms and suites are gorgeous. Each is individually decorated with fine fabrics, artwork and antiques. All have luxurious baths and a wide selection of modern facilities. Most have fireplaces. Excellent Southern Continental cuisine prepared by an award winning European chef is served in the attractive 80 seater restaurant, The Langston House. A tasty cooked breakfast can be served to guests in either their room or porch or in The Langston House itself. Serpentine brick paths lead to rolling pastures and formal gardens which feature a swimming pool and twin gazebos. The village is surrounded by 8,000 acres of prime hunting land. There are Booner and Crocket Bucks, wild quails for the wing shooter, boars that can top the scales at 500 pounds and many rare breeds. Clay pigeon shooting, riding, swimming and fishing are some of the many activities that may be practised at this fine property that combines outdoor pursuits, good accommodation and fantastic value for money. Local points of interest include The Anderson Trail and Civil War Museum. **Directions:** From Atlanta, take I-75 south to exit 41. Turn right, travel approx. 1 mile to 1st intersection. Henderson Village is on the right. Price guide (incl. breakfast): Rooms $145–$185; suites $205–$245.

Savannah

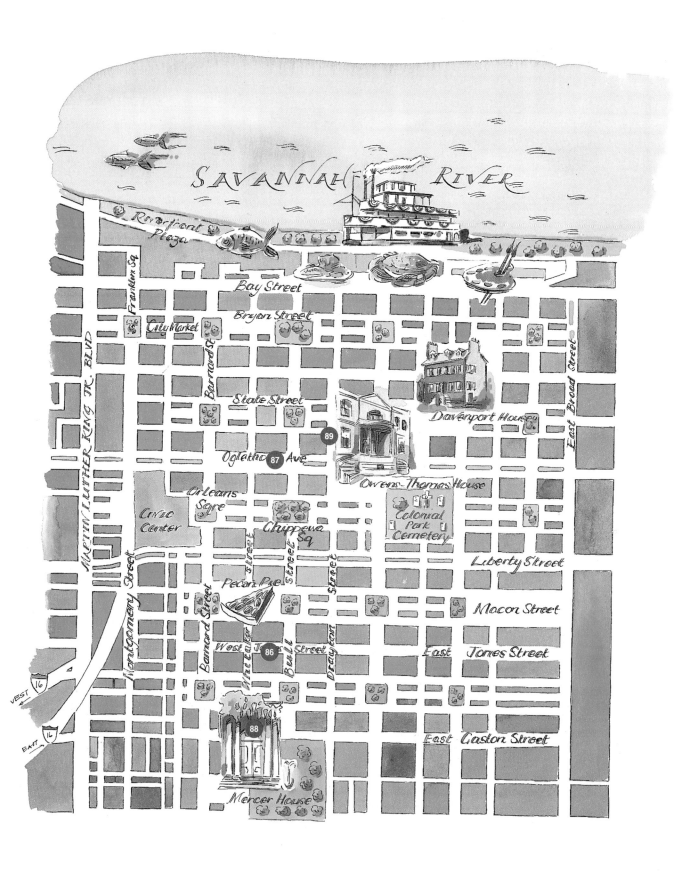

THE ELIZA THOMPSON HOUSE

5 WEST JONES STREET, SAVANNAH, GEORGIA 31401
TEL: 1 912 236 3620 FAX: 1 912 238 1920

The Eliza Thompson House, built in 1847, offers a delightful fusion of past and present times with traditions and customs of the last century and the comforts and amenities of today. Set on a quiet residential street, the house is one of the oldest inns in the heart of Savannah's historical district and is an architectural landmark. Meticulous restoration work has resulted in the superb interior, enhanced by heart pine floors and antique furnishings. Guests may stay in either the 13 stately rooms in the main house or in the Carriage House, which boasts a further 12 rooms. All the bedrooms are furnished in an exquisite style with en suite facilities and colour televisions. In addition, some main house rooms have charming fireplaces. The soft bathrobes and make-up mirrors are thoughtful extras. The breakfast is imaginative and extensive, comprising home-made recipes with fresh, local ingredients. Other delightful traditions include afternoon tea, served in the parlour, or the daily cheese and wine reception in the evening. Guests may relax in the beautifully landscaped courtyard, where the air is scented with southern fragrances and the gentle sound of the Ivan Bailey fountain may be heard. Savannah is a wonderful town to explore with many antique shops, museums and old churches nearby. **Directions:** Travel east on I-16, towards Savannah. Exit at Montgomery Street, turn right at traffic lights on Liberty Street. Turn right on Whitaker Street and left onto Jones Street. Price guide: Rooms $99–$255.

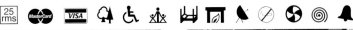

FOLEY HOUSE INN

14 WEST HULL, CHIPPEWA SQUARE, SAVANNAH, GEORGIA 31401
TEL: 1 912 232 6622 FAX: 1 912 231 1218 E-MAIL: foleyinn@AOL.COM

Savannah is steeped in history, with its port today, as in the past, an important role. The steamship Savannah, built here, was the first to cross the Atlantic. The elegance of the Old Town reflects the gracious way of life centuries ago and it is therefore an immense pleasure to enter the Foley House Inn, a town house which has been carefully and authentically restored by craftsmen, whilst discreetly introducing essential modern comforts. Today it is a prestigious and exclusive inn, offering old world courtesy. The house is approached by a staircase and the canopied entrance features lanterns on either side. Elaborate plasterwork and shutters add to its classical charm. The interior is rather romantic with fine wall hangings, delicate chandeliers, graceful furniture, superb paintings and beautiful flowers. This style extends to the bedrooms (some situated in the adjacent Carriage House). The bathrooms are welcoming, with striking wallpapers, ornate friezes, marble surrounds and gold taps. The Parlour is where guests gather for breakfast, evening hors d'oeuvres, cocktails or a glass of fine wine. Other treats include afternoon tea, coffee and lemonade, during the summer months. The Concierge will suggest where to dine locally and arrange concert or theatre reservations. Exploring Savannah is fascinating, with its waterfront, old churches, parks, museums and galleries. **Directions:** Street parking only. The inn occupies a corner of Chippewa Square. Price guide: Rooms $165–$275.

MAGNOLIA PLACE 1878

503 WHITTAKER STREET, SAVANNAH, GEORGIA 31401
TEL: 1 912 236 7674 FAX: 1 912 236 1145 E-MAIL: bbmagnolia@prodigy.net

With magnificent views of the imposing Forsyth Park in Savannah, the Magnolia Place Inn is an exclusive family-run inn, dedicated to showering its guests with lavish attention. Following a recent and extensive refurbishment, its gothic steamboat façade is now an impressive monument to Georgia's river history. The individually designed and named bedrooms compromising the two upper floors of the building all have access to lovely balconies and private terraces. Two special courtyard suites, engulfed by the fragrant gardens, have their own sitting room areas and kitchens, and are ideal for travelling families. Some rooms have delicately-painted fireplaces and Jacuzzis, whilst all have king and queen size beds. The Inn has a strong oriental theme throughout, with priceless antiques, Eastern porcelains and Japanese kimonos adorning the walls. There is also a strong butterfly motif running through the Inn and its gardens, with a cabinet displaying a magnificent collection of rare British butterflies in the lounge. Owners Rob and Jane Sales and Kathy Medlock create a relaxed, convivial and laid-back atmosphere, and the service is second to none. A home-made breakfast comprising a subtle blend of European and American flavours, is served in the privacy of the bedrooms, the parlour or in the pretty secluded courtyard at the heart of the inn. **Directions:** From I16, go to Liberty Street, then right onto Whitaker Street. Price guide: Rooms $175–$265; suite $180–$270.

THE PRESIDENT'S QUARTERS

225 EAST PRESIDENT STREET, SAVANNAH, GEORGIA 31401
TEL: 1 912 233 1600 FAX: 1 912 238 0849

Residing on Oglethorpe Square, these authentic Federal-style town houses were constructed by the estate of Andrew Gordon Low in 1855. Fashioned in the likeness of Savannah's Davenport House and as a neighbour of the renowned Owens-Thomas House, The President's Quarters opened its doors in 1987 after a careful restoration. With a long history of famous inhabitants and guests such as Robert E. Lee, each room is individually decorated celebrating 19 Presidents known to have enjoyed Savannah's southern hospitality. The spacious guest rooms feature regal wallcoverings and carefully chosen historic colours exclusive to grand homes of Savannah. Selected suites have balconies, romantic loft bedrooms and hand-painted ceilings. The inn is renowned for its fine service and hospitality. Those accustomed to pampering will enjoy the thoughtful extras such as soft bathrobes, a chilled bottle of wine and fresh fruit. Other delights include breakfast served in the rooms, sumptuous afternoon hors d'oeuvres and a nightly turndown service with bedside cordials and local sweets. Concierge service is available 24 hours for dining and entertainment suggestions and reservations. The night-life of River Street is only 3 blocks away! The many quaint shops will please those with an interest in curio. **Directions:** Take I-16 to Montgomery, right on Oglethorpe, left on Abercorn, right on York. Off-street parking. Price guide: Rooms $137–$157; suite $177–$250.

MELHANA PLANTATION

301 SHOWBOAT LANE, THOMASVILLE, GEORGIA 31792
TEL: 1 888 920 3030 FAX: 1 912 226 4585

Melhana Plantation was originally developed as a quail hunting plantation and now comprises 30 historic buildings set in 50 acres. Impressive moss-laden oaks and sweet-smelling magnolias line the entrance to the main house, where elegantly-appointed suites are available to guests. All feature king or queen-sized beds, cable channel television, Jacuzzi tubs and fresh flowers. Generous breakfasts, served in the elegant dining room or garden loggia, include delicious breads baked in the kitchen. Afternoon tea is provided in the Hogan Room. There is world class fine dining in the restaurant featuring excellent southern regional cuisine with white glove service. A heated indoor swimming pool and fitness centre are among the many leisure facilities available, while sightseeing opportunities in the surrounding area abound. Thomasville boasts many architecturally significant structures, including the Museum at Pebble Hill Plantation. The Thomas County Museum of History offers a view of south-western Georgia in the past. The Showboat Theatre, an original theatre for films and shows, must not be missed. **Directions:** From 1-75 take exit 4 to Highway 84 west to Thomasville. From Thomasville travel south on Highway 319 to Melhana Plantation. The inn is located approximately 6 miles south of Thomasville on Highway 319 south. Price guide: Suites $250–$450.

THE RHETT HOUSE INN

1009 CRAVEN STREET, BEAUFORT, SOUTH CAROLINA 29902
TEL: 1 843 524 9030 FAX: 1 843 524 1310 US TOLL FREE: 1 888 480 9530 E-MAIL: rhetthse@hargray.com

Dating back to 1820, The Rhett House Inn was once an in-town plantation house; its huge verandahs and white columns still recall the charm and romance of the Old South. All the rooms are individually and exquisitely furnished with every amenity to provide the ultimate in comfort and convenience. Many have Queen or King-size beds, fireplaces and whirlpool bath tubs. Ideally designed for a romantic getaway, guest rooms in the recently renovated historic cottage feature private entrances and porches. A blend of American and English antiques fill the living room, which is the perfect place to relax and read a book. Healthy and delicious breakfasts include fresh fruits, pancakes, savoury French toast and eggs – all served with freshly brewed coffee. Gourmet picnics, available on request, are perfect for the beach, or waterfront and in the evening there is no better way to unwind than by enjoying a glass of wine or a home-made dessert on the verandah. Although biking is the preferred way of sightseeing, the lovely town of Beaufort can also be explored by foot and carriage tours. The welcoming staff are always happy to help arrange golf, tennis, swimming, fishing and kayaking. Hunting Island, Charleston and Savannah are all within easy reach. **Directions:** From the north, 1-95 exit 33 to Beaufort. From the south, 1-95 exit 8 to Beaufort. Follow the signs. Price guide: Rooms $150–$225.

Charleston Harbour

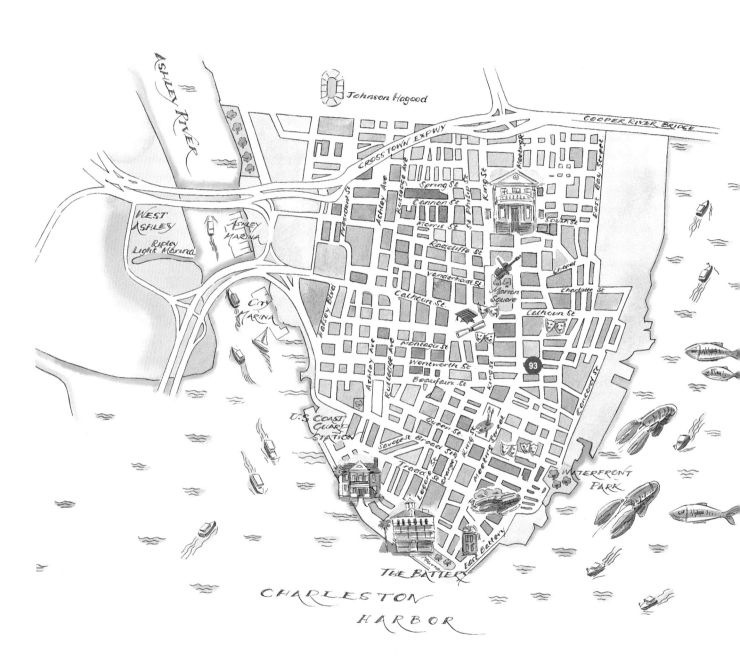

WENTWORTH MANSION

149 WENTWORTH STREET, CHARLESTON, SOUTH CAROLINA 29401
TEL: 1 843 853 1886 FAX: 1 843 720 5290 E-MAIL: mgr@wentworthmansion.com

Situated in the historic city of Charleston, the Wentworth Mansion evokes the image of America's Gilded Age. This magnificent residence is furnished in a most elaborate manner, with marble fireplaces and beautifully fashioned woodwork. Built in 1886, the house has undergone an extensive restoration, resulting in an excellent property offering fine accommodation and a refined ambience. The spacious bedrooms are adorned with fine antiques and contain luxurious whirlpools and king-size beds. Guests may relax with a book and enjoy the tranquil atmosphere of the Rodgers Library or laze on the sun porch of the Harleston Lounge, sipping a light apéritif. A stunning view of the Charleston skyline may be seen by climbing the spiral staircase up to the towering cupola. Daily events include European style breakfast buffet, afternoon tea, wine tastings and evening turndown service. The hosts recreate the same standard of cuisine and service in the restaurant, Circa 1886 in the carriage house. Guests may use the nearby fitness centre and practise a number of sports close by such as tennis and golf. **Directions:** On I–26 take exit Meeting Street, turn right on Meeting Street, then right on to John Street. Turn left onto King Street, then right onto Wentworth Street. The Wentworth Mansion is on the left, before the flashing traffic lights. Price guide: Rooms $295–$495; suites $495–$695.

LITCHFIELD PLANTATION

KINGS RIVER ROAD, PAWLEYS ISLAND, SOUTH CAROLINA 29585
TEL: 1 843 237 9121 FAX: 1 843 237 1041

Dramatically situated at the heart of a former rice plantation, Litchfield is a beautifully preserved country inn. Visitors are immediately struck by the magic of the location, as the quarter mile avenue to the main house is flanked by century-old oak trees which form an enchanting tunnel to this languid South Carolina hideaway. Guests can stay in the luxurious suites within the main house, or choose the seclusion of one of the many villas dotted around the 600-acre estate. These gorgeously designed and individually decorated retreats benefit from spacious lounges and huge bathrooms, some with Jacuzzis tubs. The Carriage House, an attractive low country-style building is the venue for excellent continental cuisine complemented by seasonal specialities, prepared by cordon bleu chefs. Tennis courts adorn the estate, while the large heated pool has excellent views of the rice fields. Guests can relax at the 3 storey beach house, moor their yachts at the marina, or take relaxing trips along the coast. The region attracts golf fanatics and the inn has ten of South Carolina's most celebrated golf courses at its doorstep. Deep sea and sport fishing, trips to historic Charleston and river cruises are among the other delights available to visitors. **Directions:** From Charleston, take the road towards Myrtle Beach, take the right fork at Jct17, and the check-in centre is on the right. Price guide: Rooms from $186; suites from $268–$540.

North Carolina and Virginia

THE GREYSTONE INN

LAKE TOXAWAY, NORTH CAROLINA 28747
TEL: 1 828 966 4700 FAX: 1 828 862 5689 E-MAIL: Greystone@citcom.net

A stay at this unique inn is to join a superbly hosted private house party. The Greystone Inn is built near the site of the legendary Toxaway Inn. The setting is idyllic, overlooking the lake and surrounded by luxuriant, verdant gardens. The Inn is a beautiful mansion, built as a private house – the architecture having European overtones. It has been lovingly transformed into a hotel with modern facilities yet old world charm and courtesy prevail. The guest rooms, those in the adjacent Hillmont annex facing the waterside, and the Lakeside Suites are spacious and romantic, furnished with antiques and period pieces, all with charming drapes. The bathrooms are twentieth century, with

Jacuzzis. The sun porch where tea is served is evocative of the past, having wicker furniture, and the salons are gracious. Cocktails are sipped in the traditional Library or on the Terrace. Dining is an occasion – inspired interpretations of classical Southern dishes accompanied by mellow wines. Croquet, golf, tennis, fishing, many water sports, hiking and picnics in the lovely countryside, swimming in the pool or lake, relaxing in the spa or just appreciating the tranquility – the days are full. **Directions:** Take US64 from Brevard, after 20 miles the Inn is signed on the right. Price guide: Rooms $275–$420; suite $350–$540.

THE FEARRINGTON HOUSE

2000 FEARRINGTON VILLAGE CENTER, PITTSBORO, NORTH CAROLINA 27312
TEL: 1 919 542 2121 FAX: 1 919 542 4202 E-MAIL: fhouse@fearrington.com

Fearrington Village was the inspiration of the Fitch Family who in 1974 purchased a 640 acre farm dating back to 1786. The barn and silo still stand and cows graze in the meadow. Rebuilt after a fire in the 1920's, the house became a restaurant in 1980, with accommodation available next door. It is a beautiful residence, with white walls, green shutters and classical pillars surrounded by well-kept gardens blooming with colourful plants and fine old trees. The charming bedrooms are extremely comfortable, peaceful and very light - filled with old English pine furniture and bowls of fresh flowers. Guests take tea in the elegant Garden House or relax in the Sun Room leading onto the terrace and rose gardens. Cuisine is an important criterion at Fearrington House and the famous popular restaurant is renowned for its magnificent Southern specialities, crafted and beautifully presented by the talented kitchen team, and its selection of distinguished wines. Dining is not merely a meal, it is an experience as guests feast by candlelight. Smoking is discouraged in the restaurant. The village is intriguing, with its aura of self-containment. It has craft and garden shops, its own bank, market café, medical and fitness centres; also tennis, croquet, riding and swimming and golf is not far away. **Directions:** From Durham Raleigh Airport take Route 40 to Chapel Hill, then Route 15-501 South to Fearrington Village. Price guide: Rooms $175–$350.

THE ORCHARD INN

HIGHWAY 176, BOX 725, SALUDA, NORTH CAROLINA 28773
TEL: 1 828 749 5471 FAX: 1 828 749 9805 E-MAIL: orchard@saluda.tds.net

Those seeking the air of opulence and the highest quality of hospitality will be rewarded by staying at the Orchard Inn, set astride a spur of the Warrior Mountains. Nestling amidst 12 acres of enticingly forested land offering majestic views of the surrounding area, the Orchard Inn is as beautiful and simple on the inside as the wonders that abound on the outside. With soft natural tones and sublimely comfortable furniture, once inside, guests, like the Railway men for whom the inn was originally built, may put aside their troubles and simply relax. Both rooms or private cottages are available, each one unique in its appearance, spacious, with a warm appeal offering every convenience necessary in homely surroundings. All feature period pieces and antique furnishings and additional comforts include queen size four-poster beds, whirlpool baths and fireplaces. The dining room looks out across an awe-inspiring view of the surrounding mountains and serves sumptuous French Provincial cuisine, a true sensory extravaganza. At the Orchard Inn, one can hike, bike, go rambling, walk with the expert naturalist and discover the flora and fauna, or simply sit back and relax amidst the beauty of the great American outdoors. **Directions:** I-85 from Atlanta towards Charlotte, take exit onto I-26 towards Asheville, then exit number 28 to Saluda and The Orchard Inn. Price guide: Rooms $119–$195.

PINE CREST INN

200 PINE CREST LANE, TRYON, NORTH CAROLINA 28782
TEL: 1 828 859 9135 E-MAIL: info@pinecrestinn.com

Situated at the foot of the Blue Ridge Mountains, this traditional English-style inn was once a popular haunt for some of America's finest 20th century authors including F Scott Fitzgerald and Ernest Hemingway. Its beautiful location makes Pine Crest Inn an ideal choice for enthusiasts of outdoor pursuits. The interior is furnished in a quaint style with stone fireplaces, wooden floors and oriental rugs. The charming British owners have aimed to create a "home away from home" ambience, with books to read beside the fire, games to play and areas for guests to commune. The choice of accommodation is delightfully varied with rooms, suites and cottages; all individually decorated. There is a wide array of amenities such as cable television, telephones, bathrobes and sherry. Guests relax with a drink in the Fox and Hounds Bar before dining in the superb restaurant; serving imaginative dishes and a fine selection of wines. The Pine Crest Inn is renowned for its excellent cuisine and a breakfast is the highlight of every morning, with blueberry muffins, Belgian waffles, eggs Benedict and other specialities. After a hearty meal, guests may wish to ramble through the surrounding woods or explore the many nearby hiking trails. Volleyball may be practised on site whilst golf, tennis, swimming and riding is arranged nearby. **Directions:** From I-26, exit 36 to Tryon. Follow Rte 108/176 to town of Tryon. Turn on New Market Rd. Follow signs to Inn. Price guide: Rooms $140–$180; suite $180–$540.

THE SWAG COUNTRY INN

2300 SWAG ROAD, WAYNESVILLE, NORTH CAROLINA 28786
TEL: 1 828 926 0430 FAX: 1 828 926 2036 E-MAIL: letters@theswag.com

Nestling on a 5,000 foot mountain, The Swag Country Inn boasts an outstanding natural setting. A deep valley of farmhouses and fields loom beyond the attractive front porch and mountain peaks are visible in the distance. The charming owners have instilled a warm and welcoming atmosphere that is present throughout and, as a result, the inn is reminiscent of a family home rather than a hotel. The beautiful handcrafted interiors reflect the ancient Appalachian mountains, reminding the inn's guests of the beautiful location. The natural materials, hand-picked fieldstone, huge hand-hewn poplar logs, hickory bark-covered furniture and native wormy chestnut panelling, all add grace to The Swag. Breakfasts are magnificent –

try the blueberry pancakes. Superb picnics can be arranged. Guests dine together by candlelight, enjoying a sumptuous 4-course meal, as conversation flows. The Swag is a veritable paradise for nature-lovers seeking the finest amenities in a remote yet breathtaking setting on the boundary of the Great Smoky Mountains National Park. When not following the wilderness trails, relax in a hammock, or lounge in the spa, play croquet or fish in the streams. **Directions:** Interstate 40 to exit 20. Exit onto state highway 276. 2.8 miles to The Swag sign. Right on Grindstone Road. Right on Hempill Road. About 4 miles to inn's gate, 2.5 miles up the private driveway. Price guide (inc. all meals): Rooms $240–$525 for two persons.

CLIFTON - THE COUNTRY INN & ESTATE

1296 CLIFTON INN DRIVE, CHARLOTTESVILLE, VIRGINIA 22911
TEL: 1 804 971 1800 FAX: 1 804 971 7098 US TOLL FREE: 1 888 971 1800 E-MAIL: reserve@cstone.net

Enter an estate steeped in history and secluded in some of the most refreshing and beautiful land imaginable. Clifton - the Country Inn and Estate, an eighteenth century manor house, is an exquisite example of Federal and Colonial style architecture and elegance set against a stunning 40 acre environment. Once inside, this superbly designed inn continues to exude a dignified and stylish air, with simple furniture that is none the less comfortable and a subtle yet warm colour scheme. The rooms are the height of grandeur, decorated exuberantly with plenty of space in which to recline and while away the hours. Each room looks out across Clifton's finely kept lawns, gardens or private

lake. Dinner is prepared with the very freshest of ingredients, incorporated to provide a feast for all the senses. With the choice of the historic dining room, or the verandah, a candle lit dinner at Clifton, along with its renowned selection of wine from their private cellar, is a gastronomic experience to remember. Guests can hike and bike, swim or picnic, or simply let the old world beauty transport you to a charming paradise in modern times. **Directions:** 5 miles East of downtown Charlottesville, Clifton is just off 250 East on State Route 729, Shadwell, Virginia. Price guide (incl. breakfast): Rooms $165–$450.

Maryland, New York State and Pennsylvania

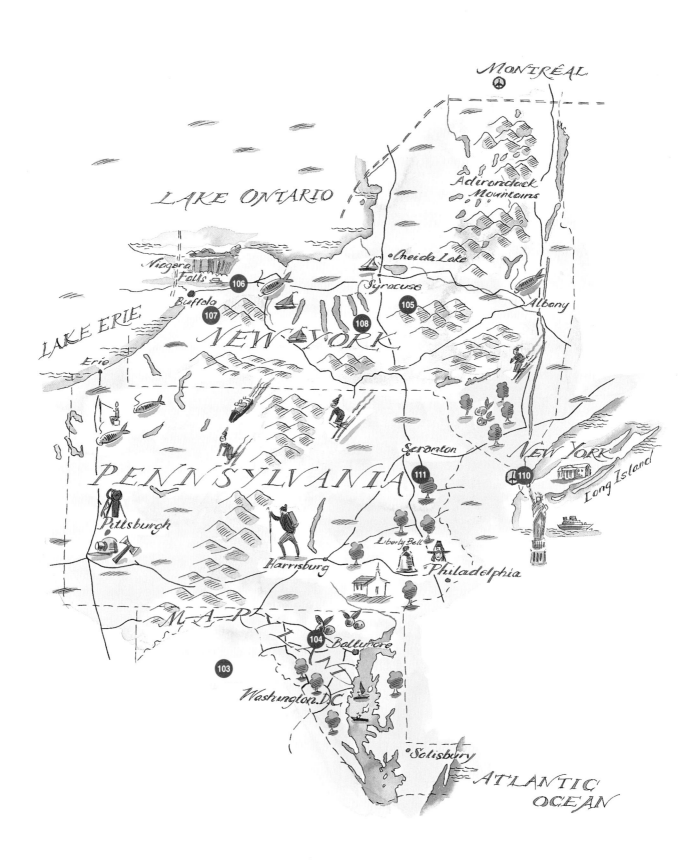

TYLER SPITE HOUSE

112 WEST CHURCH STREET, FREDERICK, MARYLAND 21701
TEL: 1 301 831 4455

Tyler Spite House is a most delightful inn with a peculiar name which tells you nothing about the charming qualities of this up-to-date hostelry but the name does commemorate its interesting origin. The celebrated eye-surgeon, John Tyler, to thwart a scheme by the town planners, had the building put up virtually overnight in the direct path of the envisaged road extension. The law protected substantial buildings and thus the road-scheme was "spited". The historic inn was taken over in 1989 by Bill and Andrea Myer who have made it a wonderful place to stay while conserving and even embellishing the fine old décor that has given this stately mansion its unique appeal and character. The bedrooms are lavishly comfortable. Breakfasts are served bountifully but formally in the elegant dining room or often, in summer weather, outside on the patio among the flowers by the swimming pool. A rewarding tour of Frederick can be made on foot or uniquely by horse-drawn carriage. Afterwards, high tea is the speciality at the weekend, served in style either in the music room or the library. During the summer months, guests may indulge in strawberries in the garden. **Directions:** From Route 70 follow Market Street into the Historic District, turning left into 2nd Street, then left into Record Street and onward to Church Street. Price guide: Rooms $140–$250.

ANTRIM 1844

30 TREVANION RD, TANEYTOWN, MARYLAND 21787

TEL: 1 410 756 6812 FAX: 1 410 756 2744 TOLL FREE: 1 800 858 1844 E-MAIL: antrim1844@prodigy.net

The great plantation houses in Maryland that survived the Battle of Gettysburg are nostalgic of a magical period in America's history. This is the era that Dorothy and Richard Mollett have recreated for their guests at Antrim 1844. Their loving and meticulous restoration of the classic Greek revivial mansion reflects long hours of research. Antiques and authentic wallhangings have been imported from Europe, fabrics are rich, mirrors have ornate gilt frames and the handsome portraits are illuminated by brilliant candelabra. The romantic guest rooms have pristine delicate linens and the luxurious suites are in imaginatively transformed outhouses. Wooden butlers outside each door offer newspapers in the morning and roses at night! On warm evenings guests dine on the enchanting verandah overlooking the formal gardens, on cooler nights in the fascinating Smokehouse Restaurant. The five-course menu is fabulous and the cellar holds magnificent wines. Strolling in the 23 acre estate is therapeutic, the pool has a picturesque gazebo and gentle exercise includes croquet, lawn bowling, target golf and tennis There are special facilities for corporate events and the Pavilion is an elite setting for private celebrations. **Directions:** Route 140 east to Taneytown, cross railroad tracks and bear right at fork. After 150' turn right, parking is signed. Price guide: Rooms $175; suite $300.

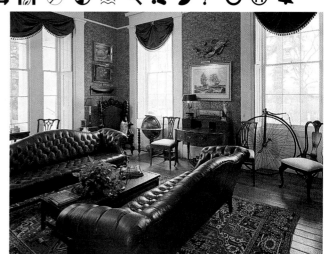

THE BREWSTER INN

6 LEDYARD AVENUE, CAZENOVIA, NEW YORK 13035
TEL: 1 315 655 9232 FAX: 1 315 655 2130

Surrounded by secluded lawned grounds, The Brewster Inn stands elegantly on the southern shore of Cazenovia Lake close to a quaint village which was founded in 1793. It is a perfect venue for carefree relaxation. The inn was built as the summer home for financier Benjamin Brewster who, with John D. Rockefeller, Sr, established the Standard Oil Company. Its elegance is enhanced by rich décor, fine drapes and impressive woodwork, including solid mahogany and antique quartered oak. Guests choose from bedrooms in the main inn or in the completely renovated carriage house. Each one has a private bath, air conditioning, television and telephone. Four rooms have Jacuzzi baths and there is one three-room de luxe suite.

The attractive dining rooms offer dinner menus of superb, classic American cuisine to please every palate. The inn's intimate Tap Room is an excellent spot in which to recline and converse with the other guests. After a complimentary Continental breakfast guests can enjoy a leisurely stroll along the inn's extensive shoreline, swim in the clear lake waters, fish off the private dock or browse around Cazenovia's many shops. Lorenzo is also worth a visit, as are the beautiful grounds of Cazenovia College and the picnic area at the nearby, spectacular Chittenango Falls. **Directions:** The Brewster Inn is on US Route 20, 20 miles east of Syracuse. Price guide: Rooms $130–$140; suite $140–$200.

ASA RANSOM HOUSE

10529 MAIN STREET (ROUTE 5), CLARENCE, NEW YORK 14031–1684
TEL: 1 716 759 2315 FAX: 1 716 759 2791 E-MAIL: innfo@asaransom.com

Built as a grist mill in 1803, by Asa Ransom, a silversmith, this fine property has been restored and refurbished and the result is a distinctive inn renowned for its charm and character. Set in the heart of Clarence, Asa Ransom House is situated in a peaceful location ideal for those seeking a tranquil ambience. Guests relax in the comfortable library and enjoy a game of chess, checkers or a large jigsaw puzzle. Alternatively, the fine selection of books will delight readers, who may recline in a soft chair beside the fire. The owners' attention to detail is evident in the superb bedrooms, decorated with antique and period furnishings. All offer en suite facilities, television and air conditioning whilst many have fireplaces and balconies. Freshly baked muffins and pastries, fresh fruit and seasonal entrées comprise the delicious breakfast. The Asa Ransom House is renowned for its excellent cuisine and as lunch is served on Wednesdays and afternoon tea on Thursdays, guests are advised to reserve a table! The dining rooms are beautifully furnished and the dishes, made with the finest seasonal produce, are complemented by a good wine list. Pastimes include browsing the giftshop, strolling in the herb garden or antique hunting in the quaint shops close by. Lancaster Opera House is nearby; Niagara Falls is only 44km distant. Toronto is 2 hours away. **Directions:** Travellers from the east must take I-90 leaving at exit 48A, whilst those from the north must leave at exit 48A. Price guide: Rooms $95–$270.

ROYCROFT INN

40 SOUTH GROVE STREET, EAST AURORA, NEW YORK 14052
TEL: 1 716 652 5552 FAX: 1 716 655 5345 E-MAIL: mbaugat@roycroftinn.com

The Roycroft Inn is in every sense an American National Landmark. It was founded over a hundred years ago by the philosopher and writer Elbert Hubbard to provide congenial accommodation for devotees of the local Arts and Craft movement. His influence and memory live on at the Roycroft, thanks largely to the Margaret L Wendt Foundation who enabled the inn to be renovated and reopened in 1995 in a style worthy of the founder's highest beliefs and aspirations. The décor and furniture are either original or authentic reproduction examples of the celebrated movement of which the inn is a shrine. The bedrooms at the Roycroft conform to the original structure whilst enhancing and conserving the historic character of the entire building. All rooms are furnished in traditional Roycroft style and feature modems, televisions and video equipment. The Roycroft inn restaurant is open for lunches, dinners and on Sunday for brunch. In summer there is dining out of doors. Private facilities are available for meetings and parties for as few as 10 or as many as 200 people. Attractions in the locality are museums, golf courses, nature walks, tennis and in season, many downhill and cross-country skiing areas. **Directions:** From Buffalo follow Route 190 south to Route 90 heading west. Take exit 54 to Route 400 and exit onto route 20A East Aurora, becoming Main Street. Pass through village, turn left into South Grove Street. Price guide: Suite $130–$230.

Benn Conger Inn

206 WEST CORTLAND STREET, GROTON, NEW YORK 13073
TEL: 1 607 898 5817 FAX: 1 607 898 5818

Step into the world of a notorious gangster of the early twentieth century, in the breathtaking surroundings of New York's Finger Lakes region. Live the high life and enjoy all the hospitality that the late twentieth century has to offer. The Benn Conger Inn is a picturesque stately home that has lost none of its grand ambience in the seventy years that it has been in existence. Set amidst eighteen acres of superbly kept land, this 'safe-haven' for gangsters has become an elegant and stylish retreat for the more discerning guest. The interior complements the style of the overall design, furnished with immaculate features of the era that are as comfortable as they are beautiful. The rooms are impressive, incorporating imported linens with period furnishings to transport guests back into the opulent history of the inn. Dinner may be sampled in one of three dining rooms that are as luxurious as the rest of the building; open fireplaces, Mediterranean cuisine and a vast selection of quality wines all work together to provide a remarkable experience for the connoisseur. There are numerous activities available here, from horseback riding to skiing, whilst the less active guest may simply take a stroll around the gardens and admire the beautiful lawns. **Directions:** Approximately 10 miles from Cortland on Route 222. Price guide (incl. breakfast): Rooms $90–$120; suites $180–$220.

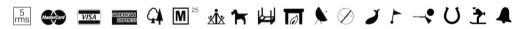

New York City

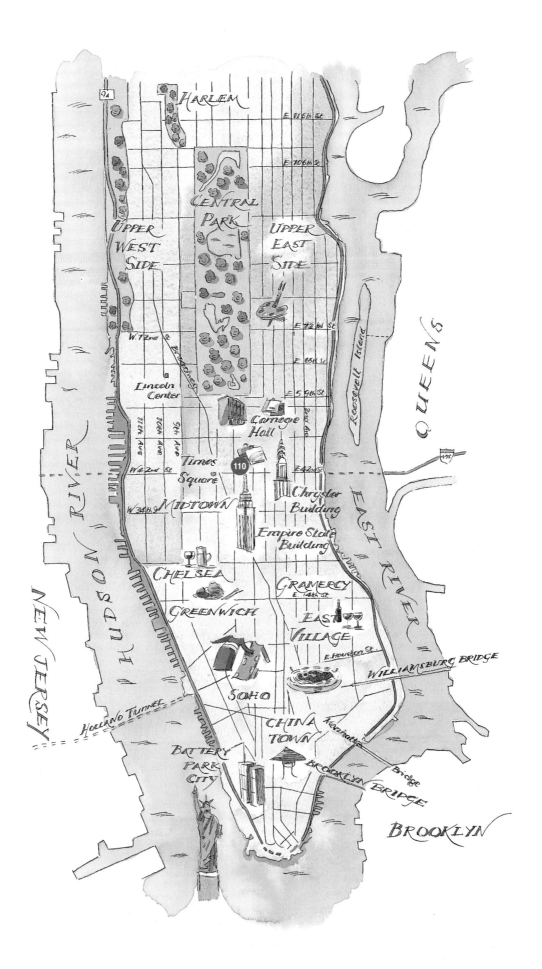

THE IROQUOIS

49 WEST 44TH STREET, NEW YORK, NEW YORK 10036
TEL: 1 212 840 3080 FAX: 1 212 398 1754 UK TOLL FREE: 00 800 525 48000

Arriving guests at The Iroquois are greeted by the impressive, recently restored 1923 French limestone façade and mahogany front doors. Inside, the décor is truly elegant, created by a subtle fusion of European furnishings and New York minimalism. The 114 rooms are decorated in pale shades of green and cream and feature every modern convenience. There are also nine individually furnished suites highlighting the city's themes such as Broadway, fashion and artists. Reflecting his career before the celebrated 'Rebel Without a Cause', the James Dean Suite is adorned with memorabilia from 1951 to 1953 when the actor lived in the building. Additional comforts include soft slippers, Frette linen and the nightly turndown service with Belgian chocolates. The Library is the essence of comfort and houses a diverse collection of works including a selection of classics by Dickins, Steinbeck and Twain. Breakfast may be enjoyed in the Drawing Room, and the Restaurant opens late 1999 under the direction of acclaimed Chef Troy Dupuis. Central station and the boutiques on 5th Avenue are within walking distance. Evening activities include the theatres on Broadway and the convivial Soho area with its restaurants and exciting nightlife. **Directions:** The hotel is situated on 44th Street, between 5th and 6th Avenues. Price guide: Rooms from $255; suite from $450.

THE FRENCH MANOR

HUCKLEBERRY RD (RTE 191), SOUTH STERLING, PENNSYLVANIA 18460
TEL: 1 717 676 3244 FAX: 1 717 676 9786 E-MAIL: thesterlinginn@ezaccess.net

This exquisite French château was built by wealthy Mr Hirshhorn in 1932, a replica of one he owned and loved in the South of France. It is built in local fieldstone, with an imported Spanish slate roof, standing high on a hilltop affording magnificent vistas. This is a luxurious hotel. The interior reflects the skills of craftsmen from Southern Europe and the architecture is magical – "pecky" cypress interior and great hall, Romanesque arched entranceway, vaulted ceilings and large stone fireplaces. The guest rooms are enormous, with canopied beds, graceful Louis XV style furnishings and efficient 'period' bathrooms; some suites have private balconies, fireplaces and Jacuzzi tubs. Guests sip apéritifs on the verandah then feast on an array of authentic aromatic French dishes accompanied by superb wines in the vaulted ceiling dining room. (Reservations are recommended). Triple sheeting, complimentary cheese and fruit platters and a nightly turndown service are some of the many additional touches that greet guests at the Manor. The French Manor has a country cousin, The Sterling Inn, and residents share its indoor pool, spa and many sporting facilities. The château estate has trails for hiking, biking and cross country ski-ing. The neighbourhood offers golf, galleries, parks and antique shops. **Directions:** The Manor is on Route 191, Huckleberry Road. Price guide (B&B): Rooms $120–$195; suites $185–$240.

Hildon Ltd., Broughton, Hampshire SO20 8DG, ☎ 01794 - 301 747

New Jersey and Delaware

THE INN AT MONTCHANIN VILLAGE

ROUTE 100 AND KIRK ROAD, MONTCHANIN, DELAWARE 19710
TEL: 1 302 888 2133 FAX: 1 302 888 0389 US TOLL FREE: 1 800 269 2473 E-MAIL: inn@montchanin.com

Listed on the national register of historic places, the village of Montchanin is steeped in history and was once a part of Winterthur. It was named after Alexandrine de Montchanin, the grandmother of the founder of the DuPont Gunpowder Company. The inn comprises 11 carefully restored buildings, consisting of 27 guest rooms and suites, all of which are beautiful period reproductions. Every amenity required by the discerning traveller has been provided including gorgeous marble baths. Guests may stroll through the gardens before traversing 'Privy Lane' which complements this charming historic property. The former blacksmith's shop has been transformed into Krazy Kat's; a rather fanciful restaurant serving delicious cuisine. Recently described as "a whimsical dining room with an eclectic menu", the flavours are complemented by an award-winning wine list. Set in the heart of the Brandywine valley, museums such as Winterthur, Hagley, Brandywine River and the art and natural history museums of Delaware abound. Other attractions include Longwood Gardens, Nemours Mansion and Gardens and the Delaware River Front Art Center. The village is equidistant from New York and Washington, 5 miles NW of Wilmington and 25 minutes from Philadelphia Airport. **Directions:** The inn is off Route 100 North and can be accessed from Route 202. Price guide: Deluxe Rooms from $190; suites $190–$500.

BOARDWALK PLAZA HOTEL

OLIVE AVENUE & THE BOARDWALK, REHOBOTH BEACH, DELAWARE 19971
TEL: 1 302 227 7169 FAX: 1 302 227 0561 E-MAIL: bph@boardwalkplaza.com

Built in 1990 and equipped with every modern amenity, guests at the Boardwalk Plaza are transported back to Victorian times and the service afforded by the attentive staff is one reminiscent of bygone years. Set in Delaware's premier resort town of Rehoboth Beach, upon walking through the lobby, guests are welcomed by lively parrots, caged or not! The accommodation comprises a varied selection of rooms and suites, all of which are bedecked with interesting antiques or fine period reproductions. The friendly owners have collected many pieces over the years to enhance the rooms and recreate the elegance and authentic character of the Victorian age. Victoria's Restaurant is situated adjacent to the thriving boardwalk, with a view of the Atlantic from every table, and here, diners may sample an array of tasty dishes made with fresh produce such as broiled crab cakes, stuffed lobster and tempting fillets. Rehoboth Beach is a particularly convivial area with special events and festivals throughout the year. Other activities within the area include boating, fishing, kayaking and simply lazing on the beach. **Directions:** From route 1 south, turn left off route 1 onto route 1A which becomes Rehoboth Avenue, then left onto 1st street, right onto Olive Avenue to the Boardwalk. Boardwalk Plaza is on the right. Price guide: Rooms $119–$499.

QUEEN'S HOTEL

601 COLUMBIA AVENUE, CAPE MAY, NEW JERSEY 08204
TEL: 1 609 884 1613 E-MAIL: info@queenshotel.com

Owned and managed by Dane and Joan Wells, Queen's Hotel is the up and coming younger sister of her longer established relation, The Queen Victoria, situated just across the road. It began as a gambling house in 1876 and over a hundred years later, in 1995, it was the subject of major restoration and renovation. The result is a fine small hotel, combining modern conveniences with old architecture, set in the historic district of Cape May. Queen's Hotel is in an enviable position, surrounded by over 600 establishments from the Victorian era with the beach only a short walk away. The bedrooms are well-equipped with mini refrigerators, coffee makers, air conditioning and the latest bathroom and shower amenities – the luxury suites have whirlpool baths. House bicycles and beverages are complimentary. Many fine restaurants are located nearby. There are also interesting shops and various entertainments including concerts, a food and wine festival and a Victorian Christmas in December. The surrounding area is one of the most renowned bird-watching areas in North America. Fishing, golf, riding and tennis are also practised close by. **Directions:** Drive south on the Garden State Parkway to exit 0, continue straight over bridge to Lafayette Street. At first stop light turn left into Madison. Proceed 3 blocks, turn right at water tower into Columbia Avenue, go ½ mile to first stop light. The hotel is on the right. Price guide: Rooms $90–$255.

INN AT MILLRACE POND

PO BOX 359, HOPE, NEW JERSEY 07844
TEL: 1 908 459 4884 FAX: 1 908 459 5276 E-MAIL: millrace@epix.net

The Inn at Millrace Pond comprises a series of historic buildings gathered round the first ever erected in the little village of Hope, founded in 1769. The superb work of restoration of these original structures has resulted in the creation of a most attractive inn, set in an exceptionally serene location. It is the focal point of the surrounding landscape and of the community. The original mill no longer works, but in the tavern room its relics are on show and the millrace still flows, creating an authentic old world scene. The inn prides itself on its reputation for generous hospitality. In the award-winning restaurant, candlelit dinners are served from an imaginative menu featuring delicacies such as pan seared duck with thyme, peach sauce and baked brie puff pastry. The bedrooms are interestingly furnished and decorated, ideally equipped for comfort and easy living. Energetic visitors can play tennis or golf, go walking, jogging or cycling. Those whose tastes are more idle will enjoy the shops and antique galleries in the nearby towns. During the warmer months, it is said that Charlie, the owner, sometimes takes guests out in his 1921 Cadillac! **Directions:** Leave Route 80 at exit 12, follow Route 521 southward, then left in Hope along Route 519. The Mill will be on your left. Price guide: Rooms $110–$160.

TO DISCOVER

1400

OF THE FINEST RECOMMENDATIONS

IN 40 COUNTRIES

VISIT OUR WEBSITE

www.johansens.com

Connecticut, Massachusetts and Rhode Island

RIVERWIND INN

209 MAIN STREET, DEEP RIVER, CONNECTICUT 06417
TEL: 1 860 526 2014 FAX: 1 860 526 0875

Conveniently placed in the Connecticut River Valley, the Riverwind Inn is a fascinating place in which to stay. The old mid-nineteenth century mansion, authentically refurbished just over ten years ago, offers a delightful blend of modern facilities and authentic works of art. Every modern comfort and convenience is offered whilst the venerable architecture, both interior and exterior, is complemented by the inn's eclectic array of collectors' items. These comprise antique animal mounts, books, ornaments, quilts and other pieces of American folk art. The bedrooms are beautiful; individually decorated with antique furnishings and providing guests with the latest amenities. A nourishing complimentary breakfast is served according to the Southern buffet tradition and includes a variety of delectable specialities such as Smithfield ham and home-baked biscuits. There are several restaurants nearby which offer exquisite dishes, made with fresh regional produce and the famous local seafood. Places to visit within close proximity are Mystic Seaport, Hammonasset Beach, Gillette Castle, the Goodspeed Opera House, the Ivoryton Playhouse and the Essex steam train/riverboat. **Directions:** From New York City follow I95 Northward to Route 9, leave Route 9 at exit 4. Go left on to Route 154. The inn is on the right. Price guide: Rooms $95–$175.

HOMESTEAD INN

420 FIELDPOINT ROAD, GREENWICH, CONNECTICUT 06830
TEL: 1 203 869 7500 FAX: 1 203 869 7502

The Homestead was built as a private home. Sixty years later, after extensive architectural renovation, it became an inn, but it was not until 1978 that it became the outstandingly handsome property that it is today, perfectly sited in the Belle Haven area. The restaurant Thomas Henkelmann has a reputation for excellence that reaches far beyond the affluent and pleasant environment in which it is situated. Wine connoisseurs will be delighted with the sensational selection of clarets and burgundies on the wine list. The food too is of a similar, classic style. The temptations of the wonderful entrées should not distract diners from leaving room for the final pièce de resistance – Henkelmann's desserts and cheese dishes. The bedrooms, all of the highest quality, are in the old mansion and also in the annexes. The inn is particularly suitable for top quality meetings in secluded conducive surroundings. Places to visit locally include the Bruce Museum in Greenwich, New York City, Yale University at New Haven, the Whitney Museum in Stamford and the Cavalier Art Gallery. Golf and tennis are practised nearby. **Directions:** From New York City leave Route 1–95 at exit 3. Turn left at foot of ramp. Continue to 2nd light, then turn left into Horseneck Lane. At the end of the road turn left into Field Point Road. The inn is on your right. Price guide: Rooms $160–$220; suite $250–$395.

THE BOULDERS INN

EAST SHORE ROAD (ROUTE 45), NEW PRESTON, CONNECTICUT 06777
TEL: 1 860 868 0541 FAX: 1 860 868 1925

This enchanting Inn is in the Berkshire Hills with spectacular views of Lake Waramaug. The sound of water lapping on the shore and the sight of this lovely Victorian house will add to guests' anticipation of a perfect stay. The hotel has just seventeen guest rooms, all filled with a melange of antiques and country furniture, patchwork quilts and cushions adding colour. Six rooms in the main inn, three are in the Carriage House and others are in four guest cottages behind the Inn with their own decks overlooking the Lake. Several of the cottages have double whirlpool baths. The lounge at the foot of the elegant staircase is the focal point of The Boulders, where guests gather for apéritifs.

The big sofas are in joyous floral chintz, the polished floors gleam and charming ornaments add a personal touch. Residents change for dinner as it is a memorable occasion, for not only has the restaurant won much acclaim for its imaginative interpretation of New England dishes, but the wine list has also won many awards. The Inn has its own beach, a private trail to Pinnacle Mountain, its own boats and canoes, bikes, a games room and skating on the lake in winter. Golf, riding, antique hunting and exploring nearby villages are alternative activities. **Directions:** From New Milford, Rt. 202 to New Preston, turning left onto Route 45 to Boulders Inn. Price guide: Rooms and suites $190–$395.

A CAMBRIDGE HOUSE

2218 MASSACHUSETTS AVENUE, CAMBRIDGE, MASSACHUSETTS 02140–1836
TEL: 1 617 491 6300 FAX: 1 617 868 2848 E-MAIL: InnACH@AOL.com

A Cambridge House is a most prestigious Inn offering impeccable service. The house is glorious, Colonial revival built in 1892 and its fin de siècle grace has been meticulously restored. This is a most superior bed and breakfast establishment, nothing but the best clearly being the rule (also no smoking) The guest rooms are exquisite, delicately patterned papers and fragile toiles, lots of cushions and bolsters, period furniture, porcelain ornaments and fresh flowers all creating a romantic ambience. Breakfast is a nourishing experience served early for professional guests and later for those on vacation – fresh fruits and/or seductive pastries, and also waffles/omelettes cooked to order for those who want it.

Every evening, distinguished guests gather in the parlour, an elegant room filled with burnished antiques and gleaming silver, relaxing over delicious fresh hors d'oeuvres, with jazz playing quietly in the background. Both Boston and Cambridge have excellent restaurants, famous universities, a busy waterfront, harbour cruises, galleries, theatres, bookstores, museums and diverse sporting facilities not too far away. **Directions:** The hotel has a parking lot – Boston's airport is 20 minutes away. The rapid transit subway is recommended for visitors heading for campuses or financial and high technology districts. Price guide: Rooms $99–$275.

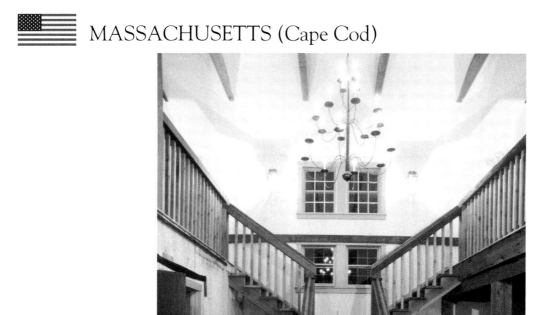

WEDGEWOOD INN

83 MAIN STREET, ROUTE 6A, YARMOUTH PORT, MASSACHUSETTS 02675
TEL: 1 508 362 5157 FAX: 1 508 362 5851 E-MAIL: info@wedgewood–inn.com

Yarmouth Port flourished in Cape Cod in the 19th century, and Main Street, the most fashionable street in this historic town, is the address of the Wedgewood Inn, a fine colonial house built in 1812. The mansion is lovely, with its white facade, green shutters and graceful lines, and stands in formal gardens, ablaze with chrysanthemums in the Autumn. The interior is faultless – polished floors, attractive wall coverings, colourful rugs, nautical prints, comfortable chairs, flowers and intriguing bibelots. The lounges have a warm elegance. The guest rooms, three in the Carriage Barn, are romantic with traditional quilts, wooden bedsteads and luxurious bathrooms. Some have garden patios and others a private, sheltered terrace. In winter the aroma of burning wood fires adds to the joy of staying here. Breakfast and afternoon tea are served in the sunny dining room, but the Inn does not have a licence – residents should 'bring their own', and hosts, Milt & Gerrie Graham, will suggest where to dine in the evenings. Guests enjoy the beaches, swim, fish, sail, play golf and tennnis, explore the Cape on bikes and hunt for antiques. Nantucket and Martha's Vineyard are close by. **Directions:** Interstate 3, over Sagamore Bridge on Route 6, exit 7, turning right, at halt sign right onto Route 6A, finding Inn 75yds on right. Price guide: Rooms $135–$155; suite $135–$195

THE CAPTAIN'S HOUSE INN

369–377 OLD HARBOR ROAD, CHATHAM, CAPE COD, MASSACHUSETTS 02633
TEL: 1 508 945 0127 FAX: 1 508 945 0866

What better name for a fine hotel in Chatham, still a busy port today with yachtsmen, private craft and its fishing fleet. Captain Harding, a famous sailor in the 1800s, built this graceful white neo-classic home and some guest rooms are named after the ships he skippered. The inn, surrounded by splendid old trees, is peaceful and secluded. The interior has period wallpapers, Queen Anne chairs, Williamsburg antiques and Oriental rugs on polished floors – a grand country house ambience with a no smoking rule. The guest quarters are extremely comfortable and wonderfully different, each with its own elegant Colonial style. Luxurious suites are in the Carriage House beyond the English Garden, The Stables, or the romantic Captain's Cottage. Disabled travellers have not been forgotten. The dining room is exquisite with floor length windows, hanging plants and pristine linen. A delicious breakfast starts the day; a full English afternoon tea appears at 4 o'clock. The friendly hosts have a list of recommended restaurants for dinner. The Inn has a croquet lawn and bikes to borrow. Chatham has its fascinating harbour, a Friday night band, sailing, fishing, galleries, golf and glorious sunsets. **Directions:** Route 28 to Chatham Centre, continuing towards Orleans. After ½ mile the Inn is on the left. Price guide: Rooms $165–$275; suite $200–$350.

PLEASANT BAY VILLAGE RESORT MOTEL

ROUTE 28, CHATHAM, MASSACHUSETTS 02633
TEL: 1 508 945 1133 FAX: 1 508 945 9701

Chatham is a delightful seaside town on Cape Cod Peninsula and Pleasant Bay Village is an appropriate name for this superb motel resort complex. Pleasant Bay has easy access to thirteen coves and sandy beaches. Guests mostly maintain an independent lifestyle, but meet in the restaurant or round the pool. The residential buildings are well spaced out, with playgrounds close by. Six acres of landscaped gardens have a dramatic waterfall as the central feature. Families may prefer to stay in the 'Efficiencies', which have a kitchen and dining alcove, or the bedroom suites, which also have outdoor tables, chairs, chaise longues and barbecues. The rooms vary in size, some having patios. All are pristine, with comfortable modern furniture. Breakfast is served in the handsome dining room. A light lunch is available poolside. The motel has a beer and wine licence for dinner. Evening meals in Chatham are great, most restaurants having Cape Cod lobster on the menu. Exploring Martha's Vineyard, playing golf, swimming, enjoying the beaches, browsing in galleries, biking, whale-watching and summer concerts fill the day. **Directions:** On Cape Cod take Route 6 to Exit 11, left after extra ramp, then left onto Pleasant Bay Road, and right onto Route 28. The Resort is 1 mile further on the right. Price guide: Rooms $135–$415.

DEERFIELD INN

108 OLD MAIN STREET, DEERFIELD, MASSACHUSETTS 01342
TEL: 1 413 774 5587 FAX: 1 413 775 7221 E-MAIL: frontdesk@deerfieldinn.com

Step back in time and stay in this select country inn in the centre of Deerfield, a three hundred years old New England village, nominated a National Historic Landmark. The Inn is an enchanting, classical building with its tall pillars and balcony over the entrance. The drawing rooms are elegant, with lovely curtains draped round the tall sash windows, yielding sofas and chairs and old rugs. The guest rooms are gorgeous – decorated in soft colours, with antique wooden bedsteads. Some are in the South Wing, reached by a covered walkway. All are wondrously peaceful and inviting. The host, Karl Sabo, trained as a chef, also has a great interest in wines, which is displayed in the renowned restaurant, an exquisite room with graceful chandeliers and authentic period furniture. Breakfast is generous, country-style and dinner is by candlelight. The menu is cosmopolitan New American and the cellar houses some great vintages. Non-smoking prevails throughout the Inn. Deerfield is ideal for discreet strategy meetings and magical for special celebrations. The fourteen 'museum' dwellings in the village should be visited. Nearby golf, tennis, hiking, cycling, and white water rafting occupy athletic residents; others may go antique hunting. **Directions:** Exits 24/25/26 from Interstate 91, then routes 5 and 10, marked to Historic Deerfield. Price guide: Rooms $128–$241.

THE WHALEWALK INN

220 BRIDGE ROAD, EASTHAM (CAPE COD), MASSACHUSETTS 02642
TEL: 1 508 255 0617 FAX: 1 508 240 0017 E-MAIL: whalewak@capecod.net

Whales have always had an important role in Cape Cod, and this prestigious 1830's mansion was built by one of the famous Whaling Masters. It is in the unspoiled Outer Cape, near the forty mile long National Seashore. Dick and Carolyn Smith have enjoyed restoring their distinguished house, collecting authentic 19th century antiques and giving meticulous attention to the minutest detail. The romantic guest rooms are immaculate and inviting, with delicate drapes in soft colours. All are light and airy and the luxurious suites have charming sitting rooms. Guests relax on the colourful patio or in the pleasant sitting room, which has original contemporary paintings hung on the walls. Breakfast is an inspired feast – "put your diet on vacation" is one of the inn's maxims, although the light repast is equally delicious. The inn is unlicensed, but hors d'oeuvres are served each evening. Good places to dine are nearby. Residents are able to watch whales, follow the nature trails, explore the sandy beaches and salt marshes,swim, sail, bike through the lovely countryside, play golf and tennis, hunt antiques or visit Martha's Vineyard, a nearby island. **Directions:** Having crossed Sagamore Bridge, follow Route 6 past exit 12 to the Orleans rotary. Take third exit onto Rock Harbour Road, find Bridge Road on right and watch for Whalewalk Inn sign, also on right. Price guide: Rooms $160–$275; suite $225–$275.

OCEAN VIEW INN & RESORT

171 ATLANTIC ROAD, GLOUCESTER, MASSACHUSETTS 01930
TEL: 1 978 283 6200 FAX: 1 978 283 1852 E-MAIL: oviar@shore.net

Step into the beautifully manicured, spectacularly quaint world that is the Ocean View Inn and Resort. Situated in Gloucester, Massachusetts, this elegant resort is a stunning turn of the century estate that simply inspires. Located on 5½ acres of prime New England oceanfront land and surrounded by lush green lawns, this English Tudor resort is a truly romantic venue. The sixty two rooms are well appointed combining spaciousness with comfort that would be hard to surpass. The dining room offers a spectacular view of the Atlantic and the gourmet food is no less enticing, offering a variety of sumptuous dishes including mouth-watering seafood, fresh from the ocean. There are many opportunities for sporting pursuits, from taking a dip in one of the pools, fishing nearby or having a game of billiards on the antique pool table. For those interested in the wonders of the sea, the whales basking off the coast may be seen. Those seeking a more challenging activity may enjoy a round of golf at the nearby courses. There are many historic attractions within the locality and the Maritime Trail is fascinating. **Directions:** From Boston, New York, I-95 and all points: Route 128 North to end (2nd light). Left on Bass Avenue, right on Atlantic Road, 1.3 miles on right. Price guide: Rooms $69–$240.

WHEATLEIGH

HAWTHORNE ROAD, LENOX, MASSACHUSETTS 01240
TEL: 1 413 637 0610 FAX: 1 413 637 4507

Wheatleigh, an enchanting Florentine palazzo in the elite Berkshires, between New York and Boston, is today a country house hotel. Built as a wedding present from a wealthy father to his beautiful daughter in 1893, its romantic ambience is rivalled only by its perfection. Surrounded by 22 acres of well manicured gardens, parkland and tall trees, it also offers peace and privacy – ideal for an important summit meeting. The Tiffany lanterns at the gate, a fountain in front of the elaborate canopied entrance leading into the impressive Great Hall, with its graceful archways, stately columns, carved balustrades, a fine grand piano, sparkling chandelier and beautiful flowers confirm that Wheatleigh is both

unique and cherished. The guestrooms, mostly overlooking the lake, are delightfully eccletic, 20th century comforts and necessities merging easily with fine period furniture and luxurious fabrics. The splendour of the dining room – Chippendale chairs, Waterford crystal and exquisite china – is matched by the inspired French dishes with American overtones and magnificent wines served by the impeccable staff. Guests can enjoy the fitness room, play tennis, swim, ski in winter, stroll in the gardens, enjoy golf nearby, hunt for antiques and in the evenings appreciate concerts at Tanglewood, home of the Boston Symphony Orchestra. **Directions:** Route 183 leads to Lenox. Price guide: Rooms $215–$725

SEACREST MANOR

99 MARMION WAY, ROCKPORT, MASSACHUSETTS 01966
TEL: 1 978 546 2211

This historic building is situated at the heart of the charming hamlet of Rockport, a town dramatically perched on the Cape Ann peninsula in the north east of Massachusetts, commanding unbelievable views of the austere Atlantic Ocean. A small and intimate inn, the Seacrest Manor is surrounded by a 2-acre sculpted garden and is stunningly positioned on a tree-lined residential shoreline drive. The inn is reminiscent of a slower, less hectic era. Several of the comfortably decorated rooms have decks overlooking the tranquil grounds and the 'Twin Lights' lighthouses on Thatcher's Island in the ocean beyond. Traditional home-cooked breakfasts are served in an earthy dining room, with a crackling log fire illuminating dark mornings. Rockport is a positive haven for marine fanatics and maritime activities abound. Visitors can embark on whale watching cruises or view the spectacular coastline from a yacht. The Seacrest Manor can also organise deep-sea fishing and sea kayaking expeditions. The town is a hive of activity, with concerts and festivals celebrating the region's unique heritage all year around. If Rockport's many shops and restaurants are not enough, Boston is a mere hour's drive away. **Directions:** From Boston, take the Interstate 93 north to Interstate 95 east. Then take State Route 128 east to Route 127 North into Rockport. Price guide (incl. breakfast and tea): Rooms $120–$148; suite $204–$216.

CLIFFSIDE INN

2 SEAVIEW AVENUE, NEWPORT, RHODE ISLAND 02840
TEL: 1 401 847 1811 FAX: 1 401 848 5850 US TOLL FREE: 1 800 845 1811 E-MAIL: cliff@wsii.com

In the 19th century East Coast tycoons built magnificent weekend retreats in fashionable Rhode Island. Today Newport is a major yachting centre. Cliffside Inn is the epitome of the style and grace of the late 19th century, standing on a tree lined avenue, close to the famous Cliff Walk and the Gilded Age mansions. The interior is sumptuous Victoriana – the spectacular carved stairway, the elaborate (and comfortable) sofas, the lamps and chandeliers, self portraits of the esteemed previous owner, painter Beatric Turner, adorning the walls, grand antique sideboards, even the plants in the patios and decks are evocative of that era. Past residents might not approve of the no-smoking regime, however. The guest rooms are glorious, wonderfully peaceful, romantic floral fabrics at the windows and covering the generous-sized beds. The opulent bathrooms are a joy! Three of the luxurious suites are in the adjoining delightful Seaview Cottage. A lavish breakfast is served and a fabulous Victorian tea is offered later in the day. There is no bar, but guests may bring their own. Guests stroll along the cliffs, go to the beach, sail, play tennis, golf or fish nearby and explore Newport's fascinating old buildings and shops. **Directions:** Seaview Avenue is off Memorial Boulevard (Route 138). Abundant parking. Price guide: Rooms and suites $205–$500.

Maine, New Hampshire and Vermont

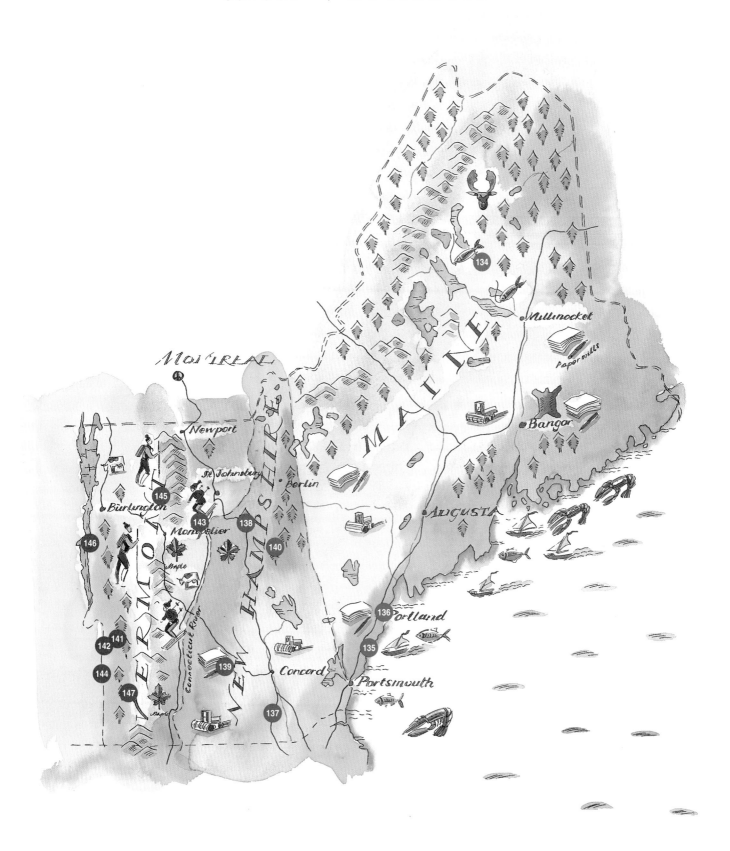

THE LODGE AT MOOSEHEAD LAKE

UPON LILY BAY ROAD, BOX 1167, GREENVILLE, MAINE 04441
TEL: 1 207 695 4400 FAX: 1 207 695 2281 E-MAIL: innkeeper@lodgeatmooseheadlake.com

The North Woods of Maine have a rugged beauty, dense forests, and more moose than anywhere else in New England. The Lodge is typical Cape Cod colonial, in brown shingle. The façade may be rustic, the interior is not. Roger and Jennifer Cauchi have great style – their imaginative use of colour, light, raw materials and local folklore has created a friendly ambience with sophisticated overtones. The spectacular views over the lake are focus points. The guest rooms have handcarved Queen-sized beds, with individual themes. They are all luxuriously appointed and every bathroom has a Jacuzzi. Attention to detail includes concealed television and full ice-buckets! Guests recount their day over drinks in the charismatic Great Room, adjacent to the charming dining room which has a wall of windows overlooking the shimmering water. There is also a minute Library, the snug Toby Room and colourful Moosehead Games Room. Breakfast is a small feast, dinner a candlelit gastronomic experience. Activities – moose safaris, fly fishing, canoeing, seaplane expeditions, exploring national parks, boating on the lake; winter sports when the snows come. **Directions:** Interstate 95N to Newport then Route 7 North, then Route 23 North to Route 15 North. Price guide: Rooms $175–$295; suites $250–$395.

KENNEBUNKPORT INN

DOCK SQUARE, KENNEBUNKPORT, MAINE 04046
TEL: 1 207 967 2621 FAX: 1 207 967 3705

Built in 1899 by a sea captain, the Kennebunkport Inn is an attractive federal-style property, located in the centre of the village. The 19th century mansion affords beautiful views across the estuary and the surrounding New England landscape. Situated in either the mansion itself or the attached River House, the 34 bedrooms are individually appointed with antiques and fine furnishings. All offer en suite facilities and modern amenities including televisions. Guests may relax in the convivial bar, enhanced by a piano bar, and indulge in a pre-dinner drink. A refined ambience envelopes the exquisite dining room where the attentive staff serve regional specialities. The very best of fresh local produce such as Maine lobster is used to create the imaginative dishes. A variety of sports is available nearby and these include golf, tennis, deep sea fishing and riding. More leisurely pursuits such as rambling along the sandy beaches or exploring the rocky coastline may also be enjoyed. The Old Port at Portland, LL Bean store and other discount outlets are within easy driving distance. A fine array of boutiques, galleries and craft shops are only footsteps away. **Directions:** Leave I-95 at exit 3. Then turn left onto Route 35. Left at Route 9, over the bridge into Dock Square. Price guide: Rooms $99.50–$289; all inclusive plan from $99 per person.

BLACK POINT INN RESORT

510, BLACK POINT ROAD, PROUTS NECK, MAINE 04074
TEL: 1 207 883 4126 FAX: 1 207 883 9976 E-MAIL: bpi@nlis.net

Maine has been a privileged summer vacation resort for over a century, the rich and famous having built magnificent homes along the Atlantic coastline. Prouts Neck peninsula has remained elite, and Black Point Inn has been offering exceptionally fine hospitality for 120 years. A gorgeous Victorian mansion, with the sea in sight from all sides, it radiates old world charm and courtesy. The dress code is jackets and ties for men after 6pm and whites for tennis The gardens are formal, scented by pine, roses and the balmy sea air, the ambience is leisurely yet sophisticated. The charming guest rooms are spacious, simply furnished, comfortable and have gorgeous views. Authentic antiques, brocaded sofas and beautiful flowers create an aura of peace in the parlours. Tea is served daily at 4pm. Cocktails taste superb when you are seated in a wicker rocking chair on the mahogany porch before feasting on fabulous New England dishes – including Maine lobster – and mellow wines from the large cellar. The impeccable restaurant overlooks the Ocean. The Inn has indoor and outdoor freshwater pools, 16 tennis courts, bikes and three miles of private beach. Excellent golf and sailing are nearby, also a fascinating bird sanctuary. Skiing can be arranged. The dress code is jackets for men after 7pm. **Directions:** Exit 6 off I95 (Maine Turnpike) to Route 1 North, right on Route 207 (Black Point Road) 6km to hotel. Price guide (dinner, bed : Rooms $300–$550 double occupancy.

BEDFORD VILLAGE INN & RESTAURANT

2 VILLAGE INN LANE, BEDFORD, NEW HAMPSHIRE 03110
TEL: 1 603 472 2001 FAX: 1 603 472 2379

An imposing colonial-style building dating from the early 1800's, the Bedford Village Inn has acquired a reputation that draws food-lovers from across the land and beyond. Set amidst the rolling New Hampshire pastureland with a sculpted garden, visitors will take a long langorous stroll as a prelude to a gastronomical voyage that will linger in the memory. Louisiana-born chef, Chris Ward, is fast becoming recognised as one of the best chefs in the country. Trained by the London Savoy's world-renowned Jean Lafonte, he has developed an individual style derived from classical French cuisine. Visits to the inn are particularly popular during the summer months, when the herb garden and the nearby organic farms and fishing villages are at their most bountiful. Visitors should not miss the specialities of the house, which include pan-seared Atlantic salmon and Chardonnay-braised lamb. After dinner, guests can relax in the convivial surroundings of the Tap Room, an English pub, serving traditional local beers: a hearty counterpoint to the wine cellar containing over 400 of the world's finest wines. Sunday mornings yield particular treats, with the inn literally buzzing with the brunch crowd, who have come to consider the imaginative fare as one of the highlights of their week. **Directions:** From 101w go to first lights (intersection of 101 and 114) turn left to continue on 101w. Turn right after next lights into Village Inn lane. Price guide: Suite $185–$285.

ADAIR

80 GUIDER LANE, BETHLEHEM, NEW HAMPSHIRE 03574
TEL: 1 603 444 2600 FAX: 1 603 444 4823 E-MAIL: adair@connriver.net

This fine creation has a tradition steeped in the legal practise and has, as a result, entertained many distinguished guests including supreme court justices, presidents and actors for a number of years. After successfully defending Edward Doheny in the Teapot Dome Cases, Frank Hogan built Adair in 1927 and then gave it to his only daughter, Dorothy Adair Hogan, on the occasion of her marriage to a Washington attorney. The interior is the essence of comfort and features period antiques, soft lighting and plush club chairs which combine to form a most relaxing ambience. Each named after a local mountain, the nine en suite bedrooms are appointed in a luxurious manner and many afford mountain views. The cuisine at Adair is excellent with hot entrées such as fruit filled French toast with Vermont cob-smoked bacon at breakfast and freshly baked cakes and cookies at teatime. The seasonal restaurant serves delicious recipes made with the best of local produce. There are several PGA 18-hole golf courses within the locality, great downhill and cross-country skiing may be enjoyed and the hiking trails are truly invigorating. For the less energetic guest, several local museums, outlet stores and antique shops are within easy reach. **Directions:** Leave I-93 at exit 40. Turn right, the entrance is on the left. From Route 302, Adair is 3 miles west of Bethlehem Village on the right. Price guide (incl. breakfast): Rooms $145–$195; suite $210–$245; cottage $295.

COLBY HILL INN

3 THE OAKS, PO BOX 779, HENNIKER, NEW HAMPSHIRE 03242
TEL: 1 603 428 3281 FAX: 1 603 428 9218 US TOLL FREE: 1 800 531 0330

Nestling in the hills of New Hampshire and surrounded by classic New England scenery, Colby Hill Inn is located just half a mile from the small college town of Henniker. The 18th century house is the centrepiece of a five-acre farm and comprises traditional barns, a restored carriage house, rolling fields, lush perennial gardens, and a swimming pool. While each of its 16 individually-decorated guest rooms offers a range of modern amenities to guarantee a comfortable stay, some feature the added attraction of a working fireplace. The friendly hosts have created an informal and very relaxed atmosphere; the only written rule refers to the resident dog, "please don't feed Delilah, she's had too many cookies". Guests are invited to enjoy the solitude provided by the inn's many nooks and crannies or gather by the parlour fire or over a puzzle in the games room. The popular restaurant's menu features over a dozen entrées and a choice of desserts including sumptuous home-made treats and evening drinks. The inn is only a 90 minutes' drive from Boston and Manchester airports, ideal for those touring New England. Leisure activities include downhill and cross-country skiing, hiking, bicycling, kayaking, visiting the many beaches and exploring the small shops and old book stores. **Directions:** 17 miles west of Concord off routes 202/9. Go ½ mile south on route 114 to blinking light and village centre. Turn right. The inn is ½ mile on right. Price guide: Rooms $85–$185; suites $275–$315.

INN AT THORN HILL

THORN HILL ROAD, JACKSON, NEW HAMPSHIRE 03846
TEL: 1 603 383 4242 FAX: 1 603 383 8602 E-MAIL: thornhll@ncia.ne

Jackson can only be reached through the 'Honeymoon Covered Bridge' – a delightful introduction to this enchanting village and the inn stands high above it, looking across to the dramatic Presidential Mountain Range. This idyllic retreat was built in 1895 and Victoriana is the theme throughout the Main Inn, with its lace curtains and fine antiques. The Parlour has a grand piano and board games, cards and books await guests' pleasure. The romantic guest rooms have old world charm and have been totally renovated and now feature gas fireplaces and spas. Other accommodation is country style in The Carriage House while three recently renovated cottages offer more privacy. The cosy Bar resembles a small pub, alternatively residents relax in the charming lounges or settle in the wicker chairs on the porch overlooking the gardens and mountains. The restaurant is joyous, the aroma of marvellous home cooking pervading the air. Hungry diners appreciate the rich seasonal dishes, fabulous soups and glorious pastries, accompanied by fine wines. In summer the inn has a pool; tennis, golf and riding are nearby. The Appalachian Mountain Club gives hikers and climbers good routes. In winter Jackson offers cross country and downhill skiing, skating and sleigh rides. **Directions:** From Montreal, Can-10 to Can-55, I-91 to I-93, Exit 40, take Route 302 to Route 16 North to Jackson. Price guide: Rooms $190–$345.

MOUNTAIN TOP INN & RESORT

MOUNTAIN TOP ROAD, CHITTENDEN, VERMONT 05737
TEL: 1 802 483 2311 FAX: 1 802 483 6373 E-MAIL: info@mountaintopinn.com

Mountain Top, known as 'Vermont's best kept secret' is a marvellous resort, famous for its cross country ski-ing but also delightful in summer – and the Inn plays an important role in its success. This is an enchanting small hotel – as it name suggests, at the top of a mountain, so the views are spectacular all the year round. Purpose built, it has every modern comfort. The spacious guest rooms are charming, decorated in soft colours, with country style furniture, and the bathrooms are efficient. Some are in the adjacent cottages and chalets. The lounges are also simplistic and attractive, looking out onto the mountains and the games room is the social centre. The elegant restaurant has big picture windows, and offers New England cooking at its best. Good wines are listed. The Inn is no smoking throughout. Mountain Top has its own ski instructors and shop. Skating and sleighrides are other popular winter diversions. In summer the Golf School is active, with tuition for all handicaps. The enormous estate has excellent facilities for shooting, riding, fishing, tennis, swimming, while the lake has a sandy beach and opportunities for water sports. Also Vermont must be explored. **Directions:** Route 7, then Route 4, left onto Meadowlake Drive and follow road to the very top. Price guide: Rooms $168–$226; suite $226–$268.

TULIP TREE INN

49 DAM ROAD, CHITTENDEN, VERMONT 05737
TEL: 1 802 483 6213 FAX: 1 802 483 2623 US TOLL FREE: 1 800 707 0017 E-MAIL: ttinn@sover.net

Deep in seclusion, surrounded by the lush green backdrop that has made Vermont known throughout the world, the Tulip Tree Inn is a hideaway for the more discerning holidaymaker. A country house that is redolent of style, guests could almost walk right past it, nestled as it is in a veritable forest of foliage. Once inside, a tranquil ambience relaxes the visitors with simple yet refined furniture providing a comfortable environment in which to escape the hectic pace of a modern lifestyle. The nine bedrooms are superbly designed in their own individual way, elegantly styled to make each stay as comfortable as possible. They all feature every necessity that today's traveller may desire.

Dinner is more of an experience than just a meal; served by candlelight whilst classical music plays soothingly in the background. The food is sumptuous and wholesome, prepared using only the freshest of ingredients. Guests can indulge in some horse-riding, visit the many museums nearby or peruse the glassworks. For those wishing to immerse themselves in the glorious natural surroundings, why not take a stroll around the stunning grounds, go hiking in the mountains and if all else fails simply relax in style at this beautiful resting spot. **Directions:** North or East of Rutland, follow signs from Route 4 or 7. Price guide (incl. breakfast & dinner): Rooms $159–$399.

RABBIT HILL INN

48 LOWER WATERFORD ROAD, VERMONT 05848
TEL: 1 802 748 5168 FAX: 1 802 748 8342 E-MAIL: info@RabbitHillInn.com

Rabbit Hill Inn is a luxurious and historical escape from the pressures of today's busy world. The property is truly romantic: from the soft strains of music welcoming visitors as they step across the entrance porch to the restful glow of candles pervading the bedrooms as they retire for the night. Innkeepers Brian and Leslie Mulcahy are dedicated to pampering guests in a stylish and comfortable environment. Overlooking the beautiful White Mountains and the Connecticut River Valley, the Inn was built in 1795 to serve the needs of travellers journeying between Canada and the New England harbours. The property has been completely restored and modernised but has retained many of its classic features, antique furnishings and its historical atmosphere. The stylish bedrooms are enhanced by original artworks, whirlpool baths and magnificent King and Queen-sized canopy beds. The whimsical use of rabbits is delightful: from bunny-shaped butter to sculpted rabbits tucked into the beams, these animals are scattered throughout. Guests relax in the parlours or the Snooty Fox Pub before indulging in the superb cuisine offered in the candlelit dining room. The exquisite dishes are made with fresh ingredients and include produce from the Inn's own greenhouse and garden. On site activities include canoeing, hiking and sledding. **Directions:** From I93 north, exit 44, onto Rt18 north, 2 miles to the inn. Price guide (incl. breakfast, tea, dinner & all service charges): Rooms $210–$295; suites $275–$370.

1811 HOUSE

PO BOX 39, ROUTE 7A, MANCHESTER VILLAGE, VERMONT 05254
TEL: 1 802 362 1811 FAX: 1 802 362 2443 US TOLL FREE: 800 432 1811 E-MAIL: info@1811house.com

Pretty Manchester Village is proud of its enchanting inn, the 1811 House which has extensive gardens filled with daffodils in Spring and its own Scottish pub appreciated as much by the locals as by the hotel guests! Loving restoration work has resulted in the joyous interior of this Federal house – a fine collection of American and English antiques sits well on rich Persian carpets, handsome paintings adorn the walls while silver photograph frames and other memorabilia add a personal touch. Discreet air conditioning controls the atmosphere. It is a non-smoking house. The attractive guest rooms are filled with gracious period furniture, and many have spectacular views of the Green Mountains. A few bedrooms are in the adjacent cottage. Marnie and Bruce Duff, good Scottish names, have their individual skills. Marnie is a superb cook and her breakfasts are fabulous. Bruce is a great gardner. He is also 'mine host' of the traditional 'snug' which offers good company, well-kept ale and 63 malt whiskies. The parlour is an elegant rendezvous, the library peaceful and residents relax over a game of snooker in the games room. Restaurants abound for dinner, and in the day antique shops, boutiques, galleries, museums, fishing, cycling, good golf, tennis are but a selection of local activities. **Directions:** On the historic Route 7A. Price guide: Rooms $120–$230; suite $230.

THE MOUNTAIN ROAD RESORT

STOWE, VERMONT 05672

TEL: 1 802 253 4566 **FAX:** 1 802 253 7397 **UK FREEPHONE** 0800 894 581 **E-MAIL: stowevt@aol.com**

The Mountain Road Resort is a vibrant, cosmopolitan and stylish hotel surrounded by seven acres of landscaped gardens. The complex is pristine and the accommodation includes commodious bedrooms with comfortable country-style furnishings, air conditioning, modern bathrooms and many gas-powered fireplaces. There are also luxurious studios and split level suites with full kitchens, large windows and Jacuzzis. No smoking is the rule. A lavish continental breakfast is served in The Library. There is no restaurant but afternoon refreshments are served. Children have a Games Room. Billy's Wine Bar has excellent vintages, several beers, 'munchable' snacks and Ben & Jerry's ice cream. The Mountain Road has a 'Dine Around' option and the Stowe Trolley transports guests into town – babysitters available. The Resort has a splendid outdoor pool, tennis and boules – indoors a marvellous Aqua-Centre with fitness facilities. The sun terraces are great for doing nothing! Special green fees have been organised at local golf clubs and other summer sports are tennis, canoeing, fishing, hiking and riding. Winter sports include downhill and cross-country skiing. Boat trips on Lake Champlain and gondola rides up the mountain are leisure activities. Internet: www.stowevtusa.com **Directions:** Interstate 89 to Junction 10, then Route 100 to Stowe. Price guide: Rooms $109–$210; suites $215–$395.

BASIN HARBOR CLUB

ON LAKE CHAMPLAIN, VERGENNES, VERMONT 05491
TEL: 1 802 475 2311 FAX: 1 802 475 6545 US TOLL FREE: 1 800 622 4000 E-MAIL: info@basinharbor.com

Upon arriving at this delightful New England resort, set on a cove on Lake Champlain, guests abandon the pressures of a modern existence and relax in this haven of seclusion. Basin Harbor has been in the hands of the Beach family for four generations and the warmth and hospitality of a past era is still offered here today. Three guest houses and 77 cottages lie in the 700 acres of beautiful grounds. Log fires, wooden floors and soft rugs featured throughout the property. All of the cottages are individually decorated with simple floral patterns and comfortable furnishings; many offer a view of either the lake or the waterfront. After a day of golf or other outdoor pursuits, hearty appetites are truly satisfied in the attractive Main Dining Room.

Traditional American cuisine fuses with more unusual flavours, creating dishes such as Dijon-garlic marinated grilled shrimp with thyme beurre blanc and pan-roasted breast of duck with raspberry bordelaise. The excellent wine list has been thoughtfully compiled. Sporting activities include canoeing, kayaking, sailing, water-skiing and hiking. Trips to the Ben and Jerry factory, Burlington's Church Street and Lake Champlain Maritime Museum are popular excursions. **Directions:** Take Interstate 89 to exit 1 at Woodstock. Take route 4 to Rutland, then North onto route 7 to Vergennes. Take 22A through Vergennes, turn right onto Basin Harbor Road for six miles. Price guide: Rooms $119–$210; suite $200–$425.

WINDHAM HILL INN

WEST TOWNSHEND, VERMONT 05359
TEL: 1 802 874 4080 FAX: 1 802 874 4702

The first settlers came to Vermont in 1720, and how thrilled they would have been had this enchanting country house inn been at the end of their journey. The Green Mountains country is some of the most spectacular in New England, whether snowclad in winter or lush and green in summer. Today's travellers arriving at this haven, with its welcoming facade, relax instantly. The parlours are inviting, filled with antiques, jewel coloured oriental rugs on the polished wood floors, and comfortable locally made furniture. The Music Room has an 1888 Steinway! The pristine guest rooms have big beds and some have decks or window seats. Some are in the attractive White Barn, adjacent to the Main House. The dress code is casual, a little smarter for the delicious five-course candle-lit dinner in the Frog Pond Dining Room, and many of the excellent wines listed are available by the glass. In winter guests skate on the pond, ski downhill or cross country; in summer they use the hotel pool and tennis court, golf, maybe take a picnic and and follow – on foot, bike or horse – the main trails through forests and flower filled meadows. South Vermont is fascinating: country fairs, art and craft shows, picturesque villages, antique dealers, music festivals. **Directions:** Route 30, at West Townshend turn off opposite county store, finding Windham Hill sign 1¼ miles on. Price guide: Rooms $180–$305

Canada

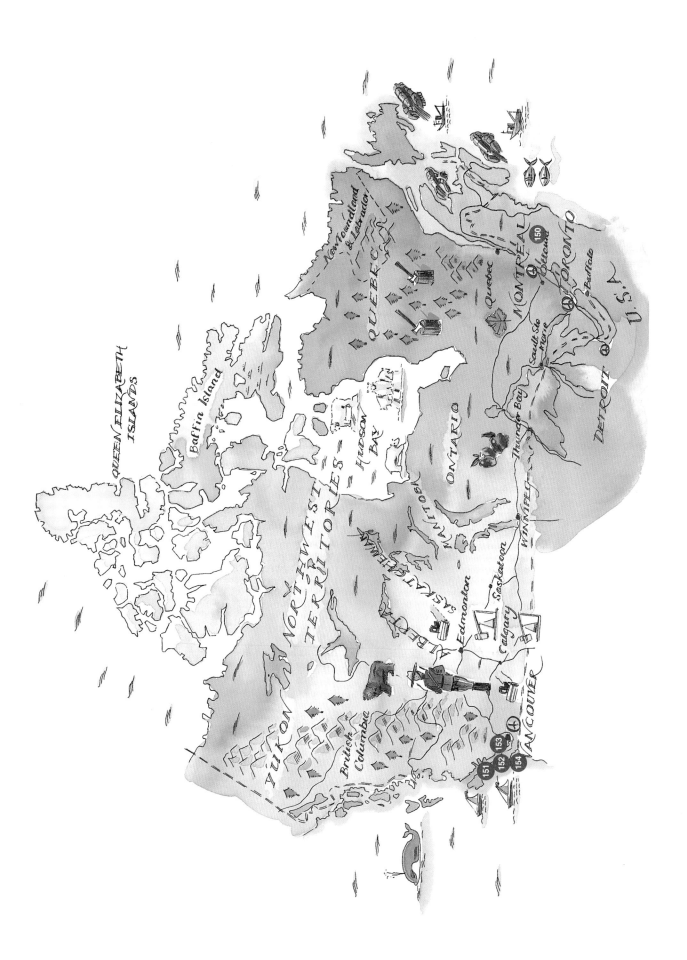

AUBERGE RIPPLECOVE INN

700 RIPPLECOVE ROAD, AYER'S CLIFF, QUEBEC, CANADA
TEL: 1 819 838 4296 FAX: 1 819 838 5541 E-MAIL: info@ripplecove.com

Founded in 1945 by the Stafford family as a summer fishing lodge, the Auberge Ripplecove Inn is the epitome of style, grace and sophistication. Dramatically perched on the shores of Lake Massawippi and surrounded by verdant woodland, this Inn is a luxurious yet homely hideaway only hours away from the thriving metropolises of Montreal and Quebec City. Set on a 12-acre estate, the Auberge Ripplecove Inn has a heated pool, two private beaches and offers a variety of recreational activities all year round. During the summer months, visitors can enjoy some of the richest fresh-water fishing in the Americas, while in winter the frozen lake provides an opportunity to practise one of Canada's most popular sports – ice-skating. There are also five Alpine centres in close proximity. The 25 individually designed rooms have been magnificently furnished and many benefit from their own private balcony and double whirlpools. Befitting a lodge in the heart of francophile Quebec, the fare is a unique blend of French and international, served by a dedicated and professional staff in a Victorian dining room. **Directions:** From Montreal, take route 10 in the direction of Magog. Turn left at exit 121 onto route 55. Turn left at exit 21, following route 141 until Ayer's Cliff, where the Auberge is signposted. Price guide (incl. breakfast & dinner): Rooms $110–$190; suite $190–$225.

SEASIDE LUXURY RESORT BED & BREAKFAST

8355 LOCHSIDE DRIVE, SIDNEY, BRITISH COLUMBIA, CANADA
TEL: 1 250 544 1000 FAX: 1 250 544 1001 US TOLL FREE: 1 888 900 2732 E-MAIL: callus@travellersinn.com

Created to provide its guests with unsurpassed warmth, luxury and privacy, this exclusive property enjoys a superb location. Situated in 3 acres of the finest ocean front on Vancouver Island and surrounded by magnificent beaches, the Seaside Luxury Resort is ideal for those seeking complete seclusion and privacy. The interior is furnished in a stylish manner and no detail has been overlooked. Each of the luxurious suites offers glorious views of the ocean, private bathrooms, satellite televisions and patio doors opening out onto the sundeck. The Diamond Suite features a Jacuzzi hot tub. Continental breakfasts are served in the privacy of the guests' own rooms or in the dining room. Fitness enthusiasts may use the Swedish designed indoor heated pool, hot tub and the fitness area. Outdoor activities are also provided and these include crabbing, fishing charters, whale-watching, sea kayaking and canoeing. For the less energetic, the beach front is perfect for strolling and admiring the spectacular sunrises whilst bird-watchers will be fascinated with the resident bald eagle, nesting beside the house. Honeymoons, reunions and other private functions can be held at the Resort. Whether they seek a private hideaway or wish to join other friends; all guests are promised a most memorable stay. **Directions:** Turn off HWY 17 onto Mt Newton Cross Road, then left on Lochside Drive, 15 mins from Victoria. Price guide: Rooms $99– $250.

THE WEDGEWOOD HOTEL

845 HORNBY STREET, VANCOUVER, BRITISH COLUMBIA, V6Z 1V1
TEL: 1 604 689 7777 FAX: 1 604 608 5348 US/CDA TOLL FREE 1 800 663 0666 E-MAIL: info@wedgewoodhotel.com

The Wedgewood, situated on Vancouver's stylish Robson Square, is a charming boutique-style hotel offering the latest modern amenities and excellent service. The refined interior is the height of European elegance. The hotel offers an interesting selection of individually appointed bedrooms which feature floral arrangements, original antiques, fine tapestries and other pieces of art. All rooms feature balconies, while the penthouse suites offer fireplaces, wet-bars, Jacuzzis and scenic garden terraces. The Wedgewood offers extraordinary dining in its popular restaurant, Bacchus, with its inspired modern French cuisine using the freshest of local ingredients as well as products from around the world. The extensive wine list will please the most particular of connoisseurs while the richly furnished cigar room with its rare selection of cigars, ports, double malt whiskies and cognacs is a perfect accompaniment. Advance reservations are highly recommended! The Piano Lounge offers an exciting and well-attended cocktail hour and after-theatre "Rendez-vous". Other delights include traditional afternoon tea and weekend brunch. The hotel's central location offers every leisure activity within walking distance from shopping, fine dining to entertainment, sightseeing and markets. **Directions**: The hotel is situated downtown, 30 minutes from Vancouver International Aiport. Price guide: Rooms Cdn$200–$360; suites Cdn$400–$660.

THE WEST END GUEST HOUSE

1362 HARO STREET, VANCOUVER, BRITISH COLUMBIA V6E 1G2
TEL: 1 604 681 2889 FAX: 1 604 688 8812 E-MAIL: wegh@idmail.com

Those wishing to explore the exciting city of Vancouver will be pleased with location of the West End Guest House. This delightful property offers warmth and character whilst exuding old world charm. Following a careful refurbishment, the interior of the house has been updated and offers many modern amenities alongside old Victorian furnishings. The bedrooms, varying in size, are all individually decorated with diverse colour schemes. A beautiful fireplace forms the centrepiece of the Parlour and the sun deck, verandah and small garden, are ideal places to recline and enjoy the relaxing atmosphere. Gourmet breakfasts comprising freshly baked pastries, cereals, fruit and daily entrées are served in the main floor salons whilst home-made cookies or tarts await the guests at turndown. Activities include visiting art galleries and museums, shopping and dining in the many restaurants within the area. The interesting civic areas of Granville Island, Chinatown, Gastown and Yaletown are worth a visit. **Directions:** From Vancouver International Airport, take Grant McConachie Way following signs to Vancouver over Arthur Lang Bridge. Take the Granville Street exit, follow Granville to bridge and exit at Seymour Street and then left to Robson Street. Exit left at Broughton Street, the hotel is one block on the left. Price guide: Rooms $150 Cdn–$225 Cdn.

DASHWOOD MANOR

1 COOK STREET, VICTORIA, BRITISH COLUMBIA V8V 3W6

TEL: 1 250 385 5517 FAX: 1 250 383 1760 TOLL FREE: 1 800 667 5517 E-MAIL: reservations@dashwoodmanor.com

This grand Edwardian house, its half timbering and large gables reflecting the Tudor revival period of the early 20th century has been imaginatively transformed into a unique bed and breakfast residence. Dashwood Manor, named after its owner Derek Dashwood, is in a magnificent position, right across the road from the shore of lovely Vancouver Island, with spectacular views over the Strait of Juan de Fuca, yet only minutes walk through verdant Beacon Hill Park to the centre of Victoria. All the accommodation is in self-contained suites, each equipped with a small kitchen offering a simple yet satisfying breakfast. Guests appreciate the privacy offered and the elegance of the rooms, some having chandeliers, fireplaces, balcony or Jacuzzi, others hideaway beds in the attractive living rooms. All have Queen beds with traditional floral quilts and period piece furniture. Budget suites do not look over the Ocean, however the grandest suites do. Early risers may see whales, seals and sea otters close to the beach while eagles soar in the sky and birdsong fills the air. The waterfront is fascinating with big ships, yachts and windsurfers all on the move. Downtown Victoria has excellent restaurants, fine museums and traditional buildings, harbour trips and good sports facilities. **Directions:** The Manor is on the corner of Cook Street and Dallas Road, right on the coast. Price guide: Rooms $175 Cdn–$385 Cdn.

Bermuda and Caribbean

ROSEDON HOTEL

PO BOX HM 290, HAMILTON HMAX, BERMUDA
TEL: 1 441 295 1640 FAX: 1 441 295 5904 E-MAIL: rosedon@ibl.bm

Originally built in 1903 by an expatriate English family, this stunningly refurbished colonial hotel provides a quiet, friendly and relaxed atmosphere in sensational surroundings. Enclosed by bountiful tropical gardens the Rosedon Hotel is a tranquil sanctuary only minutes from the bustling town of Hamilton. Suffused with the atmosphere of colonial splendour, the main house is beautifully decorated in a traditional style and is festooned with antique furniture. The Bermudian-style rooms are all spacious and well-appointed, and have balconies overlooking the swimming pool. Breakfast and lunch are served on the poolside patio, while light dinners are available on request. With Hamilton just a short stroll away, visitors can enjoy the many shops and department stores that the capital boasts, as well as its sociable nightlife. Undoubtedly Bermuda's chief asset is its beautiful coastline and visitors do not forget the peerless beaches and the crystal clear ocean, into which the nearby aquarium gives an invaluable insight. The Rosedon Hotel also organises introductions to all the island's championship golf courses and provides transportation to a South Shore Beach and Tennis Club. Conveniently located for the business traveller, the hotel has placed a data port in each room and does not charge for local calls. **Directions:** A short walk from Hamilton. Price guide (incl. breakfast): Rooms $190–$260.

FOURWAYS INN

PO BOX PG 294, PAGET PG BX, BERMUDA
TEL: 1 441 236 6517 FAX: 1 441 236 5528 E-MAIL: fourways@ibl.bm

Fourways is a glorious, relaxing hideaway nestling in the centre of this sunshine island. It combines privacy, elegance and warmth with convenience and excellent value for money. Every guest can feel pampered. Ten intimate cottages with shady terraces are scattered over hillside gardens which are emblazoned with brightly coloured hibiscus blossoms, tropical flowers, tall palms and manicured lawns. They are well-appointed and have every amenity from air conditioning, a kitchenette, spacious bathroom, mini bar and cable television to a safety deposit box. The cottages, each named after a ship, surround a magnificent fresh water heated swimming pool where cool drinks can be enjoyed in the shade of overhanging palms and matching green coloured umbrellas. Fourways is renowned for its gastronomic dining. Its award winning restaurant, housed in a luxurious 18th century residence refurbished for elegant dining, is one of Bermuda's best. Every dish is served with gourmet perfection and enhanced by a list of over 500 fine wines. There is also a fresh pastry and bread shop on site. Guests can enjoy free facilities at nearby Stonington Beach and tee times can be arranged at all of the islands championship golf courses which are no further than a 20 minutes drive away. **Directions:** Fourways is in the centre of the island, a ten minutes taxi ride or ferry crossing from Hamilton. Price guide: Rooms $150–$230; suites $190–$325.

HARMONY CLUB ALL INCLUSIVE

PO BOX 299, PAGET, BERMUDA PG BX
TEL: 1 441 236 3500 FAX: 1 441 236 2624

Surrounded by gorgeous colours under a cloudless blue sky, Bermuda's first all-inclusive resort is a glorious hideaway nestling in the heart of this sunshine island. Harmony Club combines privacy, casual elegance and gracious warmth with convenience, quality and excellent value for money. It can be as lively or as restful as you want it to be and guests can pursue their favourite pastimes at their leisure. Every guest can feel pampered by the facilities, which include tennis, swimming, a sauna and a whirlpool. Two-seater scooters are provided for those wishing to explore the island. Scattered among the brightly coloured hibiscus blossoms, tropical flowers, tall palms and manicured lawns are 68 intimate, pink and white guest rooms built in traditional British cottage-style. They are delightfully appointed and have every amenity from air conditioning, bathrooms, radio and television to de luxe toiletries and tea/coffee making facilities. Superb food, generous drinks, complimentary evening cocktails and nightcaps can be enjoyed in the enchanting gardens. The attractions of Bermuda are close at hand and special packages, including green fees and transportation, can be arranged for golfing enthusiasts. **Directions:** The resort is nine miles from the airport and two miles from Hamilton city centre. Harmony Club provides airport transfers for all their guests. Price guide: De luxe double rooms $311–$431.

THE NEWSTEAD HOTEL

27 HARBOUR ROAD, PAGET PG02, BERMUDA
TEL: 1 441 236 6060 FAX: 1 441 236 7454 E-MAIL: reservation@newsteadhotel.com

Sunshine yellow under a sparkling white roof the gracious, classical colonial style Newstead Hotel stands regally on a gently terraced hillside overlooking Hamilton Harbour and the beautiful outer islands of Bermuda. It is an enchanting manor house incorporating the traditional and modern in an exquisitely manicured garden setting of quiet tranquillity. Most of the bedrooms have been recently refurbished with cheerful prints and the finest fabrics and furniture. All have private terraces and enjoy panoramic views over the harbour, the garden or the superb freshwater swimming pool surrounded by lounges and sun umbrellas. The hotel's kitchens produce the best of American and European cuisine which diners can enjoy on the Harbour Terrace after leisurely sunset cocktails prior to dancing under the stars. There are two clay tennis courts and a putting green. Guests can also enjoy the privileges of The Elbow Beach Hotel, taking advantage of the most spectacular beach on the island. Windsailing, waterskiing and scuba diving amenities and major golf courses are within easy reach. **Directions:** Overlooking Hamilton Harbour a short ferry ride from the town centre. Price guide: Rooms from $275; suites from $375.

SURF SIDE BEACH CLUB

90 SOUTH SHORE ROAD, WARWICK, BERMUDA
TEL: 1 441 236 7100 FAX: 1 441 236 9765

Surf Side is a sunny hideaway overlooking Bermuda's unique South Shore, surrounded by five acres of landscaped hillside terraces and walkways above beautiful, white-sanded beaches and coves. Scattered among the colourful hibiscus blossoms, tall palms and manicured lawns are 37 cottages, apartment-style units and penthouses. Each has its own sea view and is designed for privacy. Guests are provided with every home comfort, from tastefully furnished bedrooms and lounges to fully-fitted kitchens and either a secluded garden patio or a wide, plant-bedecked balcony where the only sound is that of breaking waves. With a natural ambience created by the moon, stars, soft tropical breezes and delicate scent of flowers, the Palms Restaurant and Bar serves outstanding cuisine and island cocktails beside the pool. Views from the pool's sun lounges are magnificent. The relaxed and unpretentious atmosphere which is ideal for those who love to be self-sufficient and free to discover the delights of the island. For the energetic visitor Surf Side has a fully equipped fitness centre, complete with sauna and Jacuzzi. Golf and riding are nearby. **Directions:** 3 miles west of of Hamilton. Price guide (until March 2001): Deluxe units $205; superior suite $250; Penthouse accomodation for 4 persons $350.

THE INN AT ENGLISH HARBOUR

PO BOX 187, ST JOHNS, ANTIGUA, WEST INDIES
TEL: 1 268 460 1014 FAX: 1 268 460 1603 E-MAIL: theinn@candw.ag

Set on the southern coast of Antigua's national park, in ten acres of wooded headland with its own pristine white sandy beach, this charming inn overlooks the start of the historic English Harbour. The accommodation comprises beach front rooms with private verandahs, ceiling fans and wall safes. Nestling above the beach, the cottage rooms afford a wonderful panoramic vista across the entire harbour. After sipping rum punch in the traditional Stone Bar, guests may dine by candlelight beneath the tropical night sky and sample the excellent cuisine in the Terrace Restaurant. Diners start with spicy Thai prawn and coconut soup, followed by kingfish baked in a mustard butter served on slices of squash and rice and finishing with chargrilled bananas served with homemade vanilla ice cream and caramel sauce. The extensive wine list has been carefully compiled with the flavours in mind. Complimentary activities include sunfish sailing and windsurfing, with kayaks and snorkelling gear available on site. Water-skiing, sailing, scuba diving and deep sea fishing may be arranged and a game of tennis or squash may be enjoyed only five minutes away. Other pastimes include sea bottom trawling and day trips to Barbuda, Guadeloupe and St Kitts. **Directions:** 16 miles from the airport and 12 miles from the Capital St. John. Price guide: Rooms $160–$440.

AVILA BEACH HOTEL

PENSTRAAT 130, WILLEMSTAD, CURAÇAO, NETHERLANDS ANTILLES, WEST INDIES
TEL: 599 9 461 4377 FAX: 599 9 461 1493 E-MAIL: info@avilahotel.com

Originally the governor's residence the Avila Beach Hotel is a stunning testament to Dutch-Carribean style architecture. Situated in Willemstad on the Dutch island of Curaçao, this tastefully refined hotel is an ideal escape from the pressures of a hectic lifestyle. Inside, the hotel gives way to its recent renovation and is simply breathtaking with vivid and bold colours comprising the décor. The furniture is stylish and comfortable and the magnificence of the hotel inside mirrors the beauty of the island outside. Almost every room offers a panoramic vista across the ocean as well as having a private balcony or terrace. Each is well appointed providing maximum comfort and offers every necessary convenience. Avila is renowned for its fine cuisine and diners are truly spoilt for choice with the convivial Avila Café, the elegant Belle Terrace and the informal Blues Jazz Club and Seafood Restaurant with its fantastic view of the beach. Wherever guests dine, the food is superbly prepared and exquisite to taste whilst making use of the fresh ingredients that abound both on and off shore. Guests may relax on the private beach or wander around the luxurious gardens. For the more active there is tennis, squash, golf or any number of watersports to choose from on Curaçao. **Directions:** There are regular direct flights from Miami. Local car hire companies will provide directions or taxis are readily available. Price guide: Rooms $90–$245; suite $230–$460.

HUMMINGBIRD INN

MORNE DANIEL, BOX 1901, ROSEAU, DOMINICA, WEST INDIES
TEL: 1 767 449 1042 FAX: 1 767 449 1042 E-MAIL: hummingbird@cwcom.dm

Long considered the most welcoming, charming and peaceful 'pension' in Dominica, the Hummingbird Inn is the ideal base from which to explore this unspoiled island paradise. Set amidst lush forest, the Hummingbird has breathtaking views of the ocean and the famed Rock-A-Way beach. From the wooden verandah, visitors can bask in the splendour of the tropical garden, observing the 15 bird species that frequent the region, as well as the family of iguanas that live nearby. Owner Jean Finucane has transformed this plantation-style house, which was built in 1974, into a three-bungalowed tropical hideaway, with 10 beautifully appointed bedrooms. There are ceiling fans and louvred red-cedar doors letting in fresh air. The creole and international fare, lovingly crafted from local produce, is of an exceptionally high standard and can be enjoyed on the terrace or in the stylish dining room. A variety of outdoor pursuits, from fishing and tennis to horse-riding and snorkelling, may be practised nearby. A mere two minutes from the aquiline Caribbean Ocean, the Hummingbird Inn arranges scuba diving and fishing trips, as well as hiking excursions through some to most unforgettable forests in the Caribbean. **Directions:** Located between Roseau, the capital of Dominica, and Canefield Airport, the Hummingbird Inn is a short bus journey from Roseau. Price guide (including breakfast): Rooms from US$89; suite from US$150.

MANOIR DE BEAUREGARD

CHEMIN DES SALINES 97227, STE-ANNE, MARTINIQUE, FRENCH WEST INDIES
TEL: 00 596 76 73 40 FAX: 00 596 76 93 24

Manoir de Beauregard is a handsome, solidly built 18th century manor which has been restored and renovated into an attractive inn and restaurant. It is peacefully situated just a short walk from the old village of Sainte-Anne with its market and interesting craft shops. The magnificent beach of Pointe Marin and its vast array of water sports is just 8km away and for those seeking beauty and solitude the deserted beaches fringing the south of the island are within easy reach. Visitors to the hotel receive a true West Indies welcome and excellent hospitality from the ever pleasant staff and owners, Mr and Mrs St Cyr, who do everything in their power to help guests enjoy the Creole way of life. Thick stone walls, high, beamed ceilings and marble floors help keep the manor's interior cool and relaxing. Splendid antique Creole furniture abounds and fine fabrics filter the sun's bright rays. The bedrooms, eight of which are in a garden extension, are extremely comfortable and individually designed. Lunch is available but dinner is served in the elegant, timber-roofed resturant only in the high season. The cuisine is tasty tropical with such dishes as conch fillet with green pepper sauce and the chef's speciality, coconut custard. **Directions:** A five minutes walk north from Sainte-Anne. Price guide (incl. breakfast): Rooms $140–$160; suite $180–$220.

MAGO ESTATE HOTEL

PO BOX 247, SOUFRIÈRE, ST LUCIA, WEST INDIES
TEL: 1 758 459 5880 FAX: 1 758 459 7352

Set amidst some of the Caribbean's most luscious and awe-inspiring vegetation, the Mago Estate is a secluded and unique hotel with breathtaking views of the "Piton", the landmark most often associated with St. Lucia. This tropical hideaway genuinely reanimates the soul. The surrounding lush forest boasts a plethora of indigenous trees, and visitors can bask in the mélange of colours and scents emanating from the mango, mahogany and papaya trees, as well as the unique bougainvillaea and hibiscus plants. The Mago Estate is the perfect place to imbibe the relaxed atmosphere of St. Lucia. An austere rock formation and two stunning mango trees frame the bar area, while the shangrila units all afford stunning views of the ocean and natural habitat. Individually designed with furniture imported from India, the rooms also exude the ambience of antiquity. Indeed the entire hotel is lavishly decorated, with the dining room positively festooned with Persian rugs, handcrafted furniture and antique art. The beautifully presented food, an imaginative blend of Creole, French and Thai, is simply divine. In the vicinity, visitors can enjoy the impressive Diamond and Piton Falls, the Sulphur Springs and the historic Coubarie Estate. **Directions:** Signed off the island's main road near to Soufrière Town. Price guide: Shangrila units $100–$300.

CARIBBEAN (St. Vincent)

GRAND VIEW BEACH HOTEL

VILLA POINT, BOX 173, ST VINCENT, WEST INDIES
TEL: 1 784 458 4811 FAX: 1 784 457 4174 E-MAIL: grandview@caribsurf.com

Set in eight luscious acres of tropical garden with imperious views of the Grenadine Islands, the Grand View Beach Hotel has to be ranked amongst the finest hotels in the Caribbean. Befitting a small family-run hotel, the hospitality is warm and friendly and guests are guaranteed privacy and seclusion in majestic surroundings. The colonial style house is lavishly decorated, adorned throughout with antiques and pictures reflecting its aristocratic past. The rooms, all quiet and comfortable, are bathed in soothing pastel shades, while the two Honeymoon Suites have whirlpool tubs, air-conditioning and large balconies with wonderful views of the ocean. The Grand View specialises in freshly-caught fish and lobsters and the imaginatively crafted meals are served in a sumptuous dining room with breathtaking vistas over the Great Head Bay and the forested mountains beyond. The property also offers an impressive range of amenities for a small hotel, including tennis and squash courts, a superb gym, a secluded beach for diving and snorkelling and a swimming pool complete with swim-up bar. Trips to the Grenadine Islands and Botanical Gardens can also be arranged. **Directions:** Grand View is located at Villa Point, on the South Coast of St. Vincent, five minutes from the airport, and ten minutes from Kingstown. Price guide: Rooms $104–$215; suite $125–$265.

CAMELOT INN

PO BOX 787, KINGSTOWN, THE GRENADINES, ST VINCENT, WEST INDIES
TEL: 1 784 456 2100 FAX: 1 784 456 2233 E-MAIL: caminn@caribsurf.com

Once the residence of the French governor of St.Vincent, this plantation-style historic mansion offers the visitor professional and friendly service in an ambience of regal splendour. Set amongst a garden of mango trees, as well as a vast array of tropical flowers, Camelot Inn has awe-inspiring views of the city of Kingstown and the Grenadine Islands. The 22 rooms are lavishly designed, many with balconies commanding views of Kingstown harbour below. The inn has preserved its 200 year-old cobblestone dining room, making meals there a truly singular experience. The atmosphere and sense of being part of the island's rich history are only surpassed by the quality of the fare,

an eclectic mixture of native and international, served with impeccable grace by the excellent staff and accompanied by wines of the very highest standard. Clearly the Camelot Inn is purpose-made for aficionados of watersports and a free coach is provided to shuttle visitors to the beach. Snorkelling, scuba diving, sailing and deep-sea fishing can also be arranged. A mere five minutes from Kingstown, visitors can also enjoy the vibrant nightlife of St. Vincent's capital. The famous Botanical Gardens are also close at hand. **Directions:** 10 minutes from E.T. Joshua airport and 5 minutes from Kingstown. Prices (incl. breakfast and dinner): Rooms from $175; suites from $350.

COCO REEF RESORT

CROWN POINT, TOBAGO, WEST INDIES
TEL: 1 868 639 8571 FAX: 1 868 639 8574

Tobago is perhaps the most enchanting island in the Caribbean, where verdant rainforest, historical sites and endless beaches all vie for the visitors attention. On this idyllic island, the most exclusive resort is undoubtedly the Coco Reef. Overlooking the aquiline waters of the ocean, the resort is set amongst a sculpted garden, which is nearly overwhelmed by the sheer diversity and colour of its plant life. If the beauty of the surroundings were not enough, the resort's architecture, an eclectic mixture of colonial and indigenous, is an arresting reflection of the island's rich and diverse history. The attention to detail for which the resort is renowned can immediately be discerned from the bedrooms, with their hand-hewed Saltillo tiles in every bathroom and the magnificent marble baths in the suites. The food, which benefits from the amazing quality of the local produce, also reflects the splendour of the surroundings. The array of activities to be sampled is also impressive. With three beaches nearby, visitors can indulge their love of watersports, or even take a fishing trip into some of the most fecund waters on the planet. The resort also has tennis courts, while a mere 10 minutes away is one of the Caribbean's top golf courses, Mount-Irvine Bay, designed by Robert Trent-Jones. **Directions:** Transfer time 10 minutes. Price guide: Available on request.

THE SANDS AT GRACE BAY

PO BOX 681, PROVIDENCIALES, TURKS & CAICOS, WEST INDIES
TEL: 1 649 946 5199 FAX: 1 649 946 5198 E-MAIL: resort@thesandsresort.com

A magnificently appointed suite-only beachfront resort, the Sands is truly one of the best places to unwind in the Caribbean. Opened in 1998, the resort is a testament to modern design. The entire complex is painted in the most soothing of pastel colours and designer furniture abounds. The suites are all beautifully appointed with comfortable, plush furniture blending in with traditional wicker chairs and minimalist glass and steel tables. To ensure privacy, the capacious suites have large screened terraces, as well as tiled floors to keep visitors cool in the mid-day sun. The cuisine, which has quickly gained a reputation for flair and imagination, is served on the outdoor patio. The Turks and Caicos Islands have long been considered the most idyllic, unspoiled and relaxing of the many island havens in the Caribbean and Grace Bay is the ideal location to enjoy the many splendours that the island boasts. The resort has rich and colourful gardens where guests can meander and there is a luxurious beach-side pool. The climate of the island is such that visitors can partake in all manner of watersports all year around, including snorkelling and scuba-diving among the virgin reefs as well as exceptional deep-sea fishing. **Directions:** 80 minutes from Miami by air, 15 minutes from airport via hotel transfer. Price guide: suite $220–$795.

Mexico

HOTEL VILLA DEL SOL

PLAYA LA ROPA S/N, PO BOX 84, ZIHUATANEJO 40880, MEXICO
TEL: 52 755 4 2239/3239 FAX: 52 7554 2758/4066 US TOLL FREE: 888 / 398-2645 E-MAIL: hotel@villasol.com.mx

Cross a bit of Hispanic charm and an incredible amount of natural beauty and the result is the Villa del Sol. Set like a pearl on the Pacific shoreline of Mexico at Ixtapa-Zihuatanejo, the Hotel Villa del Sol lives up to its name with dazzling sunshine, idyllic beaches and magnificent groves of flourishing palm trees that simply blanket the area in a haze of green. The rooms are expansive and stunning using designs and colours that hark back to the days of the ancient civilisations that populate the area. Those wishing to indulge in an afternoon siesta must choose one of the numerous little nooks and crannies where you can doze in comfort on a swinging chair or hanging hammock. Dinner is a mélange of flavours, with dishes drawing on irresistible Mexican tastes and using fresh seafood straight out of the Pacific. There are innumerable leisure activities at the Villa del Sol, with watersports widely available and including everything from sailing to snorkelling. For something a little more cultural, take to the cobblestone streets of Zihuatanejo and explore the fascinating surrounds with its art gallery and interesting shops. **Directions:** The hotel is 15 minutes from Ixtapa-Zihuatanejo International Airport. The airport has direct services from Los Angeles, Phoenix, New York and Mexico City. Price guide: Rooms $220; suite $300–$750.

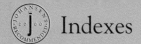

Indexes

Johansens Recommended Hotels Great Britain & Ireland 2000

LONDON

Chelsea	Chelsea Green Hotel	020 7225 7500
Chelsea	Draycott House Apartments	020 7584 4659
City	London Bridge Hotel & Apartments	020 7855 2200
Covent Garden	One Aldwych	020 7300 1000
Hendon	Hendon Hall	020 8203 3341
Kensington	Chequers of Kensington	020 7969 3555
Kensington	Harrington Hall	020 7396 9696
Kensington	The Lexham Apartments	020 7559 4444
Kensington	The Milestone Hotel	020 7917 1000
Kensington	Pembridge Court Hotel	020 7229 9977
Kensington	Twenty Nevern Square	020 7565 9555
Knightsbridge	Basil Street Hotel	020 7581 3311
Knightsbridge	The Beaufort	020 7584 5252
Knightsbridge	Beaufort House Apartments	020 7584 2600
Knightsbridge	The Cadogan	020 7235 7141
Knightsbridge	The Cliveden Town House	020 7730 6466
Knightsbridge	Number Eleven Cadogan Gardens	020 7730 7000
Lancaster Gate	Fountains	020 7706 7070
Lancaster Gate	The Hempel	020 7298 9000
Little Venice	The Colonnade Town House	020 7286 1052
Londo	Brown's Hotel	020 7493 6020
London	Sandringham Hotel	020 7435 1569
Mayfair	The Ascott Mayfair	020 7499 6868
Mayfair	Claridge's	020 7629 8860
Mayfair	The Dorchester	020 7629 8888
Mayfair	No 5 Maddox Street	020 7647 0200
Mayfair	Westbury Hotel	020 7629 7755
Portman Square	The Leonard	020 7935 2010
South Kensington	Blakes Hotel	020 7370 6701
South Kensington	Number Sixteen	020 7589 5232
Whitehall	The Royal Horseguards	020 7839 3400
Wimbledon Common	Cannizaro House	020 8879 1464
Cruise Ship	Swan Hellenic Minerva	020 7800 2227

ENGLAND

Abberley	The Elms	01299 896666
Acton Trussell	The Moat House	01785 712217
Aldeburgh	Wentworth Hotel	01728 452312
Alderley Edge	The Alderley Edge Hotel	01625 583033
Alfriston	White Lodge Country House Hotel	01323 870265
Alston	Lovelady Shield Country House Hotel	01434 381203
Altrincham	Woodland Park Hotel	0161 928 8631
Amberley	Amberley Castle	01798 831992
Ambleside	Holbeck Ghyll Country House Hotel	015394 32375
Ambleside	Langdale Hotel & Country Club	015394 37302
Ambleside	Nanny Brow Country House Hotel	015394 32036
Ambleside	Rothay Manor	015394 33605
Andover	Esseborne Manor	01264 736444
Andover	Fifehead Manor	01264 781565
Appleby-in-Westmorland	Appleby Manor Country House Hotel	017683 51571
Appleby-In-Westmorland	Tufton Arms Hotel	017683 51593
Arundel	Bailiffscourt	01903 723511
Ascot	Royal Berkshire	01344 623322
Ashbourne	Callow Hall	01335 343403
Ashbourne	The Izaak Walton Hotel	01335 350555
Ashburton	Holne Chase Hotel & Restaurant	01364 631471
Ashford	Eastwell Manor	01233 213000
Ashford-In-The-Water	Riverside House	01629 814275
Aylesbury	Hartwell House	01296 747444
Aylesbury	The Priory Hotel	01296 641239
Bagshot	Pennyhill Park Hotel	01276 471774
Bakewell	Hassop Hall	01629 640488
Banbury	Wroxton House Hotel	01295 730777
Basingstoke	Tylney Hall	01256 764881
Baslow	Fischer's	01246 583259
Baslow	The Cavendish Hotel	01246 582311
Bath	Combe Grove Manor	01225 834644
Bath	Homewood Park	01225 723731
Bath	Hunstrete House	01761 490490
Bath	Lucknam Park	01225 742777

Bath	Ston Easton Park	01761 241631
Bath	The Bath Priory Hotel and Restaurant	01225 331922
Bath	The Queensberry	01225 447928
Bath	The Royal Crescent Hotel	01225 823333
Battle	Netherfield Place Hotel	01424 774455
Battle	PowderMills Hotel	01424 775511
Beaminster	Bridge House Hotel	01308 862200
Beaulieu	The Master Builder's House	01590 616253
Beaulieu	The Montagu Arms Hotel	01590 612324
Bedford	Woodlands Manor	01234 363281
Berwick-Upon-Tweed	Marshall Meadow Country House Hotel	01289 331133
Berwick-Upon-Tweed	Tillmouth Park	01890 882255
Bibury	The Swan Hotel At Bibury	01285 740695
Birmingham	New Hall	0121 378 2442
Birmingham	The Burlington Hotel	0121 643 9191
Birmingham	The Mill House Hotel	0121 459 5800
Birmingham	The Swallow Hotel	0121 455 7073
Bishop's Stortford	Down Hall Country House Hotel	01279 731441
Blackburn	Astley Bank Hotel	01254 777700
Bolton Abbey	The Devonshire Arms Hotel	01756 710441
Bournemouth	Langtry Manor	01202 553887
Bournemouth	The Dormy	01202 872121
Bournemouth	The Norfolk Royale Hotel	01202 551521
Bovey Tracey	The Edgemoor	01626 832466
Bradford-On-Avon	Woolley Grange	01225 864705
Brampton	Farlam Hall Hotel	016977 46234
Bray-on-Thames	Chauntry House Hotel & Restaurant	01628 673991
Bray-on-Thames	Monkey Island Hotel	01628 623400
Brighton	The Old Ship Hotel	01273 329001
Bristol	Hotel Du Vin & Bistro	0117 925 5577
Bristol	Swallow Royal Hotel	0117 9255100/200
Bristol South	Daneswood House Hotel	01934 843145
Broadway	Dormy House	01386 852711
Broadway	The Lygon Arms	01386 852255
Brockenhurst	Careys Manor Hotel	01590 623551
Brockenhurst	New Park Manor	01590 623467
Brockenhurst	Rhinefield House Hotel	01590 622922
Brockenhurst	The Balmer Lawn	01590 623116
Bromsgrove	Grafton Manor Country House Hotel	01527 579007
Burford	The Bay Tree Hotel & Restaurant	01993 822791
Burnham Market	The Hoste Arms Hotel	01328 738777
Burrington	Northcote Manor Hotel	01769 560501
Bury St Edmunds	Ravenwood Hall	01359 270345
Bury St Edmunds	The Angel Hotel	01284 753926
Buxted,Near Uckfield	Buxted Park Country House Hotel	01825 732711
Buxton	The Lee Wood Hotel & Restaurant	01298 23002
Buxton	The Palace Hotel	01298 22001
Canterbury	Howfield Manor	01227 738294
Castle Combe	The Manor House Hotel	01249 782206
Chaddesley Corbett	Brockencote Hall	01562 777876
Chagford	Gidleigh Park	01647 432367
Chelmsford	Pontlands Park Country Hotel	01245 476444
Cheltenham	Hotel On The Park	01242 518898
Cheltenham	The Cheltenham Park Hotel	01242 222021
Cheltenham	The Greenway	01242 862352
Chester	Broxton Hall Country House Hotel	01829 782321
Chester	Carden Park	01829 731000
Chester	Crabwall Manor	01244 851666
Chester	Nunsmere Hall	01606 889100
Chester	Rowton Hall Hotel	01244 335262
Chester	The Chester Grosvenor	01244 324024
Chichester	The Millstream Hotel	01243 573234
Chipping Campden	Charingworth Manor	01386 593555
Chipping Campden	Noel Arms Hotel	01386 840317
Chipping Campden	The Cotswold House	01386 840330
Cirencester	The Bear of Rodborough Hotel	01453 878522
Clanfield	The Plough at Clanfield	01367 810222
Cobham	Woodlands Park Hotel	01372 843933
Colchester	Five Lakes Hotel	01621 868888
Coventry	Coombe Abbey	024 76450450
Coventry	Nailcote Hall	024 76466174
Crathorne	Crathorne Hall Hotel	01642 700398
Cuckfield	Ockenden Manor	01444 416111
Darlington	Headlam Hall	01325 730238
Dartford	Rowhill Grange	01322 615136

Dartmoor	Bel Alp House	01364 661217
Daventry	Fawsley Hall Hotel	01327 892000
Dedham	Maison Talbooth	01206 322367
Derby	Makeney Hall Country House Hotel	01332 842999
Derby	Mickleover Court	01332 521234
Derby	Risley Hall Country House Hotel	0115 939 9000
Derby	The Priest House On the River	01332 810649
Durham	Lumley Castle Hotel	0191 389 1111
Easington	Grinkle Park Hotel	01287 640515
Eastbourne	The Grand Hotel	01323 412345
Egham	Great Fosters	01784 433822
Evershot	Summer Lodge	01935 83424
Evesham	The Evesham Hotel	01386 765566
Evesham	Wood Norton Hall	01386 420007
Exeter	Combe House at Gittisham	01404 540400
Exeter	St Olaves Court Hotel	01392 217736
Falmouth	Budock Vean Golf & Country House Hotel	01326 250288
Falmouth	Meudon Hotel	01326 250541
Falmouth	Penmere Manor	01326 211411
Forest Row	Ashdown Park Hotel & Country Club	01342 824988
Fowey	Fowey Hall Hotel & Restaurant	01726 833866
Gatwick	Alexander House	01342 714914
Gatwick	Langshott Manor	01293 786680
Glossop	The Wind In The Willows	01457 868001
Grange-Over-Sands	Graythwaite Manor	015395 32001
Grasmere	Michaels Nook	015394 35496
Grasmere	The Wordsworth Hotel	015394 35592
Grayshott	Grayshott Hall Health Fitness Retreat	01428 602000
Guildford	The Angel Posting House And Livery	01483 564555
Hadley Wood	West Lodge Park	020 8216 3900
Halifax	Holdsworth House	01422 240024
Hampton Court	The Carlton Mitre Hotel	020 8979 9988
Harrogate	Grants Hotel	01423 560666
Harrogate	Hob Green Hotel & Restaurant	01423 770031
Harrogate	Rudding Park House & Hotel	01423 871350
Harrogate	The Balmoral Hotel	01423 508208
Harrogate	The Boar's Head Hotel	01423 771888
Haslemere	Lythe Hill Hotel	01428 651251
Hathersage	George Hotel	01433 650436
Hawes	Simonstone Hall	01969 667255
Hazlewood	Hazlewood Castle Hotel	01937 535353
Heathrow	Stoke Park	01753 717171
Helmsley	The Pheasant	01439 771241
Henley-On-Thames	Phyllis Court Club	01491 570500
Hockley Heath	Nuthurst Grange	01564 783972
Horsham	South Lodge Hotel	01403 891711
Hovingham	The Worsley Arms Hotel	01653 628234
Huddersfield	Bagden Hall Hotel & Golf Course	01484 865330
Hull	Willerby Manor Hotel	01482 652616
Ilkley	Rombalds Hotel	01943 603201
Ilsington	Ilsington Country Hotel	01364 661452
Ipswich	Hintlesham Hall	01473 652268
Ipswich	Swallow Belstead Brook Hotel	01473 682891
Ipswich	The Marlborough Hotel	01473 257677
Keswick	The Borrowdale Gates Hotel	017687 77204
Kettering	Kettering Park Hotel	01536 416666
Kidderminster	Stone Manor Hotel	01562 777555
King's Lynn	Congham Hall	01485 600250
Kingham	Mill House Hotel	01608 658188
Kingsbridge Estuary	Buckland-Tout-Saints	01548 853055
Knutsford	Mere Court Hotel	01565 831000
Lacock	Beechfield House	01225 703700
Lake Ullswater	Rampsbeck Country House Hotel	017684 86442
Lake Ullswater	Sharrow Bay Country House Hotel	017684 86301
Leamington Spa	Mallory Court	01926 330214
Leeds	42 The Calls	0113 244 0099
Leeds	Haley's Hotel and Restaurant	0113 278 4446
Leeds	Oulton Hall	0113 282 1000
Leicester	Sketchley Grange Hotel	01455 251133
Lewdown	Lewtrenchard Manor	01566 783 256
Lewes	Newick Park	01825 723633
Lichfield	Hoar Cross Hall Health Spa Resort	01283 575671
Lifton	The Arundell Arms	01566 784666
Loughborough	Quorn Country Hotel	01509 415050
Louth	Kenwick Park Hotel & Leisure Club	01507 608806

173

Lower Slaughter	Washbourne Court Hotel	01451 822143
Ludlow	Dinham Hall	01584 876464
Lymington	Passford House Hotel	01590 682398
Lymington	Stanwell House	01590 677123
Lyndhurst	Parkhill Country House Hotel	023 80282944
Macclesfield	Shrigley Hall Hotel Golf & Country Club	01625 575757
Maidenhead	Cliveden	01628 668561
Maidenhead	Fredrick's Hotel & Restaurant	01628 581000
Maidenhead	Taplow House Hotel	01628 670056
Maidstone	Chilston Park	01622 859803
Malmesbury	Crudwell Court Hotel	01666 577194
Malmesbury	The Old Bell	01666 822344
Malmesbury	Whatley Manor	01666 822888
Malvern	The Colwall Park Hotel	01684 540206
Malvern Wells	The Cottage In The Wood	01684 575859
Manchester	The Stanneylands Hotel	01625 525225
Manchester Airport	Etrop Grange	0161 499 0500
Marlborough	Ivy House Hotel	01672 515333
Marlow-On-Thames	Danesfield House	01628 891010
Marston	The Olde Barn Hotel	01400 250909
Matlock	Riber Hall	01629 582795
Melton Mowbray	Stapleford Park, An Outpost of The Carnegie Club	01572 787522
Middlecombe	Periton Park Hotel	01643 706885
Midhurst	The Angel Hotel	01730 812421
Midhurst	The Spread Eagle Hotel & Health Spa	01730 816911
Milton Keynes	Moore Place Hotel	01908 282000
Moreton-In-Marsh	The Manor House Hotel	01608 650501
Nantwich	Rookery Hall	01270 610016
Newbury	Donnington Valley Hotel	01635 551199
Newbury	Hollington House Hotel	01635 255100
Newbury	The Vineyard At Stockcross	01635 528770
Newcastle-Upon-Tyne	Linden Hall Hotel	01670 516611
Newmarket	Swynford Paddocks Hotel	01638 570234
Newton Aycliffe	Redworth Hall Hotel & Country Club	01388 772442
Norwich	Park Farm Hotel & Leisure	01603 810264
Norwich	Petersfield House Hotel	01692 630741
Norwich	Swallow Sprowston Manor Hotel	01603 789409
Nottingham	Langar Hall	01949 860559
Oakham	Hambleton Hall	01572 756991
Otley	Chevin Lodge Country Park Hotel	01943 467818
Ottershaw	Foxhills	01932 704500
Oxford	Fallowfields	01865 820416
Oxford	Le Manoir aux Quat' Saisons	01844 278881
Oxford	Studley Priory	01865 351203
Oxford	Weston Manor	01869 350621
Painswick	The Painswick Hotel	01452 812160
Peterborough	The Haycock	01780 782223
Polperro	Talland Bay Hotel	01503 272667
Prestbury	The Bridge Hotel	01625 829326
Preston	The Gibbon Bridge Hotel	01995 61456
Redhill	Nutfield Priory	01737 824400
Richmond-Upon-Thames	The Richmond Gate Hotel	020 8940 0061
Ross-On-Wye	Pengethley Manor	01989 730211
Ross-On-Wye	The Chase Hotel	01989 763161
Rusper	Ghyll Manor Country Hotel	01293 871571
Rutland Water	Barnsdale Lodge	01572 724678
Rye	Broomhill Lodge	01797 280421
Salcombe	Bolt Head Hotel	01548 843751
Salcombe	Soar Mill Cove Hotel	01548 561566
Salcombe	The Tides Reach Hotel	01548 843466
Salisbury	Howard's House	01722 716392
Scarborough	Hackness Grange	01723 882345
Scarborough	Wrea Head Country Hotel	01723 378211
Seaview	The Priory Bay Hotel	01983 613146
Sheffield	Charnwood Hotel	0114 258 9411
Sheffield	Hellaby Hall Hotel	01709 702701
Sheffield	Whitley Hall Hotel	0114 245 4444
Shepton Mallet	Charlton House	01749 342008
Shrewsbury	Albrighton Hall Hotel & Restaurant	01939 291000
Shrewsbury	Hawkstone Park Hotel	01939 200611
Shrewsbury	Rowton Castle	01743 884044
Sidmouth	Hotel Riviera	01395 515201
Sonning-On-Thames	The French Horn	01189 692204
South Molton	Whitechapel Manor	01769 573377
Southwold	The Swan Hotel	01502 722186
St Agnes	Rose-in-Vale Country House Hotel	01872 552202
St Albans	Sopwell House Hotel Country Club	01727 864477
St. Ives	The Garrack Hotel & Restaurant	01736 796199

St Keyne	The Well House	01579 342001
St.Mawes	The Rosevine Hotel	01872 580206
Stamford	The George Of Stamford	01780 750750
Stansted	Whitehall	01279 850603
Stonehouse	Stonehouse Court	01453 825155
Stow-on-the-Wold	Lords Of The Manor Hotel	01451 820243
Stow-On-The-Wold	The Grapevine Hotel	01451 830344
Stow-On-The-Wold	Wyck Hill House	01451 831936
Stratford-Upon-Avon	Billesley Manor	01789 279955
Stratford-Upon-Avon	Ettington Park	01789 450123
Stratford-Upon-Avon	Salford Hall Hotel	01386 871300
Stratford-Upon-Avon	Welcombe Hotel & Golf Course	01789 295252
Streatley-On-Thames	The Swan Diplomat	01491 873737
Sturminster Newton	Plumber Manor	01258 472507
Swindon	The Pear Tree at Purton	01793 772100
Taunton	Bindon Country House Hotel	01823 400070
Taunton	The Castle At Taunton	01823 272671
Taunton	The Mount Somerset Country House Hotel	01823 442500
Tavistock	The Horn Of Plenty	01822 832528
Telford	Madeley Court	01952 680068
Tetbury	Calcot Manor	01666 890391
Tetbury	The Close Hotel	01666 502272
Tewkesbury	Corse Lawn House Hotel	01452 780479
Thame	The Spread Eagle Hotel	01844 213661
Thirsk	Crab Manor	01845 577286
Ticehurst	Dale Hill	01580 200112
Torquay	The Osborne Hotel	01803 213311
Torquay	The Palace Hotel	01803 200200
Tring	Pendley Manor Hotel	01442 891891
Tunbridge Wells	Hotel Du Vin & Bistro	01892 526455
Tunbridge Wells	The Spa Hotel	01892 520331
Uckfield	Horsted Place Hotel	01825 750581
Uppingham	The Lake Isle	01572 822951
Veryan	The Nare Hotel	01872 501279
Wallingford	The Springs Hotel & Golf Club	01491 836687
Ware	Hanbury Manor	01920 487722
Wareham	The Priory	01929 551666
Warminster	Bishopstrow House	01985 212312
Warwick	The Glebe At Barford	01926 624218
Wetherby	Wood Hall	01937 587271
Weybridge	Oatlands Park Hotel	01932 847242
Weymouth	Moonfleet Manor	01305 786948
Winchester	Hotel Du Vin & Bistro	01962 841414
Winchester	Lainston House Hotel	01962 863588
Windermere	Gilpin Lodge	015394 88818
Windermere	Lakeside Hotel On Lake Windermere	0541 541586
Windermere	Langdale Chase	015394 32201
Windermere	Linthwaite House Hotel	015394 88600
Windermere	Miller Howe	015394 42536
Windermere	Storrs Hall	015394 47111
Windsor	Oakley Court	01753 609988
Windsor	Sir Christopher Wren's Hotel	01753 861354
Woburn	Flitwick Manor	01525 712242
Woburn	The Bedford Arms	01525 290441
Wolverhampton	The Old Vicarage Hotel	01746 716497
Woodbridge	Seckford Hall	01394 385678
Woodstock	The Feathers Hotel	01993 812291
Woolacombe	Watersmeet Hotel	01271 870333
Woolacombe	Woolacombe Bay Hotel	01271 870388
Yarmouth	The George Hotel	01983 760331
York	Middlethorpe Hall	01904 641241
York	Monk Fryston Hall	01977 682369
York	Mount Royale Hotel	01904 628856
York	The Grange Hotel	01904 644744

IRELAND

Adare	Adare Manor	00 353 61 396566
Belfast	The McCausland Hotel	028 9022 0200
Carrickmacross	Nuremore Hotel & Country Club	00 353 429 661438
Clonakilty	The Lodge & Spa at Inchydoney Island	00 353 23 33143
Cong	Ashford Castle	00353 92 46003
Connemara	Renvyle House Hotel	00 353 95 43511
Cork	Hayfield Manor Hotel	00 353 21 315600
Dublin	Brooks Hotel	00 353 1 670 4000
Dublin	Kildare Hotel & Country Club	00 353 1 601 7200
Dublin	Portmarnock Hotel & Golf Links	00 353 1 846 0611
Dublin	The Fitzwilliam Hotel	00 353 1 478 7000
Dublin	The Hibernian	00 353 1 668 7666
Dublin	The Merrion Hotel	00 353 1 603 0600

Galway	Connemara Coast Hotel	00 353 91 592108
Gorey	Marlfield House	00 353 55 21124
Kenmare	Sheen Falls Lodge	00 353 64 41600
Kenmare	The Park Hotel Kenmare	00 353 64 41200
Killarney	Aghadoe Heights Hotel	00 353 64 31766
Killarney	Muckross Park Hotel	00 353 64 31938
Killarney	Randles Court Hotel	00 353 64 35333
Kiltegan	Humewood Castle	00 353 508 73215
Mallow	Longueville House	00 353 22 47156
Newmarket-On-Fergus	Dromoland Castle	00 353 61 368144
Parknasilla	Parknasilla Hotel	00 353 64 45122
Rathnew	Hunter's Hotel	00 353 404 40106
Rosslare	Kelly's Resort Hotel	00 353 53 32114
Rossnowlagh	The Sand House Hotel	00 353 72 51777

SCOTLAND

Aberdeen	Ardoe House Hotel & Restaurant	01224 867355
Aberdeen	Thainstone House Hotel	01467 621643
Aberfoyle	Forest Hills	01877 387277
Angus	Letham Grange Resort	01241 890373
Auchencairn	Balcary Bay Hotel	01556 640217
Auchterarder	Auchterarder House	01764 663646
Ballantrae	Glenapp Castle	01465 831212
Ballater	Darroch Learg Hotel	013397 55443
Banchory	Raemoir House Hotel	01330 824884
Beasdale By Arisaig	Arisaig House	01687 450622
Biggar	Shieldhill-Incorporating The Mennock Valley Shoot	01899 220035
Blairgowrie	Kinloch House Hotel	01250 884237
Callander	Roman Camp Hotel	01877 330003
Craigellachie	Craigellachie Hotel	01340 881204
Dunkeld	Kinnaird	01796 482 440
Dunoon	Enmore Hotel	01369 702230
East Kilbride	Macdonald Crutherland House Hotel	01355 577000
Edinburgh	Borthwick Castle	01875 820514
Edinburgh	Channings	0131 315 2226
Edinburgh	Dalhousie Castle	01875 820153
Edinburgh	Prestonfield House	0131 668 3346
Edinburgh	The Bonham	0131 226 6050
Edinburgh	The Howard	0131 557 3500
Edinburgh	The Norton House Hotel	0131 333 1275
Edinburgh	The Scotsman	0113 244 0099
Elgin	Mansion House Hotel	01343 548811
Fort William	Glenspean Lodge Hotel	01397 712223
Gatehouse Of Fleet	Cally Palace Hotel	01557 814341
Glasgow	Carlton George Hotel	0141 353 6373
Glasgow	Gleddoch House	01475 540711
Glenshee	Dalmunzie House	01250 885224
Grantown-on-Spey	Muckrach Lodge Hotel & Restaurant	01479 851257
Gullane	Greywalls	01620 842144
Inverness	Bunchrew House Hotel	01463 234917
Inverness	Culloden House Hotel	01463 790461
Inverness	Swallow Kingsmills Hotel	01463 237166
Inverurie	Pittodrie House	01467 681444
Isle Of Skye	Flodigarry Country House Hotel	01470 552203
Kelso	Ednam House Hotel	01573 224168
Kelso	The Roxburghe Hotel & Golf Course	01573 450331
Kilchrenan by Taynuilt	Ardanaiseig	01866 833333
Kildrummy	Kildrummy Castle Hotel	019755 71288
Kinbuck	Cromlix House	01786 822125
Lochinver	Inver Lodge Hotel	01571 844496
Newton Stewart	Kirroughtree House	01671 402141
Oban	Knipoch Hotel	01852 316251
Peebles	Cringletie House Hotel	01721 730233
Perth	Ballathie House Hotel	01250 883268
Perth	Huntingtower Hotel	01738 583771
Perth	Kinfauns Castle	01738 620777
Pitlochry	Pine Trees Hotel	01796 472121
Portpatrick	Fernhill Hotel	01776 810220
St. Andrews	St. Andrews Golf Hotel	01334 472611
St Boswells	Dryburgh Abbey Hotel	01835 822261
Stirling	Stirling Highland Hotel	01786 272727
Stranraer	Corsewall Lighthouse Hotel	01776 853220
Strathpeffer	Coul House Hotel	01997 421487
Tain	Mansfield House Hotel	01862 892052
Torridon	Loch Torridon Hotel	01445 791242
Troon	Marine Highland Hotel	01292 314444
Troon	Piersland House Hotel	01292 314747
Uphall	Houstoun House	01506 853831

WALES

Aberdare	Ty Newydd Country Hotel	01685 813433
Abergavenny	Allt-Yr-Ynys Hotel	01873 890307
Abergavenny	Llansantffraed Court Hotel	01873 840678
Abersoch	Porth Tocyn Country House Hotel	01758 713303
Aberystwyth	Conrah Country House Hotel	01970 617941
Anglesey	Tre-Ysgawen Bay Hotel	01407 860301
Bala	Palé Hall	01678 530285
Barmouth	Bontddu Hall	01341 430661
Beaumaris	Ye Olde Bull's Head	01248 810329
Brecon	Llangoed Hall	01874 754525
Bridgend	Coed-Y-Mwstwr Hotel	01656 860621
Cardiff	Miskin Manor	01443 224204
Chester	St. David's Park Hotel	01244 520800
Corwen	Tyddyn Llan Country House Hotel	01490 440264
Criccieth	Bron Eifion Country House Hotel	01766 522385
Crickhowell	Gliffaes Country House Hotel	01874 730371
Dolgellau	Penmaenuchaf Hall	01341 422129
Harlech	Hotel Maes-Y-Neuadd	01766 780200
Lake Vyrnwy	Lake Vyrnwy Hotel	01691 870 692
Llandegla	Bodidris Hall	01978 790434
Llandudno	Bodysgallen Hall	01492 584466
Llandudno	St Tudno Hotel	01492 874411
Llangammarch Wells	The Lake Country House	01591 620202
Machynlleth	Ynyshir Hall	01654 781209
Pembroke	The Court Hotel & Restaurant	01646 672273
Portmeirion Village	The Hotel Portmeirion	01766 770000
St David's	Warpool Court Hotel	01437 720300
Tenby	Penally Abbey	01834 843033
Usk	The Cwrt Bleddyn Hotel	01633 450521
Wrexham	Llyndir Hall Hotel	01244 571648

CHANNEL ISLANDS

Guernsey	St Pierre Park Hotel	01481 728282
Jersey	Château La Chaire	01534 863354
Jersey	Hotel L'Horizon	01534 43101
Jersey	Longueville Manor	01534 725501
Jersey	The Atlantic Hotel	01534 744101

Johansens Recommended Traditional Inns, Hotels & Restaurants 2000

ENGLAND

Aldbury	The Greyhound Inn	01442 851228
Aldeburgh	The Dolphin Inn	01728 454994
Alfriston	Deans Place Hotel	01323 870248
Amberley	The Boathouse Brasserie	01798 831059
Ambleside	The New Dungeon Ghyll Hotel	015394 37213
Appleby-In-Westmorland	The Royal Oak Inn	017683 51463
Ashbourne	Beeches Country Restaurant	01889 590288
Ashbourne	Red Lion Inn	01335 370396
Axminster	Tytherleigh Cot Hotel	01460 221170
Badby Nr Daventry	The Windmill At Badby	01327 702363
Bamburgh	The Victoria Hotel	01668 214431
Bassenthwaite Lake	The Pheasant	017687 76234
Beckington Nr Bath	The Woolpack Inn	01373 831244
Belford	The Blue Bell Hotel	01668 213543
Bibury	The Catherine Wheel	01285 740250
Bickleigh	The Fisherman's Cot	01884 855237
Binfield	Stag & Hounds	01344 483553
Blakeney	White Horse Hotel	01263 740574
Bourton-On-The-Water	Dial House Hotel	01451 822244
Bridport	The Manor Hotel	01308 897616
Bristol	The Boars Head	01454 632581
Bristol	The New Inn	01454 773161
Broadway	The Broadway Hotel	01386 852401
Brockenhurst	The Snakecatcher	01590 622348
Burford	Cotswold Gateway Hotel	01993 822695
Burford	The Golden Pheasant Hotel	01993 823417
Burford	The Inn For All Seasons	01451 844324
Burford	The Lamb Inn	01993 823155
Burnham Market	The Hoste Arms Hotel	01328 738777
Burnley	Fence Gate Inn	01282 618101
Burnsall	The Red Lion	01756 720204
Burton Upon Trent	Boar's Head Hotel	01283 820344
Burton upon Trent	Ye Olde Dog & Partridge	01283 813030
Calver	The Chequers Inn	01433 630231
Camborne	Tyacks Hotel	01209 612424

Cambridge	The White Horse Inn	01440 706081
Carlisle	The Tarn End House Hotel	016977 2340
Castle Ashby	The Falcon Hotel	01604 696200
Chippenham	The Crown Inn	01249 782229
Chipping Sodbury	The Codrington Arms	01454 313145
Christchurch	The Lord Bute	01425 278884
Cirencester	The Eliot Arms Hotel	01285 860215
Cirencester	The New Inn at Coln	01285 750651
Clare	The Plough Inn	01440 786789
Clavering	The Cricketers	01799 550442
Cleobury Mortimer	Crown At Hopton	01299 270372
Cleobury Mortimer	The Redfern Hotel	01299 270 395
Colchester	The White Hart Hotel & Restaurant	01376 561654
Coleford	The New Inn	01363 84242
Dartmouth	The Little Admiral Hotel	01803 832572
Ditcheat	The Manor House Inn	01749 860276
Doncaster	Hamilton's Restaurant & Hotel	01302 760770
Dorchester-On-Thames	The George Hotel	01865 340404
East Witton	The Blue Lion	01969 624273
Eccleshall	The George Inn	01785 850300
Edenbridge	Ye Old Crown	01732 867896
Egton	The Wheatsheaf Inn	01947 895271
Eton	The Christopher Hotel	01753 811677
Evershot	The Acorn Inn Hotel	01935 83228
Evesham	Riverside Restaurant And Hotel	01386 446200
Evesham	The Northwick Hotel	01386 40322
Exmoor	The Royal Oak Inn	01643 851455
Falmouth	Trengilly Wartha Country Inn	01326 340332
Fifield	The Merrymouth Inn	01993 831652
Ford, Nr Bath	The White Hart	01249 782213
Fordingbridge	The Woodfalls Inn	01725 513222
Goring-On-Thames	The Leatherne Bottel Riverside Inn	01491 872667
Grimsthorpe	The Black Horse Inn	01778 591247
Grindleford	The Maynard Arms	01433 630321
Halifax/Huddersfield	The Rock Inn Hotel	01422 379721
Handcross	The Chequers At Slaugham	01444 400239
Harrogate	The Boar's Head Hotel	01423 771888
Harrogate	The Dower House	01423 863302
Harrogate	The George & Newboulds Restaurant	01765 677214
Harrogate	The Low Hall Hotel	01423 508598
Hartley Wintney	The Hatchgate	01189 32666
Hathersage	The Plough Inn	01433 650319
Hay-On-Wye	Rhydspence Inn	01497 831262
Hayfield	The Waltzing Weasel	01663 743402
Helmsley	The Feathers Hotel	01439 770275
Helmsley	The Feversham Arms Hotel	01439 770766
Hindon	The Grosvenor Arms	01747 820696
Hindon, Nr Salisbury	The Lamb at Hindon	01747 820573
Honiton	Home Farm Hotel	01404 831278
Huddersfield	The Weavers Shed Restaurant with Rooms	01484 654284
Ilchester	Northover Manor	01935 840447
Kenilworth	Clarendon House Bar Brasserie Hotel	01926 857668
Kingskerswell	The Barn Owl Inn	01803 872130
Knutsford	Longview Hotel And Restaurant	01565 632119
Ledbury	Feathers Hotel	01531 635266
Leek	The Three Horseshoes Inn	01538 300296
Long Melford	The Countrymen	01787 312356
Longleat	The Bath Arms	01985 844308
Lymington	The Angel Inn	01590 672050
Lynmouth	The Rising Sun	01598 753223
Maidstone	Ringlestone Inn	01622 859900
Malmesbury	The Horse And Groom Inn	01666 823904
Mells	The Talbot Inn at Mells	01373 812254
Newbury	The Swan Inn	01488 648271
Newby Bridge	The Swan Hotel	015395 31681
North Walsham	Elderton Lodge	01263 833547
Nottingham	Hotel Des Clos	01159 866566
Old Hunstanton	The Lodge Hotel & Restaurant	01485 532896
Oxford	Holcombe Hotel	01869 338274
Oxford	The Jersey Arms	01869 343234
Oxford	The Mill & Old Swan	01993 774441
Pelynt, Nr Looe	Jubilee Inn	01503 220312
Penistone	The Fountain Inn & Rooms	01226 763125
Petworth	Badgers	01798 342651
Petworth	The Stonemason's Inn	01798 342510
Petworth	The Swan Inn	01798 865429
Petworth	White Horse Inn	01798 869 221
Port Gaverne	The Port Gaverne Hotel	01208 880244
Preston	Ye Horn's Inn	01772 865230

Reading	The Bull at Streatley	01491 875231
Romsey	Duke's Head	01794 514450
Rugby	The Golden Lion Inn of Easenhall	01788 832265
Rye	The George Hotel	01797 222114
Saddleworth	The Old Bell Inn Hotel	01457 870130
Salisbury	The White Horse	01725 510408
Sheffield	Manor House Hotel & Restaurant	01246 413971
Sherborne	The Grange Hotel & Restaurant	01935 813463
Sherborne	The Half Moon Inn	01935 812017
Sherborne	The Walnut Tree	01935 851292
Shifnal	Naughty Nell's	01952 411412
Shipton Under Wychwood	The Shaven Crown Hotel	01993 830330
Snettisham	The Rose & Crown	01485 541382
Southport	Tree Tops Country House	01704 572430
Stafford	The Dower House	01889 270707
Stamford	Black Bull Inn	01476 860086
Stamford	The Crown Hotel	01780 763136
Stow-On-The-Wold	The Kings Head Inn & Restaurant	01608 658365
Stow-on-the-Wold	The Unicorn Hotel	01451 830257
Stratford-upon-Avon	The Coach House Hotel	01789 204109
Stroud	The Crown Inn	01285 760601
Sudbury	The Bull Hotel	01787 378494
Taunton	Greyhound Inn	01823 480227
Telford	Hadley Park House Hotel	01952 677269
Telford	The Hundred House Hotel	01952 730353
Tenterden	The White Lion Hotel	01580 765077
Thaxted	Recorders House Restaurant	01371 830438
Thirsk	Crab & Lobster	01845 577286
Thornham	The Lifeboat Inn	01485 512236
Thorpe Market	Green Farm Restaurant And Hotel	01263 833602
Tintagel	The Port William	01840 770230
Totnes	The Sea Trout Inn	01803 762274
Totnes	The Watermans Arms	01803 732214
Troutbeck	The Mortal Man Hotel	015394 33193
Upton-Upon-Severn	The White Lion Hotel	01684 592551
Warminster	The Angel Inn	01985 213225
Wells	Market Place Hotel	01749 672616
Weobley	The Salutation Inn	01544 318443
West Auckland	The Manor House Hotel	01388 834834
West Witton	The Wensleydale Heifer Inn	01969 622322
Whitewell	The Inn At Whitewell	01200 448222
Witney	The Bird in Hand	01993 868321
Wooler	The Tankerville Arms Hotel	01668 281581
Worthing	The Old Tollgate Restaurant And Hotel	01903 879494
Wroxham	The Barton Angler Country Inn	01692 630740
York	The George at Easingwold	01347 821698

SCOTLAND

Glendevon	Tormaukin Hotel	01259 781252
Inverness	Grouse & Trout	01808 521314
Isle Of Skye	Hotel Eilean Iarmain	01471 833332
Isle Of Skye	Uig Hotel	01470 542205
Kylesku	Kylesku Hotel	01971 502231
Loch Earn	Achray House on Loch Earn	01764 685231
Moffat	Annandale Arms Hotel	01683 220013
Pitlochry	The Moulin Hotel	01796 472196
Plockton	The Plockton Hotel	01599 544274
Poolewe	Pool House Hotel	01445 781272

WALES

Chepstow	The Castle View Hotel	01291 620349
Llanarmon Dyffryn Ceiriog	The West Arms Hotel	01691 600665
Llandeilo	The Plough Inn	01558 823431
Machynlleth	The Wynnstay	01654 702941
Presteigne	The Radnorshire Arms	01544 267406

CHANNEL ISLANDS

Guernsey	Les Rocquettes Hotel	01481 722176

Johansens Recommended Country Houses & Small Hotels 2000

ENGLAND

Alcester	Arrow Mill Hotel And Restaurant	01789 762419
Ambleside	Nanny Brow Country House Hotel	015394 32036
Ampleforth	Shallowdale House	01439 788325
Appleton-Le-Moors	Appleton Hall	01751 417227
Arundel	Burpham Country House Hotel	01903 882160
Atherstone	Chapel House	01827 718949
Bakewell	East Lodge Country House Hotel	01629 734474

175

Bakewell	The Peacock Hotel at Rowsley	01629 733518
Bamburgh	Waren House Hotel	01668 214581
Barnstaple	Downrew House Hotel	01271 342497
Bath	Apsley House	01225 336966
Bath	Bath Lodge Hotel	01225 723040
Bath	Bloomfield House	01225 420105
Bath	Duke's Hotel	01225 463512
Bath	Eagle House	01225 859946
Bath	Oldfields	01225 317984
Bath	Paradise House	01225 317723
Bath	The Old Priory Hotel	01761 416784
Bath	Villa Magdala	01225 466329
Bath	Widbrook Grange	01225 864750
Bath	Woolverton House	01373 830415
Belper	Dannah Farm Country Guest House	01773 550273
Beverley	The Manor House	01482 881645
Bibury	Bibury Court	01285 740337
Bicester	Bignell Park Hotel	01869 241444
Bideford	Yeoldon House Hotel	01237 474400
Biggin-By-Hartington	Biggin Hall	01298 84451
Blockley	Lower Brook House	01386 700286
Bolton	Pelton Fold Farm	01204 852207
Bolton	Quarlton Manor Farm	01204 852277
Bridgnorth	Cross Lane House Hotel	01746 764887
Brighton	The Granville	01273 326302
Broadway	Collin House Hotel	01386 858354
Broadway	The Broadway Hotel	01386 852401
Broadway	The Old Rectory	01386 853729
Brockenhurst	Thatched Cottage Hotel & Restaurant	01590 623090
Brockenhurst	Whitley Ridge & Country House Hotel	01590 622354
Buttermere	New House Farm	01900 85404
Cambridge	Melbourn Bury	01763 261151
Carlisle	Crosby Lodge Country House Hotel	01228 573618
Cartmel	Aynsome Manor Hotel	015395 36653
Castle Cary	Bond's - Bistro with Rooms	01963 350464
Chagford	Easton Court Hotel	01647 433469
Chagford	Mill End Hotel	01647 432282
Cheltenham	Charlton Kings Hotel	01242 231061
Cheltenham	Halewell	01242 890238
Chester	Green Bough Hotel	01244 326241
Chichester	Crouchers Bottom Country Hotel	01243 784995
Chichester	Woodstock House Hotel	01243 811666
Chippenham	Stanton Manor	01666 837552
Chipping Campden	The Malt House	01386 840295
Church Stretton	Mynd House Hotel & Restaurant	01694 722212
Clearwell	Tudor Farmhouse Hotel & Restaurant	01594 833046
Clovelly	Foxdown Manor	01237 451325
Coalville	Abbots Oak	01530 832 328
Combe Martin	Ashelford	01271 850469
Crediton	Coombe House Country Hotel	01363 84487
Dartmoor	Bel Alp House	01364 661217
Diss	Chippenhall Hall	01379 588180
Diss	Starston Hall	01379 854252
Doncaster	Hamilton's Restaurant & Hotel	01302 760770
Dorchester	Yalbury Cottage Hotel	01305 262382
Dorchester-On-Thames	The George Hotel	01865 340404
Dover	The Woodville Hall	01304 825256
Dover	Wallett's Court	01304 852424
Dulverton	Ashwick Country House Hotel	01398 323868
Enfield	Oak Lodge Hotel	020 8360 7082
Epsom	Chalk Lane Hotel	01372 721179
Evershot	Rectory House	0193583 273
Evesham	The Mill At Harvington	01386 870688
Exford	The Crown Hotel	01643 831554/5
Exmoor	The Beacon Country House Hotel	01643 703476
Falmouth	Trelawne Hotel-The Hutches Restaurant	01326 250226
Fenny Drayton	White Wings	01827 716100
Gatwick	Stanhill Court Hotel	01293 862166
Golant by Fowey	The Cormorant Hotel	01726 833426
Grasmere	White Moss House	015394 35295
Great Snoring	The Old Rectory	01328 820597
Hampton Court	Chase Lodge	020 8943 1862
Hamsterley Forest	Grove House	01388 488203
Harrogate	The White House	01423 501388
Hawes	Rookhurst Country House Hotel	01969 667454
Hawkshead	Sawrey House Country Hotel	015394 36387
Helston	Nansloe Manor	01326 574691
Hereford	The Bowens Country House	01432 860430
Hereford	The Steppes	01432 820424
Holt	Felbrigg Lodge	01263 837588
Ilminster	The Old Rectory	01460 54364
Ilsington	Ilsington Country Hotel	01364 661452
Isle of Wight	Rylstone Manor	01983 862806
Keswick	Dale Head Hall Lakeside Hotel	017687 72478
Keswick	Swinside Lodge Hotel	017687 72948
Kirkby Lonsdale	Hipping Hall	015242 71187
Lavenham	Lavenham Priory	01787 247404
Leominster	Lower Bache House	01568 750304
Lifton	The Thatched Cottage Country Hotel	01566 784224
Lincoln	Washingborough Hall	01522 790340
Looe	Coombe Farm	01503 240223
Lorton	Winder Hall	01900 85107
Loughborough	The Old Manor Hotel	01509 211228
Ludlow	Delbury Hall	01584 841267
Ludlow	Overton Grange Hotel	01584 873500
Luton	Little Offley	01462 768243
Lydford	Moor View House	01822 820220
Lyme Regis	Thatch Lodge Hotel	01297 560407
Lymington	Hotel Gordleton Mill	01590 682219
Lymington	Rosefield House	01590 671526
Lynton	Hewitt's Hotel	01598 752293
Maidstone	Tanyard	01622 744705
Malton	Newstead Grange	01653 692502
Maxey	Abbey House & Coach House	01778 344642
Middlecombe	Periton Park Hotel	01643 706885
Middleham	Millers House Hotel	01969 622630
Middleham	Waterford House	01969 622090
Minchinhampton	Burleigh Court	01453 883804
Morchard Bishop	Wigham	01363 877350
New Romney	Romney Bay House	01797 364747
North Walsham	Beechwood Hotel	01692 403231
Norwich	Catton Old Hall	01603 419379
Norwich	Norfolk Mead Hotel	01603 737531
Norwich	The Beeches Hotel & Victorian Gardens	01603 621167
Norwich	The Old Rectory	01603 700772
Norwich	The Stower Grange	01603 860210
Nottingham	Cockliffe Country House Hotel	01159 680179
Nottingham	L'Auberge	01949 843086
Nottingham	Langar Hall	01949 860559
Nottingham	The Cottage Country House Hotel	01159 846882
Ockham	The Hautboy	01483 225355
Oswestry	Pen-y-Dyffryn Country Hotel	01691 653700
Otterburn	The Tower	01830 520620
Owlpen	Owlpen Manor	01453 860261
Oxford	Fallowfields	01865 820416
Padstow	Cross House Hotel	01841 532391
Penrith	Temple Sowerby House Hotel	017683 61578
Penzance	The Summer House	01736 363744
Petersfield	Langrish House	01730 266941
Petworth	The Old Railway Station	01798 342346
Porlock Weir	Porlock Vale House	01643 862338
Porlock Weir	The Cottage Hotel	01643 863300
Porthleven	Tye Rock Country House Hotel	01326 572695
Portsmouth	The Beaufort Hotel	023 92823707
Preston	Pickering Park Country House	01995 600999
Pulborough	Chequers Hotel	01798 872486
Ringwood	Moortown Lodge	01425 471404
Ross-On-Wye	Glewstone Court	01989 770367
Rye	White Vine House	01797 224748
Saham Toney	Broom Hall	01953 882125
Saunton	Preston House Hotel	01271 890472
Seavington St Mary	The Pheasant Hotel	01460 240502
Sherborne	The Eastbury Hotel	01935 813131
Shipton-Under-Wychwood	The Shaven Crown Hotel	01993 830330
Shrewsbury	Upper Brompton Farm	01743 761629
Simonsbath	Simonsbath House Hotel	01643 831259
Snape	Butley Priory	01394 450046
St Ives	The Countryman At Trink Hotel	01736 797571
St Mawes	The Hundred House Hotel	01872 501336
Stanhope	Horsley Hall	01388 517239
Stanwell	Stanwell Hall	01784 252292
Staverton	Kingston House	01803 762 235
Stevenage	Redcoats Farmhouse Hotel	01438 729500
Stonor	The Stonor Arms Hotel	01491 638866
Stow-On-The-Wold	The Tollgate Inn	01608 658389
Stow-on-the-Wold	The Unicorn Hotel	01451 830257
Stratford-upon-Avon	Glebe Farm House	01789 842501
Sway	The Nurse's Cottage	01590 683402
Tarporley	Willington Hall Hotel	01829 752321
Tewkesbury	Upper Court	01386 725351
Thurlestone Sands	Heron House Hotel	01548 561308
Tintagel	Trebrea Lodge	01840 770410
Uckfield	Hooke Hall	01825 761578
Wadebridge	Trehellas House & Memories of Malaya Restaurant	01208 72700
Wareham	Kemps Country House Hotel	01929 462563
Warwick	The Ardencote Manor Hotel	01926 843111
Wells	Beryl	01749 678738
Wells	Coxley Vineyard	01749 670285
Wells	Glencot House	01749 677160
Wem	Soulton Hall	01939 232786
Wimborne Minster	Beechleas	01202 841684
Wincanton	Holbrook House Hotel	01963 32377
Windermere	Fayrer Garden House Hotel	015394 88195
Windermere	Quarry Garth Country House Hotel	015394 88282
Witherslack	The Old Vicarage Country House Hotel	015395 52381
Woodbridge	Wood Hall Country House Hotel	01394 411283
York	The Parsonage Country House Hotel	01904 728111
Yoxford	Hope House	01728 668281

IRELAND

Caragh Lake Co Kerry	Caragh Lodge	00 353 66 9769115
Cashel Co Tipperary	Cashel Palace Hotel	00 353 62 62707
Connemara	Ross Lake House Hotel	00 353 91 550109
Craughwell	St. Clerans	00 353 91 846 555
Dublin	Aberdeen Lodge	00 353 1 2838155
Dublin	Fitzwilliam Park	00 353 1 6628 280
Kilkee Co Clare	Halpins Hotel & Vittles Restaurant	00 353 65 9056032
Killarney Co Kerry	Earls Court House	00 353 64 34009
Kilmeaden	The Old Rectory - Kilmeaden House	00 353 51 384254
Letterkenny	Castle Grove Country House	00 353 745 1118
Riverstown,Co Sligo	Coopershill House	00 353 71 65108
Sligo,Co Sligo	Markree Castle	00 353 71 67800
Wicklow,Co Wicklow	The Old Rectory	00 353 404 67048

SCOTLAND

Ballater,Royal Deeside	Balgonie Country House	013397 55482
By Huntly	The Old Manse of Marnoch	01466 780873
Castle Douglas	Longacre Manor	01556 503576
Comrie	The Royal Hotel	01764 679200
Dumfries	Trigony House Hotel	01848 331211
Dunkeld	The Pend	01350 727586
Edinburgh	Garvock House Hotel	01383 621067
Fintry	Culcreuch Castle Hotel & Country Park	01360 860555
Glasgow	Nairns	0141 353 0707
Glen Cannich	Mullardoch House Hotel	01456 415460
Helmsdale	Navidale House Hotel	01431 821 258
Inverness	Culduthel Lodge	01463 240089
Inverness	Maple Court & Chandlery Restaurant	01463 230330
Isle Of Harris	Ardvourlie Castle	01859 502307
Isle of Mull	Highland Cottage	01688 302030
Isle Of Mull	Killiechronan	01680 300403
Isle of Skye	Bosville Hotel & Chandlery Seafood Restaurant	01478 612846
Kentallen Of Appin	Ardsheal House	01631 740227
Killiecrankie,By Pitlochry	The Killiecrankie Hotel	01796 473220
Kinlochbervie	The Kinlochbervie Hotel	01971 521275
Leslie	Balgeddie House Hotel	01592 742511
Loch Ness	Polmaily House Hotel	01456 450343
Lockerbie	The Dryfesdale Hotel	01576 202427
Maybole	Culzean Castle	01655 760274
Moffat	Well View Hotel	01683 220184
Nairn	Boath House	01667 454896
Oban	Dungallan House Hotel	01631 563799
Oban	The Manor House Hotel	01631 562087
Pitlochry	Knockendarroch House	01796 473473
Port Of Menteith	The Lake Hotel	01877 385258
Rothiemurchus	Corrour House Hotel	01479 810220
St. Andrews	The Argyle House Hotel	01334 473387
St. Boswell By Melrose	Clint Lodge	01835 822027
St Fillans	The Four Seasons Hotel	01764 685333
Strathtummel	Queen's View Hotel	01796 473291
Tain	Glenmorangie House at Cadbol	01862 871671
The Great Glen	Corriegour Lodge Hotel	01397 712685

WALES

Aberdovey	Plas Penhelig Country House Hotel	01654 767676
Abergavenny	Glangrwyney Court	01873 811288
Abergavenny	Llanwenarth House	01873 830289
Anglesey	Tre-Ysgawen Hall	01245 750750
Betws-y-Coed	Tan-y-Foel	01690 710507
Brecon	Old Gwernyfed Country Manor	01497 847376
Caernarfon	Ty'n Rhos Country Hotel	01248 670489
Conwy	The Old Rectory	01492 580611
Dolgellau	Plas Dolmelynllyn	01341 440273
Fishguard	Stone Hall	01348 840212
Monmouth	The Crown At Whitebrook	01600 860254
Pwllheli	Plas Bodegroes	01758 612363
Swansea	Norton House Hotel & Restaurant	01792 404891
Tenby	Waterwynch House Hotel	01834 842464
Tintern	Parva Farmhouse and Restaurant	01291 689411

CHANNEL ISLANDS

Guernsey	Bella Luce Hotel & Restaurant	01481 38764
Guernsey	La Favorita Hotel	01481 35666
Herm Island	The White House	01481 722159
Jersey	Hotel La Tour	01534 743770
Sark Island	La Sablonnerie	01481 832061

MINI LISTINGS
Johansens Recommended Hotels – Europe & The Mediterranean 2000
Here in brief are the entries that appear in full in Johansens Recommended Hotels – Europe & The Mediterranean 2000.
They are listed in order by country and town. To order Johansens guides turn to the order forms at the back of this book.

ANDORRA (ANDORRA LA VELLA)
Andorra Park Hotel
Les Canals 24, Andorra La Vella, Andorra
Tel: 376 82 09 79
Fax: 376 82 09 83

AUSTRIA (ALPBACH)
Romantik Hotel Böglerhof
Alpbach 166, 6236, Austria
Tel: 43 5336 5227
Fax: 43 5336 5227 402

AUSTRIA (ALTAUSSEE)
Landhaus Hubertushof
Puchen, 8992 Altaussee, Steiermark, Austria
Tel: 43 36 22 71 280
Fax: 43 36 22 71 28 080

AUSTRIA (BAD GASTEIN)
Hotel & Spa Haus Hirt
Kaiserhofstrasse 14, 5640 Bad Gastein,
Austria
Tel: 43 64 34 27 97
Fax: 43 64 34 27 97 48

AUSTRIA (BAD HOFGASTEIN)
Grand Park Hotel
Kurgartenstrasse 26, 5630 Bad Hofgastein,
Austria
Tel: 43 6432 63560
Fax: 43 6432 8454

AUSTRIA (BAD HOFGASTEIN)
**Kur-Sport &
Gourmethotel Moser**
Kaiser-Franz-Platz 2, 5630 Bad Hofgastein,
Austria
Tel: 43 6432 6209
Fax: 43 6432 6209 88

AUSTRIA (BAD KLEINKIRCHHEIM)
Almdorf "Seinerzeit"
Fellacher Alm, 9564 Patergassen bei Bad
Kleinkirchheim, Austria
Tel: 43 4275 7201
Fax: 43 4275 7380

AUSTRIA (BADEN BEI WIEN)
Grand Hotel Sauerhof
Weilburgstrasse 11-13, 2500 Baden bei
Wien, Austria
Tel: 43 2252 41251 0
Fax: 43 2252 48047

AUSTRIA (DÜRNSTEIN)
Hotel Schloss Dürnstein
3601 Dürnstein, Austria
Tel: 43 2711 212
Fax: 43 2711 351

AUSTRIA (GRAZ)
Schlossberg Hotel
Kaiser-Franz-Josef-Kai 30, 8010 Graz,
Austria
Tel: 43 316 80700
Fax: 43 316 807070

AUSTRIA (GRÜNAU IM ALMTAL)
Romantik Hotel Almtalhof
4645 Grünau Im Almtal, Austria
Tel: 43 7616 82040
Fax: 43 7616 820466

AUSTRIA (IGLS)
Schlosshotel Igls
Viller Steig 2, 6080 Igls, Tirol, Austria
Tel: 43 512 37 72 17
Fax: 43 512 3786 79

AUSTRIA (IGLS)
Sporthotel Igls
Hilberstrasse 17, 6080 Igls, Tirol, Austria
Tel: 43 512 37 72 41
Fax: 512 37 86 79

AUSTRIA (KITZBÜHEL)
Romantik Hotel Tennerhof
Griesenauweg 26, 6370 Kitzbühel, Austria
Tel: 43 53566 3181
Fax: 43 53566 318170

AUSTRIA (KLAGENFURT)
Hotel Palais Porcia
Neuer Platz 13, 9020 Klagenfurt, Austria
Tel: 43 463 51 1590
Fax: 43 463 51 159030

AUSTRIA (LECH)
Sporthotel Kristiania
Omesberg 331 , 6764 Lech/Arlberg, Austria
Tel: 43 55 83 25 610
Fax: 43 55 83 35 50

AUSTRIA (OBERLECH)
Hotel Goldener Berg
Lech, 6764, Austria
Tel: 43 5583 22050
Fax: 43 5583 220513

AUSTRIA (PÖRTSCHACH AM WÖRTHER SEE)
Hotel Schloss Leonstain
Leonstein 1, Pörtschach Am Wörther See,
Austria
Tel: 43 4272 28160
Fax: 43 4272 2823

AUSTRIA (SALZBURG)

Hotel Auersperg

Auerspergstrasse 61, 5027 Salzburg, Austria
Tel: 43 662 88944
Fax: 43 662 8894455

AUSTRIA (SALZBURG)

Hotel Schloss Mönchstein

Mönchsberg Park, City Center, 26-Joh, 5020
Salzburg, Austria
Tel: 43 662 84 85 55 0
Fax: 43 662 84 85 59

AUSTRIA (SALZBURG)

Schloss Haunsperg

5411 Oberalm bei Hallein, Salzburg, Austria
Tel: 43 62 45 80 662
Fax: 43 62 45 85 680

AUSTRIA (SCHWARZENBERG IM
BREGENZERWALD)

Romantik-Hotel Gasthof Hirschen

Hof 14, 6867 Schwarzenberg, Austria
Tel: 43 55 12 29 44 0
Fax: 43 55 12 29 44 20

AUSTRIA (SEEFELD)

Hotel Klosterbräu

6100 Seefeld Tirol, Austria
Tel: 43 5212 26210
Fax: 43 5212 3885

AUSTRIA (SEEFELD)

Hotel Viktoria

Geigenbühelweg 589 , 6100 Seefeld Tirol,
Austria
Tel: 43 52 12 44 41
Fax: 43 52 12 44 43

AUSTRIA (ST CHRISTOPH)

Arlberg Hospiz

6580 St Christoph, Austria
Tel: 43 5446 2611
Fax: 43 5446 3773

AUSTRIA (ST WOLFGANG AM SEE)

Romantik Hotel im Weissen Rössl

5360 St Wolfgang am See, Salzkammergut,
Austria
Tel: 43 61 38 23 060
Fax: 43 61 38 23 06 41

AUSTRIA (VELDEN)

Seeschlössl Velden

Klagenfurter Strasse 34, 9220 Velden,
Austria
Tel: 43 4274 2824
Fax: 43 4274 282444

AUSTRIA (VIENNA)

ANA Grand Hotel Wien

Kärntner Ring 9, 1010, Vienna, Austria
Tel: 43 1 515 80 0
Fax: 43 1 515 13 13

AUSTRIA (VIENNA)

Hotel im Palais Schwarzenberg

Schwarzenbergplatz 9, 1030 Vienna, Austria
Tel: 43 1 798 4515
Fax: 43 1 798 4714

AUSTRIA (ZÜRS)

Thurnhers Alpenhof

6763 Zürs/Arlberg, Austria
Tel: 43 5583 2191
Fax: 43 5583 3330

BELGIUM (ANTWERP)

Firean Hotel

Karel Oomsstraat 6, 2018 Antwerp, Belgium
Tel: 32 3237 02 60
Fax: 32 3238 11 68

BELGIUM (BRUGES)

Die Swaene

Steenhouwersdijk, 8000 Bruges, Belgium
Tel: 32 50 34 27 98
Fax: 32 50 33 66 74

BELGIUM (BRUGES)

Hotel Acacia

Korte Zilverstraat 3A, 8000 Bruges, Belgium
Tel: 32 50 34 44 11
Fax: 32 50 33 88 17

BELGIUM (BRUGES)

Hotel de Orangerie

Kartuizerinnenstraat10, 8000 Bruges,
Belgium
Tel: 32 50 34 16 49
Fax: 32 50 33 30 16

BELGIUM (BRUGES)

Hotel Hansa

N. Desparsstraat 11, 8000 Bruges, Belgium
Tel: 32 50 33 84 44
Fax: 32 50 33 42 05

BELGIUM (BRUGES)

Hotel Jan Brito

Freren Fonteinstraat 1, 8000 Bruges,
Belgium
Tel: 32 50 33 06 01
Fax: 32 50 33 06 52

BELGIUM (BRUGES)

Hotel Montanus

Nieuwe Gentweg 78, 8000 Bruges, Belgium
Tel: 32 50 33 11 76
Fax: 32 50 34 09 38

BELGIUM (BRUGES)

Hotel Prinsenhof

Ontvangersstraat 9, 8000 Bruges, Belgium
Tel: 32 50 34 26 90
Fax: 32 50 34 23 21

BELGIUM (BRUSSELS)
L'Amigo
1-3 Rue de L'Amigo, 1000 Brussels, Belgium
Tel: 32 2 547 47 47
Fax: 32 2 513 52 77

BELGIUM (FLORENVILLE)
Hostellerie Le Prieuré De Conques
Rue Florenville 176, 6820 Florenville, Belgium
Tel: 32 61 41 14 17
Fax: 32 61 41 27 03

BELGIUM (LANAKEN)
La Butte Aux Bois
Paalsteenlaan 90, 3620 Lanaken, Belgium
Tel: 32 89 72 12 86
Fax: 32 89 72 16 47

BELGIUM (MALMEDY)
Hostellerie Trôs Marets
Route Des Trôs Marets , 4960 Malmédy, Belgium
Tel: 32 80 33 79 17
Fax: 32 80 33 79 10

BELGIUM (MARCHE-EN-FAMENNE)
Château d'Hassonville
6900 Marche-en-Famenne, Belgium
Tel: 32 84 31 10 25
Fax: 32 84 31 60 27

BELGIUM (VIEUXVILLE)
Chateau de Palogne
Route du Palogne 3, 4190 Vieuxville, Belgium
Tel: 32 86 21 38 74
Fax: 32 86 21 38 76

CYPRUS (LIMASSOL)
Le Meridien Limassol
PO Box 56560, 3308 Limassol, Cyprus
Tel: 357 5 634 000
Fax: 357 5 634 222

CYPRUS (LIMASSOL)
The Four Seasons Hotel
PO Box 57222, Limassol, Cyprus
Tel: 357 5 310 222
Fax: 357 5 310 887

CZECH REPUBLIC (PRAGUE)
Hotel Hoffmeister
Pod Bruskou 7, Kralov, 11800 Prague 1, Czech Republic
Tel: 420 2 510 17 111
Fax: 420 2 510 17 120

CZECH REPUBLIC (PRAGUE)
Sieber Hotel & Apartments
Slezska 55, 130 00, Prague 3, Czech Republic
Tel: 420 224 25 00 25
Fax: 420 224 25 00 27

DENMARK (FAABORG)
Steensgaard Herregårdspension
Steensgaard, 5600 Millinge, Faaborg, Denmark
Tel: 45 62 61 94 90
Fax: 45 63 61 78 61

DENMARK (NYBORG)
Hotel Hesselet
Christianslundsvej 119, 5800 Nyborg, Denmark
Tel: 45 65 31 30 29
Fax: 45 65 31 29 58

BRITISH ISLES (AYLESBURY)
Hartwell House
Oxford Road, Nr Aylesbury, Buckinghamshire, England HP17 8NL
Tel: 44 1296 747444
Fax: 44 1296 747450

BRITISH ISLES (BAMBURGH)
Waren House
Waren Mill, Bamburgh, Northumberland, England NE70 7EE
Tel: 44 1668 214581
Fax: 44 1668 214484

BRITISH ISLES (BATH)
Lucknam Park
Colerne, Nr Bath, Wiltshire, England SN14 8AZ
Tel: 44 1225 742777
Fax: 44 1225 743536

BRITISH ISLES (BERWICK-UPON-TWEED)
Tillmouth Park
Cornhill-on-Tweed, Nr Berwick-Upon-Tweed, Northumberland, England TD12 4UU
Tel: 44 1890 882255
Fax: 44 1890 882540

BRITISH ISLES (BIRMINGHAM)
The Burlington Hotel
6 Burlington Arcade, 126 New Street, Birmingham, West Midlands, England B2 4JQ
Tel: 44 121 643 9191
Fax: 44 121 643 5075

BRITISH ISLES (BURRINGTON)
Northcote Manor
Burrington, Nr Umberleigh, Devon, England EX37 9LZ
Tel: 44 1769 560501
Fax: 44 1769 560770

BRITISH ISLES (CLANFIELD)
The Plough At Clanfield
Bourton Road, Clanfield, Oxfordshire, England OX18 2RB
Tel: 44 1367 810222
Fax: 44 1367 810596

BRITISH ISLES CHANNEL ISLANDS (JERSEY)
The Atlantic Hotel
La Moye, St Brelade, Channel Islands, England JE3 8HE
Tel: 44 1534 44101
Fax: 44 1534 44102

The Ascott Mayfair

49 Hill Street, London, England W1X 7FQ
Tel: 44 20 7499 6868
Fax: 44 20 7499 0705

Basil Street Hotel

Basil Street, London, England SW3 1AH
Tel: 44 20 7581 3311
Fax: 44 20 7581 3693

The Beaufort

33 Beaufort Gardens, Knightsbridge,
London, England SW3 1PP
Tel: 44 20 7584 5252
Fax: 44 20 7589 2834

Beaufort House Apartments

45 Beaufort Gardens, London, England SW3
1PN
Tel: 44 20 7584 2600
Fax: 44 20 7584 6532

Cannizaro House

West Side, Wimbledon Common, London,
England SW19 4UE
Tel: 44 20 8879 1464
Fax: 44 20 8879 7338

The Cliveden Town House

26 Cadogan Gardens, London, England
SW3 2RP
Tel: 44 20 7730 6466
Fax: 44 20 7730 0236

The Colonnade Town House

2 Warrington Crescent, London, England
W9 1ER
Tel: 44 20 7286 1052
Fax: 44 20 7286 1057

The Dorchester

Park Lane, Mayfair, London, England WIA
2HJ
Tel: 44 20 7629 8888
Fax: 44 20 7409 0114

Draycott House Apartments

10 Draycott Avenue, Chelsea, London,
England SW3 3AA
Tel: 44 020 7584 4659
Fax: 44 020 7225 3694

The Hempel

Hempel Garden Square, 31-35 Craven Hill
Gardens, London, England W2 3EA
Tel: 44 20 7298 9000
Fax: 44 20 7402 4666

The Leonard

15 Seymour Street, London, England W1H
5AA
Tel: 44 20 7935 2010
Fax: 44 20 7935 6700

The Lexham Apartments

32–38 Lexham Gardens, Kensington,
London, England W8 5JE
Tel: 44 20 7559 4444
Fax: 44 20 7559 4400

The Milestone

1-2 Kensington Court, London, England W8
5DL
Tel: 44 20 7917 1000
Fax: 44 20 7917 1010

Number Eleven
Cadogan Gardens

11 Cadogan Gardens, Sloane Square,
London, England SW3 2RJ
Tel: 44 20 7730 7000
Fax: 44 20 7730 5217

Number Sixteen

16 Sumner Place, London, England SW7
3EG
Tel: 44 20 7589 5232
Fax: 44 20 7584 8615

Pembridge Court Hotel

34 Pembridge Gardens, London, England
W2 4DX
Tel: 44 020 7229 9977
Fax: 44 020 7727 4982

Twenty Nevern Square

20 Nevern Square, London, England SW5
9PD
Tel: 44 20 7565 9555
Fax: 44 20 7565 9444

Swan Hellenic Minerva

77 New Oxford Street, London, England
WC1 1PP
Tel: 44 20 7800 2227
Fax: 44 20 7800 2724

Hewitt's Hotel

North Walk, Lynton, Devon, England EX35
6HJ
Tel: 44 1598 752293
Fax: 44 1598 752489

Stapleford Park

Nr Melton Mowbray, Leicestershire, England
LE14 2EF
Tel: 44 1572 787522
Fax: 44 1572 787651

BRITISH ISLES (STREATLEY-ON-THAMES)

Swan Diplomat

Streatley-On-Thames, Reading, Berkshire,
England RG8 9HR
Tel: 44 1491 873737
Fax: 44 1491 872554

BRITISH ISLES (WINDERMERE)

Miller Howe

Rayrigg Road, Windermere, Cumbria,
England LA23 1EY
Tel: 44 15394 42536
Fax:

BRITISH ISLES (WINDERMERE)

Storrs Hall

Windermere, Cumbria, England LA23 3LG
Tel: 44 15394 47111
Fax: 44 15394 47555

ESTONIA (TALLINN)

Park Consul Schlössle

Pühavaimu 13-15, EE 10123 Tallinn, Estonia
Tel: 372 699 7700
Fax: 372 699 7777

FINLAND (HÄMEENLINNA)

Hotel Vanajanlinna

13330 Harviala, Hämeenlinna, Finland
Tel: 358 3 619 65 65
Fax: 358 3 619 65 91

FRANCE (AMBOISE)

Chateau de Pray

Route De Charge, 37400, Amboise, France
Tel: 33 2 47 57 23 67
Fax: 33 2 47 57 32 50

FRANCE (AVALLON)

Château de Vault de Lugny

11 Rue de Château, 89200 Avallon, France
Tel: 33 3 86 34 07 86
Fax: 33 3 86 34 16 36

FRANCE (AVALLON)

Hostellerie de la Poste

13 place Vauban, 89200, Avallon, France
Tel: 33 3 86 34 16 16
Fax: 33 3 86 34 19 19

FRANCE (BEAULIEU-SUR-MER)

La Réserve de Beaulieu

5 Boulevard Général Leclerc, 06310
Beaulieu-sur-Mer, France
Tel: 33 4 93 01 00 01
Fax: 33 4 93 01 28 99

FRANCE (BEAUNE)

Ermitage de Corton

R.N. 74, 21200 Chorey-Les-Beaune, France
Tel: 33 3 80 22 05 28
Fax: 33 3 80 24 64 51

FRANCE (BIARRITZ)

Hôtel du Palais

Avenue de L'Impératrice, 64200 Biarrritz,
France
Tel: 33 5 59 41 64 00
Fax: 33 5 59 41 67 99

FRANCE (BILLIERS)

La Domaine de Rochevilaine

Pointe De Pen Lan, 56190 Billiers, France
Tel: 33 2 97 41 61 61
Fax: 33 2 97 41 44 85

FRANCE (BOUTIGNY NR BARBIZON)

Domaine de Belesbat

Courdimanche-sur-Essonne, 91820,
Boutigny-sur-Essonne, France
Tel: 33 1 69 23 19 00
Fax: 33 1 69 23 19 01

FRANCE (CASTRES)

Château d'Aiguefonde

81200 , Aiguefonde, France
Tel: 33 5 63 98 13 70
Fax: 33 5 63 98 69 90

FRANCE (CHAMBÉRY-LE-VIEUX)

Château de Candie

Rue du Bois de Candie, 73000 Chambéry-le-
Vieux, France
Tel: 33 4 79 96 63 00
Fax: 33 4 79 96 63 10

FRANCE (CHAMPIGNÉ)

Château des Briottières

49330 Champigné, France
Tel: 33 2 41 42 00 02
Fax: 33 2 41 42 01 55

FRANCE (CHINON)

Château de Danzay

RD 749, 37420 Chinon, France
Tel: 33 2 47 58 46 86
Fax: 33 2 47 58 84 35

FRANCE (COLMAR)

Hôtel Les Têtes

19 Rue Des Têtes, 68000 Colmar, France
Tel: 33 3 89 24 43 43
Fax: 33 3 89 24 58 34

FRANCE (CONNELLES)

Le Moulin de Connelles

39 Route d'Amfreville-Sous-Les-Monts,
27430 Connelles, France
Tel: 33 2 32 59 53 33
Fax: 33 2 32 59 21 83

FRANCE (CORSICA-PORTICCIO)

Hotel Le Maquis

BP 94, 20166 Porticcio-Corsica, France
Tel: 33 4 95 25 05 55
Fax: 33 4 95 25 11 70

FRANCE (COURCHEVEL)

Hôtel Annapurna

73120 Courchevel, 1850, France
Tel: 33 4 79 08 04 60
Fax: 33 4 79 08 15 31

FRANCE (DIVONNE-LES-BAINS)

Le Domaine de Divonne

Avenue des Thermes, 01220 Divonne-Les-
Bains, France
Tel: 33 4 50 40 34 34
Fax: 33 4 50 40 34 24

FRANCE (ÉPERNAY)

Hostellerie La Briqueterie

4 Route de Sézanne, Vinay, 51530 Epernay,
France
Tel: 33 3 26 59 99 99
Fax: 33 3 26 59 92 10

FRANCE (EZE VILLAGE)

Château Eza

Rue De La Pise, 06360 Eze Village, France
Tel: 33 4 93 41 12 24
Fax: 33 4 93 41 16 64

FRANCE (GÉRARDMER)

Hostellerie Les Bas Rupts

88400 Gérardmer, Vosges, France
Tel: 33 3 29 63 09 25
Fax: 33 3 29 63 00 40

FRANCE (GRESSY-EN-FRANCE/CHANTILLY)

Le Manoir de Gressy

77410 Gressy-en-France, Chemin des
Carrosses, France
Tel: 33 1 60 26 68 00
Fax: 33 1 60 26 45 46

FRANCE (GRIGNAN)

Manoir de la Roseraie

Route de Valreas, 26230, Grignan, France
Tel: 33 4 75 46 58 15
Fax: 33 4 75 46 91 55

FRANCE (HONFLEUR)

La Chaumière

Route du Littoral, 14600 Honfleur, France
Tel: 33 2 31 81 63 20
Fax: 33 2 31 89 59 23

FRANCE (HONFLEUR)

La Ferme Saint Siméon

Rue Adolphe-Marais, 14600 Honfleur,
France
Tel: 33 2 31 81 78 00
Fax: 33 2 31 89 48 48

FRANCE (HONFLEUR)

Le Manoir du Butin

Phare du Butin, 14600 Honfleur, France
Tel: 33 2 31 81 63 00
Fax: 33 2 31 89 59 23

FRANCE (LA GOUESNIÈRE/ST MALO)

Chateau de Bonaban

La Gouesniére, 35350, France
Tel: 33 2 99 58 24 50
Fax: 33 2 99 58 28 41

FRANCE (LANGEAIS)

Château de Rochecotte

Saint Patrice, 37130 Langeais, France
Tel: 33 2 47 96 16 16
Fax: 33 2 47 96 90 59

FRANCE (LES ISSAMBRES)

Villa Saint Elme

Corniche des Issambres, 83380 Les
Issambres, France
Tel: 33 4 94 49 52 52
Fax: 33 4 94 49 63 18

FRANCE (LYON)

La Tour Rose

22 Rue de Boeuf, 69005 Lyon, France
Tel: 33 4 78 37 25 90
Fax: 33 4 78 42 26 02

FRANCE (MADIERES-GANGES)

Chateau de Madieres

Madieres-Ganges, 34170, Ganges, France
Tel: 33 4 67 73 84 03
Fax: 33 4 67 73 55 71

FRANCE (MARTILLAC)

Les Sources de Caudalie

Chemin de Smith Haut-Lafitte, 33650,
Martillac, France
Tel: 33 5 57 83 83 83
Fax: 33 5 57 83 83 84

FRANCE (MEGÈVE)

Hôtel Mont-Blanc

Place de l'Eglise, 74120 Megève, France
Tel: 33 4 50 21 20 02
Fax: 33 4 50 21 45 28

FRANCE (MEGÈVE)

Lodge Park Hôtel

100 Route d'Arly, 74120 Megève, France
Tel: 33 4 50 93 05 03
Fax: 33 4 50 93 09 52

FRANCE (MONESTIER)

Château des Vigiers

24240 Monestier, France
Tel: 33 5 53 61 50 00
Fax: 33 5 53 61 50 20

FRANCE (PARIS)

Hôtel Buci Latin

34 Rue de Buci, 75006 Paris, France
Tel: 33 1 43 29 07 20
Fax: 33 1 43 29 67 44

FRANCE (PARIS)

Hôtel de Crillon

10 Place de la Concorde, 75008 Paris,
France
Tel: 33 1 44 71 15 00
Fax: 33 1 44 71 15 02

FRANCE (PARIS)

Hôtel de L'Arcade

9 Rue de L'Arcade, 75008 Paris, France
Tel: 33 1 53 30 60 00
Fax: 33 1 40 07 03 07

FRANCE (PARIS)

Hotel Franklin D. Roosevelt

18 rue Clement Marot, 75008, Paris, France
Tel: 33 1 53 57 49 50
Fax: 33 1 47 20 44 30

FRANCE (PARIS)

Hôtel Le Parc

55-57 avenue Raymond Poincaré, 75116,
Paris, France
Tel: 33 1 44 05 66 66
Fax: 33 1 44 05 66 00

FRANCE (PARIS)

Hôtel le Saint-Grégoire

43 Rue de l'Abbé Grégoire, 75006 Paris,
France
Tel: 33 1 45 48 23 23
Fax: 33 1 45 48 33 95

FRANCE (PARIS)

Hôtel Le Tourville

16 Avenue de Tourville, 75007 Paris, France
Tel: 33 1 47 05 62 62
Fax: 33 1 47 05 43 90

FRANCE (PARIS)

L'Hôtel

13 rue des Beaux Arts, 75006 Paris, France
Tel: 33 1 43 25 27 22
Fax: 33 1 43 25 64 81

FRANCE (PARIS)

L'Hôtel Pergolese

3 Rue Pergolese, 75116 Paris, France
Tel: 33 1 53 64 04 04
Fax: 33 1 53 64 04 40

FRANCE (PARIS)

La Villa Maillot

143 Avenue de Malakoff, 75116, Paris,
France
Tel: 33 1 53 64 52 52
Fax: 33 1 45 00 60 61

FRANCE (PARIS)

Le Lavoisier

21 rue Lavoisier, 75008, Paris, France
Tel: 33 1 53 30 06 06
Fax: 33 1 53 30 23 00

FRANCE (PLEVEN)

Le Manoir de Vaumadeuc

22130 Pleven, France
Tel: 33 2 96 84 46 17
Fax: 33 2 96 84 40 16

FRANCE (ROCHEFORT-SUR-MER)

Hotel De La Corderie Royale

Rue Audebert, BP 275 Rochefort S.Mer,
17300, France
Tel: 33 5 46 99 35 35
Fax: 33 5 46 99 78 72

FRANCE (ROQUEBRUNE CAP-MARTIN/MONACO)

Grand Hôtel Vista Palace

Route De La Grande Corniche, 06190
Roquebrune/Cap-Martin, France
Tel: 33 4 92 10 40 00
Fax: 33 4 93 35 18 94

FRANCE (SAINT TROPEZ)

Hôtel Sube

15 Quai Suffren, 83990 St Tropez, France
Tel: 33 4 94 97 30 04
Fax: 33 4 94 54 89 08

FRANCE (SAINT TROPEZ)

La Résidence de la Pinède

Plage de la Bouillabaisse, 83991 Saint
Tropez, France
Tel: 33 4 94 55 91 00
Fax: 33 4 94 97 73 64

FRANCE (SAINT-RÉMY-DE-PROVENCE)

Château des Alpilles

Route Départementale 31, Ancienne route
du Grés, 13210 St-Rémy-de-Provence,
France
Tel: 33 4 90 92 03 33
Fax: 33 4 90 92 45 17

FRANCE (SAINTE- MAXIME/BAY OF ST TROPEZ)

Hotel Le Beauvallon

Baie de St. Tropez, Beauvallon-Grimaud,
83120 Sainte-Maxime, France
Tel: 33 4 94 55 78 88
Fax: 33 4 94 55 78 78

FRANCE (SARLAT-VITRAC)

Domaine de Rochebois

Route du Château de Montfort, 24200
Vitrac, France
Tel: 33 5 53 31 52 52
Fax: 33 5 53 29 36 88

FRANCE (SCIEZ SUR LEMAN)

Château de Coudrée

Domaine de Coudrée, Bonnatrait, 74140
Sciez sur Leman, France
Tel: 33 4 50 7262 33
Fax: 33 4 50 72 57 28

FRANCE (SERRE-CHEVALIER)

L'Auberge du Choucas

05220, Monetier-Les-Bains, 1550 Serre-
Chevalier , France
Tel: 33 4 92 24 42 73
Fax: 33 4 92 24 51 60

FRANCE (VERVINS)

La Tour Du Roy

45 rue du Général Leclerc, 02140, Vervins,
France
Tel: 33 3 23 98 00 11
Fax: 33 3 23 98 00 72

GERMANY (BADENWEILER)

Hotel Römerbad

Schlossplatz 1, 79410, Badenweiler,
Germany
Tel: 49 76 32 70 0
Fax: 49 76 32 70 200

GERMANY (GÖTTINGEN)

Burghotel Hardenberg

37176 Nörten-Hardenberg, Germany
Tel: 49 5503 9810
Fax: 49 5503 981 666

GERMANY (MUNICH)

Hotel Königshof

Karlsplatz 25, 80335 Munich, Germany
Tel: 49 89 551 360
Fax: 49 89 5513 6113

GERMANY (NIEDERSTOTZINGEN)

Schlosshotel Oberstotzingen

Stettener Strasse 35-37 , 89168
Niederstotzingen, Germany
Tel: 49 7325 1030
Fax: 49 7325 10370

GERMANY (OBERWESEL/RHEIN)

Burghotel Auf Schönburg

55430 Oberwesel/Rhein, Germany
Tel: 49 67 44 93 93 0
Fax: 49 67 44 16 13

GERMANY (ROTHENBURG OB DER TAUBER)

Hôtel Eisenhut

Herrngasse 3-7, 91541, Germany
Tel: 49 9861 70 50
Fax: 49 9861 7 05 45

GERMANY (TRIBERG)

Romantik Parkhotel Wehrle

Gartenstr.24, 78098, Triberg, Germany
Tel: 49 7722 86020
Fax: 49 7722 860290

GERMANY (WALDECK)

Hotel Schloss Waldeck

34513 Waldeck, Germany
Tel: 49 5623 5890
Fax: 49 5623 589289

GERMANY (WASSENBERG)

Hotel Burg Wassenberg

Kirchstrasse 17, 41849 Wassenberg,
Germany
Tel: 49 2432 9490
Fax: 49 2432 949100

GERMANY (WERNBERG-KÖBLITZ)

Hotel Burg Wernberg

Schlossberg 10, 92533 Wernberg-Köblitz,
Wernberg-Köblitz, Germany
Tel: 49 9604 9390
Fax: 49 9604 939139

GIBRALTER

The Rock Hotel

3 Europa Road, Gibralter
Tel: 350 73 000
Fax: 350 73 513

GREECE (ATHENS)

Hotel Pentelikon

66 Diligianni Street, 14562 Athens, Greece
Tel: 30 1 62 30 650/656
Fax: 30 1 8010 314

GREECE (CRETE)

St Nicolas Bay Hotel

72100 Agios Nicholaos, Crete, Greece
Tel: 30 841 25 041
Fax: 30 841 24556

GREECE (EVRITANIA-KARPENISSI)

Hotel Club Montana

36100 Karpenissi, Greece
Tel: 30 237 80400
Fax: 30 237 80409

GREECE (SAMOS ISLAND)

Doryssa Bay Hotel-Village

Pythagorion 83103, Samos Island, Aegean
Island, Greece
Tel: 30 273 613 60
Fax: 30 273 614 63

GREECE (SANTORINI ISLAND)

Esperas Traditional Houses

Oia Santorini, 84702, Greece
Tel: 30 286 71088
Fax: 30 286 71613

HUNGARY (BUDAPEST)

Danubius Hotel Gellért

St.Gellért Tér 1, 1111 Budapest, Hungary
Tel: 36 1 185 2200
Fax: 36 1 466 6631

HUNGARY (LAKE BALATON)

Hotel Erika

Bathyany u.6, 8237, Tihany, Hungary
Tel: 36 87 44 86 44
Fax: 36 87 44 86 46

ISRAEL (JERUSALEM)

The American Colony

PO Box 19215, Jerusalem, Israel
Tel: 972 2 6279 777
Fax: 972 2 6279 779

ITALY (ASSISI)

Romantik Hotel Le Silve di Armenzano

Loc. Armenzano, 06081 Assisi, Italy
Tel: 39 075 801 90 00
Fax: 39 075 801 90 05

ITALY (BREUIL-CERVINIA)

Hotel Bucaneve

Piazza Jumeaux 10, 11021 Breuil-Cervinia,
Italy
Tel: 39 0166 949119/948386
Fax: 39 0166 948308

ITALY (CASTELLINA IN CHIANTI)

Romantik Hotel Tenuta Di Ricavo

Localita Ricavo 4, 53011 Castellina In
Chianti, Italy
Tel: 39 0577 740221
Fax: 39 0577 741014

ITALY (CASTELLO DI MONTEGRIDOLFO)

Palazzo Vivani Castello Di Montegridolfo

Via Roma 38, Montegridolfo 47837, Italy
Tel: 39 0541 855350
Fax: 39 0541 855340

ITALY (COMO)

Albergo Terminus

Lungo Lario Trieste 14, 22100 Como, Italy
Tel: 39 031 329111
Fax: 39 031 302550

ITALY (COMO)

Hotel Villa Flori

Via Cernobbio 12, 22100 Como, Italy
Tel: 39 031 573105
Fax: 39 031 570379

ITALY (ETNA)

Hotel Villa Paradiso Dell' Etna

Via per Viagrande 37, 95037 SG La Punta,
Italy
Tel: 39 095 751 2409
Fax: 39 095 741 3861

ITALY (FERRARA)

Albergo Annunziata

Piazza Repubblica 5, 44100 Ferrara, Italy
Tel: 39 0532 20 11 11
Fax: 39 0532 203233

ITALY (FERRARA)

Ripagrande Hotel

Via Ripagrande 21, 44100 Ferrara, Italy
Tel: 39 0532 765250
Fax: 39 0532 764377

ITALY (FLORENCE)

Hotel J &J

Via Mezzo 20, 50121 Florence, Italy
Tel: 39 055 26312
Fax: 39 055 240282

ITALY (ISCHIA)

Hotel Miramare E Castello

Via Pontano 9, 80070 Ischia (NA), Italy
Tel: 39 081 991333
Fax: 39 081 984572

ITALY (ITALIAN RIVIERA)

Hotel Punta Est

17024 Via Aurelia 1, Finale Ligure, Italy
Tel: 39 019 600 611
Fax: 39 019 600 611

ITALY VENICE (LIDO)

Albergo Quattro Fontane

30126, Lido di Venezia, Italy
Tel: 39 041 5260227
Fax: 39 041 5260726

ITALY (LUCCA)

Locanda l'Elisa

Via Nuova per Pisa, 1952, 55050 Massa
Pisana, Lucca, Italy
Tel: 39 0583 379737
Fax: 39 0583 379019

ITALY (MADONNA DI CAMPIGLIO)

Hotel Lorenzetti

Via Dolomiti Di Brenta 119, 38084
Madonna Di Campiglio (TN), Italy
Tel: 39 0 465 44 1404
Fax: 39 0 465 44 14104

ITALY (MANTOVA)

Albergo San Lorenzo

Piazza Concordia 14, 46100 Mantova, Italy
Tel: 39 0376 220500
Fax: 39 0376 327194

ITALY (MILAN)

Hotel Auriga

Via Pirelli 7, 20124 Milan, Italy
Tel: 39 02 66 98 58 51
Fax: 39 02 66 98 06 98

ITALY (NOVI LIGURE)

Relais Villa Pomela

Via Serravalle 69, 15067 Novi Ligure (AL),
Italy
Tel: 39 0143 329910
Fax: 39 0143329912

ITALY (PIEVESCOLA)

Hotel Relais La Suvera

53030 Pievescola, Siena, Italy
Tel: 39 0577 960 300
Fax: 39 0577 960 220

ITALY (PORTO ERCOLE)

Il Pellicano

Aeralita Cala Dei Santi, 58018 Porto Ercole
(GR), Italy
Tel: 39 0564 858111
Fax: 39 0564 833418

ITALY (PORTOBUFFOLÉ-TREVISO)

Romantik Hotel Villa Giustinian

Via Giustiniani 11, 31019 Portobuffolé-Treviso, Italy
Tel: 39 0422 850244
Fax: 39 0422 850260

ITALY (POSITANO)

Romantik Hotel Poseidon

Via Pasitea 148, 84017 Positano, Italy
Tel: 39 089 81 11 11
Fax: 39 089 87 58 33

ITALY (RIMINI)

Il Grand Hotel Di Rimini

Parco Federico Fellini, 47900 Rimini, Italy
Tel: 39 0541 56000
Fax: 39 0541 56866

ITALY (ROME)

Hotel Farnese

Via Alessandro Farnese 30, (Angolo Viale Giulio Cesare), 00192 Rome, Italy
Tel: 39 06 321 25 53
Fax: 39 06 321 51 29

ITALY (ROME)

Hotel Giulio Cesare

Via Degli Scipioni 287, 00192 Rome, Italy
Tel: 39 06 321 0751
Fax: 39 06 3211736

ITALY (ROME)

Romantik Hotel Barocco

Piazza Barberini 9, 00187 Rome, Italy
Tel: 39 0 6 4872001
Fax: 39 0 6 485994

ITALY (ROME-PALO LAZIALE)

La Posta Vecchia

Palo Laziale, 00055 Ladispoli, Rome, Italy
Tel: 39 06 9949 501
Fax: 39 06 994 9507

ITALY (SALERNO-SANTA MARIA DI CASTELLABATE)

Hotel Villa Sirio

Via Lungomare De Simone 15, 84072 Santa Maria di Castellabate, Italy
Tel: 39 0974 961 099
Fax: 39 0974 960 162

ITALY (SATURNIA)

Hotel Terme Di Saturnia

58050 Saturnia, Grosseto, Italy
Tel: 39 0 564 601061
Fax: 39 0 564 601266

ITALY (SESTRI LEVANTE)

Grand Hotel Villa Balbi

Viale Rimembranza 1, 16039 Sestri Levante, Italy
Tel: 39 0185 42941
Fax: 39 0185 482459

ITALY (SORRENTO)

Grand Hotel Cocumella

Via Cocumella 7, 80065 Sant'Agnello, Sorrento, Italy
Tel: 39 081 878 2933
Fax: 39 081 878 3712

ITALY (SORRENTO)

Grand Hotel Excelsior Vittoria

Piazza Tasso 24, Sorrento-(Napoli), Italy
Tel: 39 081 80 71 044
Fax: 39 081 87 71 206

ITALY (SOUTH TYROL MARLING-MÉRAN)

Romantic Hotel Oberwirt

St Felixweg 2, 39020 Marling/Méran, Italy
Tel: 39 0473 44 71 11
Fax: 39 0473 44 71 30

ITALY (SOUTH TYROL-MAULS)

Romantik Hotel Stafler

Mauls 10, 39040 Freienfeld, Italy
Tel: 39 0472 771136
Fax: 39 0472 77 1094

ITALY (SOUTH TYROL NOVA LEVANTE)

Posthotel Weisses Rössl

Via Carezza 30, 39056 Nova Levante (BZ), Dolomites, Italy
Tel: 39 0471 613113
Fax: 39 0471 613390

ITALY (SOUTH TYROL-VÖLS AM SCHLERN)

Romantik Hotel Turm

Piazza Della Chiesa 9, Fié Allo Scilari, Bolzano, Italy
Tel: 39 0471 725014
Fax: 39 0471 725474

ITALY (TAORMINA MARE)

Hotel Villa Sant' Andrea

Via Nazionale 137, 98030 Taormina Mare, Italy
Tel: 39 0942 23125
Fax: 39 0942 24838

ITALY (TAORMINA)

Hotel Villa Diodoro

Via Bagnoli Croci 75, 98039 Taormina (ME), Italy
Tel: 39 0942 23312
Fax: 39 0942 23391

ITALY (TAORMINA-SICILY)

Grande Albergo Capotaormina

Via Nazionale 105, 98039 Taormina, Italy
Tel: 39 0942 576015
Fax: 39 0942 54014

ITALY (TORINO)

Hotel Victoria

Via N.Costa 4, 10123 Torino, Italy
Tel: 39 011 56 11 909
Fax: 39 011 56 11 806

ITALY (TUSCAN RIVIERA)

Hotel Villa Undulna

Viale Marina, 54030 Cinquale Di
Montignoso, Italy
Tel: 39 0585 807788
Fax: 39 0585 807791

ITALY (VARESE LAKE - MALPENSA)

Romantik Hotel Locanda Dei Mai Intees

Via Nobile Claudio Riva 2, 21022 Azzate
(VA), Italy
Tel: 39 0332 457223
Fax: 39 0332 459339

ITALY (VENICE)

Hotel Metropole

San Marco- Riva Degli Schiavoni 4149,
30122 Venice, Italy
Tel: 39 041 52 05 044
Fax: 39 041 52 23 679

ITALY (VENICE)

Villa Condulmer

31020 Zerman Di Mogliani Veneto, Treviso,
Italy
Tel: 39 041 45 71 00
Fax: 39 041 45 71 34

ITALY (VICENZA-ARCUGNANO)

Hotel Villa Michelangelo

Via Sacco 19, 36057 Arcugnano (Vicenza),
Italy
Tel: 39 0444 550300
Fax: 39 0444 550490

LATVIA (RIGA)

Hotel de Rome

Kalkuiela 28, LV 1050 Riga, Latvia
Tel: 37 1 708 7600
Fax: 37 1 708 76 06

LATVIA (RIGA)

Hotel Konventa Seta

Kaleju Iela 9/11, LV 1050 Riga, Latvia
Tel: 371 708 7501
Fax: 371 708 7515

LUXEMBOURG (LUXEMBOURG CITY)

Hotel Albert Premier

2A rue Albert 1er, 1117, Luxembourg
Tel: 352 442 4421
Fax: 352 447 441

LUXEMBOURG (REMICH)

Hotel Saint Nicolas

31 Esplanade, 5533 Remich, Luxembourg
Tel: 352 69 8888
Fax: 352 69 8869

MONACO (MONTE-CARLO)

Hotel Hermitage

Square Beaumarchais BP277, MC 98005,
Monaco
Tel: 377 92 16 40 00
Fax: 377 92 16 38 52

MONACO (MONTE CARLO)

Monte Carlo Beach Hotel

Avenue Princesse Grace, 06190
Rôquebrune-Cap-Martin, France
Tel: 33 4 93 28 66 66
Fax: 33 4 93 78 14 18

MOROCCO (MARRAKECH)

Les Deux Tours

Douar Abiad-Circuit de la Palmeraie,
Municipalite An-Nakhil, Marrakech BP
513, Morocco
Tel: 212 4 32 95 27
Fax: 212 4 32 95 23

THE NETHERLANDS (AMSTERDAM)

Ambassade Hotel

Herengracht 341, 1016 AZ Amsterdam, The
Netherlands
Tel: 31 20 5550222
Fax: 31 20 5550277

THE NETHERLANDS (AMSTERDAM)

The Canal House Hotel

Keizersgracht 148, 1015 CX Amsterdam,
The Netherlands
Tel: 31 20 6225182
Fax: 31 20 6241317

THE NETHERLANDS (AMSTERDAM)

Seven One Seven

Prinsengracht 717, 1017 JW Amsterdam,
The Netherlands
Tel: 31 20 4270717
Fax: 31 20 4230717

THE NETHERLANDS (BEETSTERZWAAG)

Bilderberg Landgoed Lauswolt

Van Harinxmawrg 10, 924 CJ Beetsterzwaag,
The Netherlands
Tel: 31 512 381245
Fax: 31 512 381496

THE NETHERLANDS (BERGAMBACHT)

Hotel De Arendshoeve

Molenlaan 14, 2861 LB Bergambacht, The
Netherlands
Tel: 31 182 35 1000
Fax: 31 182 35 1155

THE NETHERLANDS (DRUNEN)

Hotel De Duinrand

Steegerf 2, 5151 RB Drunen, The
Netherlands
Tel: 31 416 372 498
Fax: 31 416 374 919

THE NETHERLANDS (LATTROP)

Hotel De Holtwenjde

Spiekweg 7, 7635 LP Lattrop, The
Netherlands
Tel: 31 541 229 234
Fax: 31 541 229 445

THE NETHERLANDS (OISTERWIJK)

Hotel Restaurant de Swaen

De Lind 47, 5061 HT Oisterwijk, The
Netherlands
Tel: 31 135 23 3233
Fax: 31 135 28 58 60

THE NETHERLANDS (OOTMARSUM)
Hotel de Wiemsel
Winhofflaan 2, 7631 HX Ootmarsum, The Netherlands
Tel: 31 541 292 155
Fax: 31 541 293 295

THE NETHERLANDS (VOORBURG)
Restaurant-Hotel Savelberg
Oosteinde 14, 2271 EH Voorburg, The Netherlands
Tel: 31 70 387 2081
Fax: 31 70 387 7715

NORWAY (BALESTRAND)
Kvikne's Hotel
6898 Balestrand, Norway
Tel: 47 57 69 11 01
Fax: 47 57 69 15 02

NORWAY (BERGEN)
Grand Hotel Terminus
Zander Kaaesgt 6, PO Box 1100 Sentrum, 5001 Bergen, Norway
Tel: 47 55 31 16 55
Fax: 47 55 31 85 76

NORWAY (DALEN)
Dalen Hotel
Postboks 123, 3880 Daleni Telemark, Norway
Tel: 47 35 07 70 00
Fax: 47 35 07 70 11

NORWAY (HONEFOSS)
Grand Hotel Honefoss
Stabellsgate 8, 3500 Honefoss, Norway
Tel: 47 32 12 27 22
Fax: 47 32 12 27 88

NORWAY (LOFTHUS IN HARDANGER)
Hotel Ullensvang
5787 Lofthus in Hardanger, Norway
Tel: 47 53 66 11 00
Fax: 47 53 66 15 20

NORWAY (MOSS)
Hotel Refsnes Gods
P.O Box 236, 1501, Moss, Norway
Tel: 47 69 27 83 00
Fax: 47 69 27 83 01

NORWAY (OSLO)
First Hotel Bastion
Postboks 27, Sentrum, Skippergaten 7, 0152 Oslo, Norway
Tel: 47 22 47 77 00
Fax: 47 22 33 11 80

NORWAY (SANDANE)
Gloppen Hotel
6860 Sandane, Norway
Tel: 47 57 86 53 33
Fax: 47 57 86 60 02

NORWAY (SANDNES/STAVANGER)
Kronen Gaard Hotel
Vatne, 4300 Sandnes, Norway
Tel: 47 51 62 14 00
Fax: 47 51 62 20 23

NORWAY (SOLVORN)
Walaker Hotell
6879 Solvorn, Norway
Tel: 47 576 84 207
Fax: 47 576 84 544

NORWAY (VOSS)
Fleischer's Hotel
5700 Voss, Norway
Tel: 47 56 52 05 00
Fax: 47 56 32 05 01

PORTUGAL (ARMAÇAO DE PERA)
Vilalara Thalasso
Praia das Gaivotas, 8365 Armaçao De Pera, Portugal
Tel: 351 82 32 00 00
Fax: 351 82 31 49 56

PORTUGAL (CARVOEIRO)
Casa Domilu
Estrada De Benagil, Apartado 250, 8400 Praia Do Carvoeiro, Lagoa, Portugal
Tel: 351 82 358 409
Fax: 351 82 358 410

PORTUGAL (FARO)
La Réserve
Santa Bárbara de Nexe, 8000 Faro, Algarve, Portugal
Tel: 351 89 999474
Fax: 351 89 999402

PORTUGAL (FARO)
Monte do Casal
Cerro do Lobo, Estoi , 8000 Faro, Algarve, Portugal
Tel: 351 89 990140
Fax: 351 89 991341

PORTUGAL (LAGOS)
Romantik Hotel Vivenda Miranda
Porto de Mós, 8600 Lagos, Algarve, Portugal
Tel: 351 82 763 222
Fax: 351 82 760 342

PORTUGAL (LISBON)
Hotel Tivoli Lisboa
Av da Liberdade 185, 1250 Lisbon, Portugal
Tel: 351 1 319 89 00
Fax: 351 1 319 89 50

PORTUGAL (MADEIRA)
Quinta Da Bela Vista
Caminho Do Avista Navios 4, 9000 Funchal, Madeira, Portugal
Tel: 351 91 764 144
Fax: 351 91 765 090

PORTUGAL (PINHAO)
Vintage House Hotel
Lugar da Ponte, 5085 Pinhao, Portugal
Tel: 351 54 730 230
Fax: 351 54 730 240

PORTUGAL (REDONDO)
Convento de Sao Paulo
Aldeia Da Serra, 7170, 18 Redondo,
Portugal
Tel: 351 66 989 160
Fax: 351 66 999 104

PORTUGAL (SINTRA)
Hotel Palacio de Seteais
Rua Barbosa de Bocage,10, Seteais, 2710
Sintra, Portugal
Tel: 351 1 923 32 00
Fax: 351 1 923 42 77

PORTUGAL (SINTRA)
Quinta de Sao Thiago
2710 Sintra , Portugal
Tel: 351 1 923 29 23
Fax: 351 1 923 43 29

SPAIN (ALMUÑECAR)
Hotel Suites Albayzin Del Mar
Avenida Costa Del Sol, 23 18690
Almuñecar, (Granada), Spain
Tel: 34 958 632 161
Fax: 34 958 631 237

SPAIN (ARCOS DE LA FRONTERA)
Hacienda El Santiscal
Avda. del Santiscal 129, 11630 Arcos de la
Frontera, Spain
Tel: 34 956 708 313
Fax: 34 956 708 268

SPAIN (BARCELONA)
Hotel Claris
Pau Claris 150, 08009 Barcelona, Spain
Tel: 34 93 487 62 62
Fax: 34 93 215 79 70

SPAIN (BARCELONA)
Hotel Colon
Avenida de la Catedral 7, 08002, Barcelona,
Spain
Tel: 34 93 301 14 04
Fax: 34 93 317 29 15

SPAIN (BARCELONA)
The Gallery
Rosselló 249, 08008, Barcelona, Spain
Tel: 34 93 415 99 11
Fax: 34 93 415 91 84

SPAIN (CAMPRODON)
Hotel Grevol
Carretra Camprodon A Setcases 17869,
Llanars, Spain
Tel: 34 972 74 10 13
Fax: 34 972 74 10 87

SPAIN (EL ROCIO ALMONTE)
El Cortijo de los Mimbrales
Crta del Rocio A483, KM20, 21750
Almonte (Huelva), Spain
Tel: 34 959 44 22 37
Fax: 34 959 44 24 43

SPAIN (IBIZA)
Pikes
San Antonio De Portmany 07820, Isla De
Ibiza, Balearic Islands, Spain
Tel: 34 971 34 22 22
Fax: 34 971 34 23 12

SPAIN (LLORET DE MAR)
Hotel Rigat Park
Playa de Fenals, 17310 Lloret de Mar, Costa
Brava, Spain
Tel: 34 972 36 52 00
Fax: 34 972 37 04 11

SPAIN (MADRID)
Villa Real
Plaza De Las Cortes 10, 28014 Madrid ,
Spain
Tel: 34 91 420 37 67
Fax: 34 91 420 25 47

SPAIN (MALAGA)
La Posada Del Torcal
29230 Villanueva de la Concepción, Malaga,
Spain
Tel: 34 9 5 203 11 77
Fax: 34 9 5 203 10 06

SPAIN (MALLORCA)
Gran Hotel Son Net
Castillo Son Net, 07194 Puigpunyent,
Mallorca, Balearic Islands, Spain
Tel: 34 971 147 000
Fax: 34 971 147 001

SPAIN (MALLORCA)
Hotel Monnaber Nou
Possessio de Monnaber Nou, 07310,
Campanet, Mallorca, Balearic Islands, Spain
Tel: 34 971 877 176
Fax: 34 971 877 127

SPAIN (MALLORCA)
Hotel Vistamar De Valldemosa
Ctra. Valldemosa, Andratx Km 2, 07170
Valldemosa , Mallorca, Balearic Islands,
Spain
Tel: 34 971 61 23 00
Fax: 34 971 61 25 83

SPAIN (MALLORCA)
Read's
Ca'n Moragues, 07320 Santa Maria,
Mallorca, Balearic Islands, Spain
Tel: 34 971 140 262
Fax: 34 971 140 762

SPAIN (MARBELLA)
Hotel Los Monteros
29600 Marbella, Malaga, Spain
Tel: 34 952 82 38 46
Fax: 34 952 82 58 46

SPAIN (MARBELLA)

Hotel Puente Romano

P.O Box 204, 29600 Marbella, Malaga,
Spain
Tel: 34 952 82 09 00
Fax: 34 952 82 26 43

SPAIN (MARBELLA)

Marbella Club Hotel

Boulevard Príncipe Alfonso von Hohenlohe
s/n, 29600 Marbella, Malaga, Spain
Tel: 34 95 282 22 11
Fax: 34 95 282 98 84

SPAIN (MARBELLA/ESTEPONA)

Las Dunas Suites

Ctra de Cádiz Km163.5, 29689 Marbella-
Estepona, (Malaga), Spain
Tel: 34 95 279 43 45
Fax: 34 95 279 48 25

SPAIN (MIJAS-COSTA)

Hotel Byblos Andaluz

29640 Mijas Golf, Apt.138., Fuengirola
(Malaga), Spain
Tel: 34 95 246 02 50
Fax: 34 95 258 63 27

SPAIN (OVIEDO)

Hotel de la Reconquista

Gil de Jaz 16, 33004 Oviedo, Principado de
Asturias, Spain
Tel: 34 98 524 11 00
Fax: 34 98 524 11 66

SPAIN (PALS)

Hotel La Costa

Avenida Arenales de Mar 3, 17526 Platja de
Pals, Costa Brava, Spain
Tel: 34 972 66 77 40
Fax: 34 972 66 77 36

SPAIN (PUERTO DE SANTA MARIA-CÁDIZ)

Monasterio de San Miguel

Calle Larga 27, 11500 El Puerto de Santa
Maria, Cádiz, Spain
Tel: 34 956 54 04 40
Fax: 34 956 54 26 04

SPAIN (SALAMANCA)

Hotel Rector

Rector Esperabe 10, Apartado 399, 37008
Salamanca, Spain
Tel: 34 923 21 84 82
Fax: 34 923 21 40 08

SPAIN (SEVILLE)

Cortijo Aguila Real

Crta.Guillena-Burguillos, KM4, 41210
Guillena, Seville, Spain
Tel: 34 95 578 50 06
Fax: 34 95 578 43 30

SPAIN (SEVILLE)

Hacienda Benazuza

41800 Sanlúcar la Mayor, Seville, Spain
Tel: 34 95 570 33 44
Fax: 34 95 570 34 10

SPAIN (SITGES)

Hotel Estela Barcelona

Avda. Port d'Aiguadolc s/n, 08870 Sitges
(Barcelona), Spain
Tel: 34 938 11 45 45
Fax: 34 938 11 45 46

SPAIN (SOTOGRANDE/SAN ROQUE)

The San Roque Club Suites Hotel

CN340, KM127,5, 11360 Sotogrande/San
Roque, (Cádiz), Spain
Tel: 34 956 61 30 30
Fax: 34 956 61 30 12

SPAIN (TARRAGONA)

Hotel Termes Montbrío Resort, Spa & Park

Carrer Nou,38, 43340 Montbrío Del Camp,
Tarragona, Spain
Tel: 34 9 77 81 40 00
Fax: 34 9 77 82 62 51

SPAIN (TENERIFE)

Gran Hotel Bahia Del Duque

38660 Adeje, Costa Adeje, Tenerife South,
Canary Islands, Spain
Tel: 34 922 74 69 00
Fax: 34 922 74 69 25

SPAIN (TENERIFE)

Hotel Botánico

Avda. Richard J. Yeoward 1, Urb Botánico,
38400 Puerto de la Cruz, Tenerife, Canary
Islands, Spain
Tel: 34 922 38 14 00
Fax: 34 922 38 15 04

SPAIN (TENERIFE)

Hotel Jardin Tropical

Calle Gran Bretana, 38670 Costa Adeje,
Tenerife, Canary Islands, Spain
Tel: 34 922 74 60 00
Fax: 34 922 74 60 60

SPAIN (TENERIFE)

Hotel San Roque

C/. Esteban de Ponte 32, 38450 Garachico,
Tenerife, Canary Islands, Spain
Tel: 34 922 13 34 35
Fax: 34 922 13 34 06

SPAIN (VILADRAU)

Xalet La Coromina

Carretera De Vic S/N, 17406, Viladrau,
Spain
Tel: 34 93 884 92 64
Fax: 34 93 884 81 60

SWEDEN (ÅRE)

Hotell Åregården

Box 6, 83013 Åre, Sweden
Tel: 46 647 178 00
Fax: 46 647 179 60

SWEDEN (BORGHOLM)

Halltorps Gästgiveri

387 92 Borgholm, Sweden
Tel: 46 485 85 000
Fax: 46 485 85 001

SWEDEN (GOTHENBURG)

Hotel Eggers

Drottningtorget, Box 323, 401 25
Gothenburg, Sweden
Tel: 46 31 80 60 70
Fax: 46 31 15 42 43

SWEDEN (LAGAN)

Toftaholm Herrgård

Toftaholm P.A., 34014 Lagan, Sweden
Tel: 46 370 440 55
Fax: 46 370 440 45

SWEDEN (SÖDERKÖPING)

Romantik Hotel Söderköpings Brunn

Box 44, Skönbergagatan 35, 614 21
Söderköping, Sweden
Tel: 46 121 109 00
Fax: 46 121 139 41

SWEDEN (STOCKHOLM)

Hotell Diplomat

Strandvägen 7C, Box 14059, 10440
Stockholm, Sweden
Tel: 46 8 459 68 00
Fax: 46 8 459 68 20

SWEDEN (TÄLLBERG)

Romantik Hotel Åkerblads

793 70 Tällberg, Sweden
Tel: 46 247 50800
Fax: 46 247 50652

SWEDEN (TANNDALEN)

Hotel Tanndalen

84098 Tanndalen, Sweden
Tel: 46 684 220 20
Fax: 46 684 224 24

SWITZERLAND (BURGDORF-BERN)

Hotel Stadthaus

Kirchbühl 2, 3402, Burgdorf-Bern,
Switzerland
Tel: 41 34 428 8000
Fax: 41 34 428 8008

SWITZERLAND (CHATEAU D'OEX)

Hostellerie Bon Accueil

1837 Chateau d'Oex, Switzerland
Tel: 41 26 924 6320
Fax: 41 26 924 5126

SWITZERLAND (KANDERSTEG)

Royal Park ***** Hotel

3718 Kandersteg, Switzerland
Tel: 41 33 675 88 88
Fax: 41 33 675 88 80

SWITZERLAND (LUCERNE/ LUZERN)

Romantik Hotel Wilden Mann

Bahnhofstrasse 30, 6000 Lucerne 7,
Switzerland
Tel: 41 41 210 16 66
Fax: 41 41 210 16 29

SWITZERLAND (LUGANO)

Villa Principe Leopoldo & Residence

Via Montalbano, 6900 Lugano, Switzerland
Tel: 41 91 985 8855
Fax: 41 91 985 8825

SWITZERLAND (MONTREUX)

Villa Kruger

Villas Dubochet 17, 1815, Clarens,
Switzerland
Tel: 41 21 98 92 110
Fax: 41 21 964 7439

SWITZERLAND (ZERMATT)

Grand Hotel Zermatterhof

3920, Zermatt, Switzerland
Tel: 41 27 966 66 00
Fax: 41 27 966 66 99

SWITZERLAND (ZOUZ)

Posthotel Engiadina

Via Maistra, 7524 Zouz, Switzerland
Tel: 41 81 85 41 021
Fax: 41 81 85 43 303

TUNISA (TUNIS)

La Maison Blanche

45 Avenue Mohamed V, 1002, Tunis, Tunisa
Tel: 216 1 849 849
Fax: 216 1 793 842

TURKEY (ISTANBUL)

Hotel Sari Konak

Mimar Mehmet Aga Cad, No.42-46 34400
Sultanahmet, Istanbul, Turkey
Tel: 90 212 638 62 58
Fax: 90 212 517 86 35

TURKEY (KALKAN)

Hotel Villa Mahal

P.K 4 Kalkan, 07960 Antalya, Turkey
Tel: 90 242 844 3268
Fax: 90 242 844 2122

TURKEY (KAS)

Club Savile

Cukurbag Yarimadasi, Kas, Antalya, Turkey
Tel: 90 242 836 1393
UK Tel: 44 20 7625 3001

TURKEY (KAS)

Savile Residence

Cukurbag Yarimidasi, Kas,Antalya, Turkey
Tel: 90 242 836 2300
Fax: 90 242 836 3054

MINI LISTINGS

Johansens Recommended Hotels & Game Lodges – Southern Africa, Mauritius, The Seychelles 2000

Here in brief are the entries that appear in full in Johansens Recommended Hotels & Game Lodges – Southern Africa, Mauritius, The Seychelles 2000.
To order Johansens guides turn to the order forms at the back of this book.

BOTSWANA (KALAHARI)

Jack's Camp

PO Box 173, Francistown, Botswana
Tel: +267 212 277
Fax: +267 213 458

BOTSWANA (OKAVANGO)

Xugana Island Lodge

C/O Hartley's Safaris, Private Bag 48 Maun,
Botswana
Tel: +267 661806
Fax: +267 660528

BOTSWANA (OKAVANGO DELTA)

Abu Camp- Elephant Back Safaris

Elephant Back Safaris, Private Bag 332,
Maun , Botswana
Tel: +267 661 260
Fax: +267 661 005

NAMIBIA (WINDHOEK)

Vingerklip Lodge

PO Box 443, Outjo, Namibia
Tel: +264 61 220 324
Fax: +264 61 221 432

SEYCHELLES (MAHE)

Fregate Island Private

PO Box 330, Victoria, Mahe , Seychelles
Tel: +248 324 545
Fax: +248 324 499

EASTERN CAPE (GRAAFF-REINET)

Andries Stockenström Guest House & Restaurant

100 Cradock Street, PO Box 55, Graaff-
Reinet 6280, Eastern Cape , South Africa
Tel: +27 49 892 4575
Fax: +27 49 892 4575

EASTERN CAPE (GRAHAMSTOWN)

Aucklands Country House

PO Box 997, Grahamstown 6140, Eastern
Cape , South Africa
Tel: +27 46 622 2401
Fax: +27 46 622 5682

EASTERN CAPE (PORT ELIZABETH)

Hacklewood Hill Country House

152 Prospect Road,Walmer, Port Elizabeth,
Eastern Cape , South Africa
Tel: +27 41 58 11 300
Fax: +27 41 58 141 55

EASTERN CAPE (PORT ELIZABETH)

Shamwari Game Reserve

PO Box 32017, Summerstrand, Port
Elizabeth 6019 , South Africa
Tel: +27 42 203 1111
Fax: +27 42 235 1224

GAUTENG (CULLINAN)

Zebra Country Lodge

PO Box 6349, Weltevreden Park, Gauteng ,
South Africa
Tel: +27 11 675 0609
Fax: +27 11 675 0610

GAUTENG (MAGALIESBURG)

De Hoek

PO Box 117, Magaliesburg 2085, Gauteng,
South Africa
Tel: +27 014 577 1198
Fax: +27 014 577 4530

GAUTENG (PRETORIA)

Rovos Rail

P.O Box 2837, Pretoria 0001, Gauteng,
South Africa
Tel: +27 12 323 6052
Fax: +27 12 323 0843

GAUTENG (ROZENHOF)

Rozenhof Guest House

525 Alexander Street, Brooklyn, Pretoria
0181, Gauteng , South Africa
Tel: +27 12 468 075
Fax: +27 12 468 085

KWAZULU-NATAL (CURRYS POST)

Old Halliwell Country Inn

PO Box 201, Howick 3290, Kwazulu , South
Africa
Tel: +27 33 330 2602
Fax: +27 33 330 3430

KWAZULU-NATAL (DURBAN)

Ridgeview Lodge

17 Loudoun Road, Berea, Durban, Kwazulu-
Natal , South Africa
Tel: +27 31 202 9777
Fax: +27 31 201 5587

KWAZULU-NATAL (LIDGETTON)

Happy Hill

Old Main Road, Lidgetton, Kwazulu-Natal
3270, South Africa
Tel: +27 33 234 4380
Fax: +27 33 234 4079

KWAZULU-NATAL (LIDGETTON)

Lythwood Lodge

PO Box 17, Lidgetton 3270, Kwazulu-Natal ,
South Africa
Tel: +27 33 234 4666
Fax: +27 33 234 4668

KWAZULU-NATAL (MAPUTALAND)

Makakatana Bay Lodge

PO Box 65, Mtubatuba 3935, Kwazulu-Natal
, South Africa
Tel: +27 35 550 4189
Fax: +27 35 550 4198

What does your paper say about you?

Jeremy Hoskins, hotelier, chooses Conqueror* Contour in Oyster, printed in colour.

Starring role. Jeremy Hoskins combed the Conqueror* range to discover the perfect texture for his hotel's letterhead. Ideal for brochures, menus, wine-lists and letterheads, as well as for all corporate and conference stationery, the colours, textures and weights of the Conqueror* range are the best in the business. For a free sample pack or advice on the Conqueror* range and where to find it, call + 44 (0) 1256 728665 or visit www.conqueror.com now. You'll get five stars for presentation.

conqueror®

★ Star quality. For a free sample pack or advice on the Conqueror* range and where to find it, call + 44 (0) 1256 728665 or visit www.conqueror.com now.

KWAZULU-NATAL (MAPUTALAND)

Ndumo Wilderness Camp

P.O Box 5219, Rivonia, Kwazulu-Natal ,
South Africa
Tel: +27 11 883 0747
Fax: +27 11 883 0911

KWAZULU-NATAL (MAPUTALAND)

Shayamoya Game Lodge

PO Box 784, Pongola 3170, Kwazulu-Natal ,
South Africa
Tel: +27 34 435 1110
Fax: +27 34 435 1008

KWAZULU-NATAL (MOOI RIVER NR GIANTS CASTLE)

Hartford House

PO Box 430, Mooi River 3300, Kwazulu-
Natal, South Africa
Tel: +27 33 263 2713
Fax: +27 33 263 2818

KWAZULU-NATAL (NOTTINGHAM ROAD)

Hawklee Country House

PO Box 27, Nottingham Road 3280,
Western Province , South Africa
Tel: +27 33 263 6209
Fax: +27 33 263 6008

KWAZULU-NATAL (PIETERMARITZBURG)

Rehoboth Chalets

276 Murray Road, Hayfields,
Pietermaritzburg 3201, Kwazulu-Natal,
South Africa
Tel: +27 33 39 62 312
Fax: +27 33 39 64 008

KWAZULU-NATAL (RORKE'S DRIFT)

Fugitives Drift Lodge & Guest House

PO Rorkes Drift 3016, Kwazulu-Natal,
South Africa
Tel: +27 34 642 1843
Fax: +27 34 123 319

KWAZULU-NATAL (SHAKA'S ROCK)

Comfort House

27 Dolphin Crescent, Shaka's Rock,
Kwazulu-Natal, South Africa
Tel: +27 322 525 5575
Fax: +27 322 525 8775

KWAZULU-NATAL (SHAKA'S ROCK)

Lalaria Lodge

25a Dolphin Crescent, Shaka's Rock,
Dolphin Coast, Kwazulu-Natal, South Africa
Tel: +32 525 5789
Fax: +32 525 8869

KWAZULU-NATAL (UMHLALI)

Isibindi Lodge

P.O. Box 275, Umhlali, Kwazulu-Natal 4390,
South Africa
Tel: +0322 947 0538
Fax: +0322 947 0659

KWAZULU-NATAL (UMHLALI)

Zimbali Lodge & Country Club

PO Box 404, Umhlali 4390, Kwazulu-Natal ,
South Africa
Tel: +27 32 2538 1007
Fax: +27 32 2538 1019

KWAZULU-NATAL (UNDERBERG)

Penwarn Country Lodge

PO Box 253, Underberg, Kwazulu-Natal,
South Africa
Tel: +27 33 7011 777
Fax: +27 33 7011 341

MOZAMBIQUE (BENGUERRA ISLAND)

Benguerra Lodge

Sales Office, Benguerra Island Holidays, 89
Houghton Drive,Houghton 2041,
Johannesburg , South Africa
Tel: +27 11 483 27 34
Fax: +27 11 728 37 67

MPUMALANGA (SABI SAND)

Idube Game Reserve

Mpumalanga, South Africa
Tel: +27 11 888 3713
Fax: +27 11 888 2181

MPUMALANGA (HAZYVIEW)

Casa Do Sol

PO Box 57, Hazyview 1242, Mpumalanga,
South Africa
Tel: +27 13 737 8111
Fax: +27 13 737 8166

MPUMALANGA (KRUGER NATIONAL PARK)

Chitwa Chitwa Game Lodges

Head Office & Central Reservations, P.O
Box 781854 Sandton , Gauteng 2146, South
Africa
Tel: +011 883 1354 /784 8131
Fax: +011 783 1858

MPUMALANGA (MALELANE)

Buhala Country House

PO Box 165, Malelane 1320, Mpumalanga,
South Africa
Tel: +27 13 790 4372
Fax: +27 13 790 4306

MPUMALANGA (NELSPRUIT)

Annandale House

27 Rocket Street,PO Box 12597, Nelspruit,
Mpumalanga , South Africa
Tel: +27 82 7745 833
Fax: +27 13 74 49397

MPUMALANGA (NELSPRUIT)

The Rest Country Lodge

The Rest Road,PO Box 5900, Nelspruit,
Mpumalanga , South Africa
Tel: +27 13 744 9991/2
Fax: +27 13 744 9991/2

MPUMALANGA (TIMBAVATI)

Kings Camp

PO Box 427, Nelspruit 1200, Mpumalanga,
South Africa
Tel: +27 13 793 3633
Fax: +27 13 793 3634

MPUMALANGA (WHITE RIVER)

Jatinga Country Lodge

PO Box 3577, White River 1240,
Mpumalanga, South Africa
Tel: +27 13 751 5059
Fax: +27 13 751 5072

MPUMALANGA (WHITE RIVER)

Leopard Hills Private Game Reserve

PO Box 3619, White River,1240,
Mpumalanga, South Africa
Tel: +27 13 737 6626
Fax: +27 13 737 6628

MPUMALANGA (WHITE RIVER)

Savanna Tented Safari Lodge

PO Box 3619, White River 1240,
Mpumalanga, South Africa
Tel: +27 13 751 2205
Fax: +27 13 751 2205

NORTHERN CAPE (KALAHARI)

Tswalu Private Desert Reserve

PO Box 420, Kathu 8446, Northern Cape ,
South Africa
Tel: +27 53 781 9311
Fax: +27 53 781 9316

NORTHERN PROVINCE (HOEDSPRUIT)

Garonga Safari Camp

PO Box 737, Hoedspruit 1380, Northern
Province , South Africa
Tel: +27 11 804 7595
Fax: +27 11 802 6503

NORTHERN PROVINCE (HOEDSPRUIT)

Kapama Private Game Reserve

P.O Box 912-031, Silverton, Mpumalanga ,
South Africa
Tel: +27 12 804 4840
Fax: +27 12 804 4842

NORTHERN PROVINCE (HOEDSPRUIT)

Tshukudu Game Lodge

PO Box 289, Hoedspruit 1380, Northern
Province, South Africa
Tel: +27 15 793 2476
Fax: +27 15 793 2078

NORTHERN PROVINCE (TZANEEN)

Coach House

PO Box 544, Tzaneen 0850, Northern
Province , South Africa
Tel: +27 15 307 3641
Fax: +27 15 307 1466

NORTHERN PROVINCE (WATERBERG)

Entabeni Game Reserve

PO Box 6349, Weltevreden Park 1715,
Gauteng , South Africa
Tel: +27 11 675 0609
Fax: +27 11 675 0610

NORTHERN PROVINCE (WELGEVONDEN)

Makweti Safari Lodge

Welgevonden Game Reserve, P.O Box 310 ,
Vaalwater, Northern Province 0530, South
Africa
Tel: +27 83 458 6122
Fax: +27 83 459 1153/2/1

WESTERN CAPE (CAPE TOWN)

Cape Grace Hotel

West Quay, Victoria & Alfred Waterfront,
Cape Town, Western Cape , South Africa
Tel: +27 21 410 7100
Fax: +27 21 419 7622

WESTERN CAPE (CAPE TOWN)

De Waterkant Lodge & Cottages

20 Loader Street, De Waterkant, Cape Town
8001, Western Cape , South Africa
Tel: +27 21 419 1097/77
Fax: +27 21 419 1097

WESTERN CAPE (CAPE TOWN)

Villa Belmonte Manor House

33 Belmont Avenue,Orangjezicht, Cape
Town, Western Cape , South Africa
Tel: +27 21 462 1576
Fax: +27 21 462 1579

WESTERN CAPE (CAPE TOWN-HIGGOVALE)

Kensington Place

38 Kensington Crescent, Higgovale, Cape
Town, Western Cape , South Africa
Tel: +27 21 424 4744
Fax: +27 21 424 1810

WESTERN CAPE (CAPE TOWN-SEAPOINT)

The Clarendon

67 Kloof Road,PO Box 224, Seapoint,Cape
Town, Western Cape , South Africa
Tel: +27 21 439 3224
Fax: +27 21 434 6855

WESTERN CAPE (CAPE TOWN-SEAPOINT)

Huijs Haerlem

25 Main Drive,Sea Point, PO Box
493,Green Point, Cape Town, Western Cape
, South Africa
Tel: +27 21 434 6434
Fax: +27 21 439 2506

WESTERN CAPE (CAPE TOWN-SEAPOINT)

Winchester Mansions

221 Beach Road, Seapoint, Western Cape ,
South Africa
Tel: +27 21 434 2351
Fax: +27 21 434 0215

WESTERN CAPE (CEDERBERG MOUNTAINS)

Bushmans Kloof Wilderness Reserve

PO Box 53405 Kenilworth, Cape Town,
South Africa
Tel: +27 21 797 0990
Fax: +27 21 761 5551

WESTERN CAPE (CONSTANTIA VALLEY)

Steenberg Country Hotel

PO Box 10802, Steenberg Estate, Cape
Town, Western Cape 7945, South Africa
Tel: +27 21 713 2222
Fax: +27 21 713 2221

WESTERN CAPE (FRANSCHHOEK)

La Couronne

Robertsvlei Road, Franschhoek 7690,
Western Cape , South Africa
Tel: +27 21 876 2770
Fax: +27 21 876 3788

WESTERN CAPE (FRANSCHHOEK)

Le Quartier Francais

16 Huguenot Road, PO Box 237,
Franschhoek, Western Cape , South Africa
Tel: +27 21 876 2151
Fax: +27 21 876 3105

WESTERN CAPE (GREYTON)

Greyton Lodge

46 Main Street, Greyton 7233, Western
Cape , South Africa
Tel: +27 28 254 9876
Fax: +27 28 254 9672

WESTERN CAPE (HERMON)

Bartholomeus Klip Farmhouse

PO Box 36, Hermon 7308, Western Cape ,
South Africa
Tel: +27 22 448 1820
Fax: +27 22 448 1829

WESTERN CAPE (HOUT BAY)

Tarragona Lodge

Cnr of Disa River Road & Valley Road, PO
Box 26887, Hout Bay 7872, Western Cape ,
South Africa
Tel: +27 21 790 5080
Fax: +27 21 790 5095

WESTERN CAPE (KNYSNA)

Belvidere Manor

PO Box 1195, Knynsa 6570, Western Cape ,
South Africa
Tel: +27 44 387 1055
Fax: +27 44 387 1059

WESTERN CAPE (LITTLE KAROO)

Mimosa Lodge

Church Street, Montague, Western Cape ,
South Africa
Tel: +27 23 614 23 51
Fax: +27 23 614 24 18

WESTERN CAPE (MOSSEL BAY)

Reins Nature Reserve

PO Box 298, Albertinia 6695, Western Cape
, South Africa
Tel: +27 28 735 3322
Fax: +27 28 735 3324

WESTERN CAPE (NEWLANDS)

Vineyard Hotel

Colinton Road, Newlands 7700, Cape
Town, Western Cape , South Africa
Tel: +27 21 683 3044
Fax: +27 21 683 3365

WESTERN CAPE (NORTHERN PAARL)

Roggeland Country House

PO Box 7210, Northern Paarl, Western
Cape 7623, South Africa
Tel: +27 21 868 2501
Fax: +27 21 868 2113

WESTERN CAPE (ORANJEZICHT)

No.1 Chesterfield

1 Chesterfield Road, Oranjezicht, 8001 Cape
Town, Western Cape , South Africa
Tel: +27 21 461 7383
Fax: +27 21 461 4688

WESTERN CAPE (PLETTENBERG BAY)

Hog Hollow Country Lodge

PO Box 503, Plettenberg Bay, Western Cape
6600, South Africa
Tel: +27 4457 48879
Fax: +27 4457 48879

WESTERN CAPE (PLETTENBERG BAY)

Laird's Lodge

P.O Box 657, Plettenberg Bay, Western Cape
6600, South Africa
Tel: +27 4453 27721
Fax: +27 4453 27671

WESTERN CAPE (STELLENBOSCH)

d'Ouwe Werf

30 Church Street, Stellenbosch 7600,
Western Cape , South Africa
Tel: +27 21 887 4608
Fax: +27 21 887 4626

WESTERN CAPE (STELLENBOSCH)

Lyngrove Country House

PO Box 7275, Stellenbosch 7599, Western
Cape , South Africa
Tel: +27 21 842 2116
Fax: +27 21 842 2118

WESTERN CAPE (STELLENBOSCH)

River Manor

No.6 The Avenue, Stellenbosch, Western
Cape , South Africa
Tel: +27 21 887 9944
Fax: +27 21 887 9940

WESTERN CAPE (TULBAGH)

Rijk's Ridge Country House

PO Box 340, Tulbagh 6820, Western Cape ,
South Africa
Tel: +27 23 230 1006
Fax: +27 23 230 1125

MAURITIUS

Paradis

Mauritius House, 1 Portsmouth Road,
Guildford, Surrey GU2 5BL, UK
Tel: +01483 533008
Fax: +01483 532820

MAURITIUS

Royal Palm

Mauritius House, 1 Portsmouth Road,
Guildford, Surrey GU2 5BL, UK
Tel: +01483 533008
Fax: +01483 532820

ZIMBABWE (CHIREDZI-SOUTH EAST LOWVELD)

Nduna Safari Lodge

Malilangwe Private Wildlife Reserve,
Reservations P.O Box MP845 Mount
Pleasant, Harare , Zimbabwe
Tel: +263 4 722 983
Fax: +263 4 735 530

ZIMBABWE (CHIREDZI-SOUTH EAST LOWVELD)

Pamushana

Malilangwe Private Wildlife Reserve,
Reservations P.O Box MP845 Mount
Pleasant, Harare , Zimbabwe
Tel: +263 4 722 983
Fax: +263 4 735530

ZIMBABWE (HARARE)

Meikles Hotel

Jason Moyo Avenue, PO Box 594, Harare ,
Zimbabwe
Tel: +263 4 707721
Fax: +263 4 707754

ZIMBABWE (HARARE)

Wild Geese Lodge

PO Box BW 198, Borrowdale, Harare ,
Zimbabwe
Tel: +26 34 860466
Fax: +26 34 860276

ZIMBABWE (HWANGE)

The Hide Safari Camp

27-29 James Martin Drive, PO Box ST274,
Southerton, Harare , Zimbabwe
Tel: +263 4 660554
Fax: +263 4 621216

ZIMBABWE (LAKE KARIBA)

Sanyati Lodge

Lake Kariba, Sanyati Gorge, Kariba ,
Zimbabwe
Tel: +263 4 72 22 33
Fax: +263 4 72 03 60

ZIMBABWE (JULIASDALE)

Inn on Rupurara

PO Box 337, Juliasdale, Eastern Highlands ,
Zimbabwe
Tel: +263 29 3021/4
Fax: +263 29 3025

ZIMBABWE (VICTORIA FALLS)

The Victoria Falls Hotel

P.O Box 10, Victoria Falls, Zimbabwe
Tel: +263 13 4761
Fax: +263 13 2354

ORDER FORM

Call our 24hr credit card hotline FREEPHONE 0800 269 397.

Simply indicate which title(s) you require by putting the quantity in the boxes provided. Choose your preferred method of payment and mail to Johansens, FREEPOST (CB 264), 43 Millharbour, London E14 9BR, England (no stamp needed). Your FREE gifts will automatically be dispatched with your order. Fax orders welcome on 0171 537 3594

CHOOSE FROM 7 SPECIAL GUIDE COLLECTIONS – SAVE UP TO £56

TITLE	Normal Price	PRICE	SAVE	QTY	TOTAL
OFFER ONE – The Basic Collection					
3 Johansens Guides A+B+C	£42.85	£36.00	£6.85		
OFFER TWO – The Extended Collection					
4 Johansens Guides A+B+C+G	£58.80	£46.00	£12.80		
OFFER THREE – The Full Selection					
5 Johansens Guides A+B+C+G+K PLUS Southern Africa Guide **FREE**	£71.75	£56.00	£15.75		
OFFER FOUR - The Executive Collection					
Business Meeting Venues Guide & CD-ROM M+R	£40.00	£30.00	£10.00		
OFFER FIVE - The Holiday Pack					
3 Johansens Guides D+E+F	£18.93	£9.99	£8.94		
OFFER SIX - The Digital Collection					
3 Johansens CD-ROMs N+O+P PLUS Southern Africa CD-ROM Q **FREE**	£69.85	£59.85	£10.00		
OFFER SEVEN - The Chairman's Collection					
Business Meeting Venues Guide & CD-ROMs M+R PLUS 5 Johansens Boxed Guides A+B+C+G+K, PLUS D+E+F, PLUS 3 CD-ROMs N+O+P PLUS Southern Africa Guide/CD ROM Q **FREE**, PLUS Mystery Gift **FREE**	£205.53	£149.00	£56.53		
Privilege Card PLUS The Millennium Guide		**FREE**			
1 Presentation box for offers 1, 2 and 3		£5.00	£20.00		

TOTAL 1

JOHANSENS PRINTED GUIDES 2000

CODE	TITLE	PRICE	QTY	TOTAL
A	Recommended Hotels – Great Britain & Ireland 2000	£19.95		
B	Recommended Country Houses & Small Hotels – Great Britain & Ireland 2000	£11.95		
C	Recommended Traditional Inns, Hotels & Restaurants – Great Britain 2000	£10.95		
NEW D	Recommended Holiday Cottages – Great Britain & Ireland 2000	£4.99		
E	Historic Houses, Castles & Gardens 2000	£4.99		
F	Museums & Galleries 2000	£8.95		
G	Recommended Hotels – Europe & The Mediterranean 2000	£15.95		
NEW H	Recommended Hotels – Europe & The Mediterranean 2000 (*French Language*)	£15.95		
NEW J	Recommended Hotels – Europe & The Mediterranean 2000 (*German Language*)	£15.95		
K	Recommended Hotels & Inns – North America, Bermuda & The Caribbean 2000	£12.95		
NEW L	Recommended Hotels & Game Lodges – Southern Africa, Mauritius & The Seychelles 2000	£9.95		
M	Recommended Business Meeting Venues 2000	£20.00		

JOHANSENS CD ROMs DIGITAL COLLECTION 2000

CODE	TITLE	PRICE	QTY	TOTAL
N	The Guide 2000 – Great Britain & Ireland	£29.95		
O	The Guide 2000 – Europe & The Mediterranean (*English, French, German Language*)	£22.95		
P	The Guide 2000 – North America, Bermuda & The Caribbean	£16.95		
NEW Q	The Guide 2000 – Southern Africa, Mauritius & The Seychelles	£16.95		
R	Business Meeting Venues 2000	£20.00		
S	Privilege Card 2000 (*Free with your order. Additional Cards £20 each*)	£20.00		

Postage & Packing (UK) £4.50 or £2.50 for single order and CD-ROMs
Outside UK add £5 or £3 for single orders and CD-ROMs

TOTAL 2

GRAND TOTAL 1+2+P&P

Name (Mr/Mrs/Miss)
Address
Postcode
Card No.
Exp Date
Signature

I have chosen my Johansens Guides/CD-ROMs and

☐ I enclose a cheque for £ _____ payable to Johansens

☐ I enclose my order on company letterheading, please invoice (UK only)

☐ Please debit my credit/charge card account (please tick).

☐ MasterCard ☐ Diners ☐ Amex

☐ Visa ☐ Switch (Issue Number) _____

A20

GUEST SURVEY REPORT

Your own Johansens 'inspection' gives reliability to our guides and assists in the selection of Award Nominations

Name of Hotel: _____

Location of Hotel: _____

Page No: _____

Date of visit: _____

Name of guest _____

Address of guest: _____

_____Postcode _____

Please tick one box in each category below:	Excellent	Good	Disappointing	Poor
Bedrooms				
Public Rooms				
Restaurant/Cuisine				
Service				
Welcome/Friendliness				
Value For Money				

To: Johansens, FREEPOST (CB264), 43 Millharbour, London E14 9BR

ORDER FORM

Call our 24hr credit card hotline FREEPHONE 0800 269 397.

Simply indicate which title(s) you require by putting the quantity in the boxes provided. Choose your preferred method of payment and mail to Johansens, FREEPOST (CB 264), 43 Millharbour, London E14 9BR, England (no stamp needed). Your FREE gifts will automatically be dispatched with your order. Fax orders welcome on 0171 537 3594

CHOOSE FROM 7 SPECIAL GUIDE COLLECTIONS – SAVE UP TO £56

TITLE	Normal Price	PRICE	SAVE	QTY	TOTAL
OFFER ONE – The Basic Collection					
3 Johansens Guides A+B+C	£42.85	£36.00	£6.85		
OFFER TWO – The Extended Collection					
4 Johansens Guides A+B+C+G	£58.80	£46.00	£12.80		
OFFER THREE – The Full Selection					
5 Johansens Guides A+B+C+G+K PLUS Southern Africa Guide **FREE**	£71.75	£56.00	£15.75		
OFFER FOUR - The Executive Collection					
Business Meeting Venues Guide & CD-ROM M+R	£40.00	£30.00	£10.00		
OFFER FIVE - The Holiday Pack					
3 Johansens Guides D+E+F	£18.93	£9.99	£8.94		
OFFER SIX - The Digital Collection					
3 Johansens CD-ROMs N+O+P PLUS Southern Africa CD-ROM Q **FREE**	£69.85	£59.85	£10.00		
OFFER SEVEN - The Chairman's Collection					
Business Meeting Venues Guide & CD-ROMs M+R **PLUS** 5 Johansens Boxed Guides A+B+C+G+K, **PLUS** D+E+F, **PLUS** 3 CD-ROMs N+O+P **PLUS** Southern Africa Guide/CD ROM Q **FREE**, **PLUS** Mystery Gift **FREE**	£205.53	£149.00	£56.53		
Privilege Card PLUS The Millennium Guide		**FREE**			
1 Presentation box for offers 1, 2 and 3		£5.00	£20.00		

TOTAL 1

JOHANSENS PRINTED GUIDES 2000

CODE	TITLE	PRICE	QTY	TOTAL
A	Recommended Hotels – Great Britain & Ireland 2000	£19.95		
B	Recommended Country Houses & Small Hotels – Great Britain & Ireland 2000	£11.95		
C	Recommended Traditional Inns, Hotels & Restaurants – Great Britain 2000	£10.95		
NEW D	Recommended Holiday Cottages – Great Britain & Ireland 2000	£4.99		
E	Historic Houses, Castles & Gardens 2000	£4.99		
F	Museums & Galleries 2000	£8.95		
G	Recommended Hotels – Europe & The Mediterranean 2000	£15.95		
NEW H	Recommended Hotels – Europe & The Mediterranean 2000 (French Language)	£15.95		
NEW J	Recommended Hotels – Europe & The Mediterranean 2000 (German Language)	£15.95		
K	Recommended Hotels & Inns – North America, Bermuda & The Caribbean 2000	£12.95		
NEW L	Recommended Hotels & Game Lodges – Southern Africa, Mauritius & The Seychelles 2000	£9.95		
M	Recommended Business Meeting Venues 2000	£20.00		

JOHANSENS CD ROMs DIGITAL COLLECTION 2000

CODE	TITLE	PRICE	QTY	TOTAL
N	The Guide 2000 – Great Britain & Ireland	£29.95		
O	The Guide 2000 – Europe & The Mediterranean (English, French, German Language)	£22.95		
P	The Guide 2000 – North America, Bermuda & The Caribbean	£16.95		
NEW Q	The Guide 2000 – Southern Africa, Mauritius & The Seychelles	£16.95		
R	Business Meeting Venues 2000	£20.00		
S	Privilege Card 2000 (Free with your order. Additional Cards £20 each)	£20.00		

Postage & Packing (UK) £4.50 or £2.50 for single order and CD-ROMs
Outside UK add £5 or £3 for single orders and CD-ROMs

TOTAL 2

GRAND TOTAL 1+2+P&P

Name (Mr/Mrs/Miss)

Address

Postcode

Card No.

Exp Date

Signature

I have chosen my Johansens Guides/CD-ROMs and

☐ I enclose a cheque for £ _____ payable to Johansens

☐ I enclose my order on company letterheading, please invoice (UK only)

☐ Please debit my credit/charge card account (please tick).

☐ MasterCard ☐ Diners ☐ Amex

☐ Visa ☐ Switch (Issue Number) _____

A20

GUEST SURVEY REPORT

Your own Johansens 'inspection' gives reliability to our guides and assists in the selection of Award Nominations

Name of Hotel: _____

Location of Hotel: _____

Page No: _____

Date of visit: _____

Name of guest _____

Address of guest: _____

_____Postcode _____

Please tick one box in each category below:	Excellent	Good	Disappointing	Poor
Bedrooms				
Public Rooms				
Restaurant/Cuisine				
Service				
Welcome/Friendliness				
Value For Money				

Occasionally we may allow other reputable organisations to write with offers which may be of interest.
If you prefer not to hear from them, tick this box ☐

To: Johansens, FREEPOST (CB264), 43 Millharbour, London E14 9BR